Cass...
Colloquial
French

Michel and Eleanor Levieux

A HANDBOOK
OF IDIOMATIC USAGE

Formerly *Beyond the Dictionary in French*

Cassell's Colloquial French

A HANDBOOK OF IDIOMATIC USAGE

by Michel Levieux

Licencié-ès-Lettres, Diplômé d'Etudes
Supérieures, C.A.P.E.S. (Sorbonne)
and Eleanor Levieux, B.A.
Maîtrise en traduction (Sorbonne)

Formerly *Beyond the Dictionary in French*

Completely revised

COLLIER BOOKS
MACMILLAN PUBLISHING COMPANY
New York

Previous edition entitled
Beyond the Dictionary in French
Copyright © Cassell Ltd.
1967, 1969, 1971, 1972, 1974, 1977

Macmillan Publishing Company
866 Third Avenue, New York, N.Y. 10022
Collier Macmillan Canada, Inc.

Library of Congress Cataloging in Publication Data

Levieux, Michel.
  Cassell's colloquial French.

  "Formerly Beyond the dictionary in French."
  Includes index.
  1. French language—Text-books for foreign
speakers—English. 2. French language—Conversation
and phrase books—English. 3. French language—
Spoken French. 4. French language—Usage. I. Levieux,
Eleanor. II. Title. III. Title: Colloquial French.
PC2129.E5L49 1984   443'.21   84-21382
ISBN 0-02-079420-7

10 9 8 7 6 5 4

Printed in the United States of America

Contents

Introduction

The scope of this book is, obviously, modest, since we have not aimed at writing a dictionary but at enabling the student with an already solid grounding in French to advance into more secret territory by helping him to read between the lines and fill in the gaps of a standard dictionary. To achieve this, we have attempted to place each of the terms on the following pages IN ITS CONTEXT and, usually, to give examples of its use. A word out of context is virtually useless to you, just another item to chalk up on the vocabulary list. After all, what good is the ace of spades when all the rest of the pack is missing?

When you can wield certain terms deftly, accurately, then you stand an excellent chance of avoiding the more sticky *gaffes* (q.v.) which otherwise fall to the lot of any *étranger*. Which is why we are as likely to stress what not to say—and why—as we are to suggest what you ought to say. We have been especially anxious to point out when a word is used more often than you might suspect on the basis of its twin in English, as with *obligatoire*, for example; and to stress those turns of phrase which are not likely to occur to you the first time you grope for the right expression. *S'occuper de quelque chose* is the proper translation of 'to take care of something', 'to see to something'; whereas you might be tempted to say, *prendre soin de quelque chose*—which actually means, 'to take good care of something', that is, 'to be careful of it'.

A word about our choice of words. You may expect to find certain words that do not appear; you may be taken unawares by others that have been included. Our choice has been essentially personal (and therefore, arbitrary), based on the ambushes we have heard English-speaking people run into in France or, conversely, on the stumbling blocks we have known Frenchmen to find most troublesome in learning English. No two persons and certainly no two Franco-Anglo-Saxon (*v.* ANGLO-SAXON) couples would have selected the same terms for your consideration, nor cited the same examples.

We do not pretend to give every meaning of each term, since that would force us straight back to the dictionary form instead of going beyond it; but we have tried to choose some of the meanings which seem to cause the greatest trouble or are likely to be the most useful to you. To this end, we have given some idioms or clichés, although this book is by no means a listing of 'colourful phrases'. Neither is it a hand-book of slang, *l'argot. Les expressions argotiques* are so many, so peculiar to various *milieux*—and often, so fleeting. *Langage familier*, on the other hand, has not been overlooked, since it is an integral, if not always irreproachable, part of what we aim at helping you use with confidence and understand with ease: the genuine spoken language. In this way, we have included some constructions, some forms which may displease the purists, but whose gradual absorption into modern French is a matter for simple observation. You may rest assured, none the less, that we have not included items of unduly careless, erroneous or undesirable usage. The rare instances of definitely slangy or vulgar language are pointed out as such.

Where we have felt that certain aspects of daily life require, or deserve, a more lingering look, we have grouped the appropriate terms in special categories towards the end of the book; and you will see that they range from banking to theatre-going, from driving a car to telling the time, from telephoning to renting or buying a flat.

You may be shocked at the absence of culinary terms, since France and Food form an indissoluble marriage.

But so many competent and even monumental cookbooks do exist already, and so many guide-books on what and where to eat in France have been put on the market, that we felt we might make better use of the following pages by devoting them to other things. Which is not to say that you will find no mention whatever of *restaurants*, *cafés*, *casseroles*, *la table*, or *le marché*.

Nor is this a manual of grammar. We have taken it for granted that since you are interested enough in French to look into this book, you generally know when a verb is transitive and when it is not. But now and again, where there is an exception or where we foresee confusion, we have indicated the nature of the verb. Again, with adjectives: we have given the feminine form only when it may appear irregular, or to remind you that masculine adjectives in *-eux* take *-euse* in the feminine (*paresseux*, *-euse*, 'lazy'): that those in *-er* take *-ère* (*gaucher*, *-ère*, 'left-handed'); those in *-é*, *ée* (*fâché*, *-ée*, 'angry'); in *-if*, *ive* (*compréhensif*, *-ive*, 'comprehensive' or 'understanding'); in *-nc*, *nche* (*blanc*, *-nche*, 'white'); in *-et*, *-ète* (*inquiet*, *-ète*, 'anxious'); and so on.

On the other hand we have, of course, indicated the gender of each noun and called your attention to cases of surprising or double genders.

The plan of the volume as a whole has adhered quite closely to that established in *Beyond the Dictionary in Spanish* and followed in *Beyond the Dictionary in Italian*, now renamed *Colloquial Spanish* and *Colloquial Italian* respectively. We hope that you will *not* read the book through in one sitting—only to put it away on a shelf, nor resort to it, as a reference book, only in times of stress. Instead, we hope that you will adopt it as a pleasant and very informal guide and companion.

Pronunciation

The rules of pronunciation in French are a good deal more stable and less liable to exception than they are in English. The comparative lack of tonal accent is a blessing in this respect: there is little need to look for the accented syllable, even in a word as long as—say—*irrémédiablement*. To an English-speaking person, however, used to doing just that, the relative uniformity of stress in French does not come naturally. (You might note, if it is any comfort to you, a tendency to place a light accent on the last syllable comprising a pronounced vowel: *com/MODE, ci/TERNE.*)

Certainly, you have already realized that English is (and sounds) a more concrete, blunt, synthesizing language than French—which is better adapted to abstract discussions and to analysis, being itself analytically constructed. Diplomats have long appreciated the seeming non-bluntness of French; even insults are attenuated by the time the offending adjective is set off by a *de* here, a *du* there.

Italian is often said to be a very musical language. French is more smooth-flowing and less melodic, but certainly has a definite musicality; and while the English ear can often catch it, the English tongue often finds it impossible to reproduce. Compare a news broadcast on the French radio with one on the BBC or, again, on an American network. We might take one example, more homely and perhaps over-simplified.

The British or American housewife will say, making out her shopping list: 'I need potatoes, French beans, cauliflower, radishes . . .'. And not only will her voice become less audible on the unaccented syllables but also, it will drop a few notes on each comma. Whereas when her French counterpart says, *Il me faut des pommes de terre, des haricots verts, un chou-fleur, des radis . . .*, her voice remains even, as regards stress, and rises several notes—expectantly, as it were—at each comma. Hence, schematically, if you will:

'po *ta*   'French   '*cau* li   '*rad*
     toes',   beans',   flow er',   ish es . . .'

                      terre,   verts,   fleur,
des pommes de   des haricots   un chou-

        dis . . .
des ra

To come back to pronunciation *per se*: there is the occasional trap, created by an uncertainty as to how a word is being used; rather like 'read' and 'read' in English. The words *fils* (m. sing.), meaning 'son', rhymes with 'fleece' in English; the word *fils* (m. pl.), meaning 'wires' or 'threads', is pronounced roughly, 'feel'. (See note below on final *s* and *x*.) And in turn, *un fil*, 'wire' or 'thread', is pronounced like *une file*, 'a line' or 'queue'.

As for the words ending in *-ille*, you had best learn by heart which ones pronounce the double *l*—that is, the minority of them—and which do not. *Une fille* does not, or it would sound like *un fil* and *une file*. But *une ville* does pronounce it, and sounds like *vil*. Some common cases of the silent double *l* are these: *bille, cheville, faucille, fille, gorille, grille, lentille, Manille, morille, quille* ('marble', 'ankle', 'sickle', 'girl', 'gorilla', 'gate', 'lentil', 'Manila', 'type of mushroom', 'keel'). And cases of the audible double *l* are: *Lille, mille, tranquille, ville* ('Lille', 'thousand', 'calm', 'city').

Similarly, a few of the words ending in *-il* make the *l* of that ending inaudible: *fusil, gril, sourcil* ('gun', 'grill', 'eyebrow'); and each of these forms a verb by doubling the *l*, which remains (doubly) silent: *fusiller*, *griller*, *sourciller*—'to shoot', 'grill', 'frown'. Whereas *chenil*, *cil*, *fil*, *le Nil*, and *vil* ('kennel', 'eyelash', 'wire', 'the Nile', 'vile') pronounce the *l*. Only two of these latter can form verbs: *filer* ('to spin' or 'run'); and *ciller* ('to blink'), where the double *l* reverts to silence.

Again, the select group of words ending in *-act* or *-ect* seems to cause trouble. Undoubtedly because *un acte* ('act', or 'action') takes an *e* at the end, learners of French, desperate for an analogy, either tack an *e* on to *contact*, *exact*, *infect*, *intact*, *tact* ('contact', 'exact', 'filthy', 'intact', 'tact') even when they are masculine adjectives, or else refuse to pronounce their two final consonants.

Final *s* or *x*—The *s* or *x* which serves to form the plural in French is never pronounced, except when a liaison is required with a vowel or a mute *h* coming immediately after, in which case the *s* or *x* is pronounced with a hard *z* sound: *les avions anglais*, *des gens habiles*, *les beaux arts*. Nor in general, do you pronounce a final *s* anywhere, except for deliberate liaison, as in *pas à pas* (paz a pa).[1] The most comical and classic example of an error in this respect is that committed by the person who mispronounces *un corps* ('body'), 'corpse,' thus transforming it into 'a dead body'! In fact, *corps* is pronounced like *un cor* ('horn'), as in *un cor de chasse*. In words like *un puits* ('a well'), from the Latin *puteus*; *un fonds de commerce* ('good-will'), from the Latin *fundus*; and in verb forms like *je prends* ('I take'), the *ts* or *ds* is silent.

The letter *c*—In general, *c* has a hard *k*-sound when it occurs in front of *a*, *o*, or *u*—*car*, *colle*, *culot* ('coach', 'glue', 'nerve')—or in front of any combination of

[1]Two present-day exceptions which immediately come to mind are *un fils*, as we have seen above, and *un ours*, both of which are pronounced with an audible *s*. Formerly, though, they too abided by the rule of silent *s*.

vowels beginning with one of these: *caille*, *coiffeur*, *couenne*, *coalition*, *cou*, *cuir*, *cœur* ('quail', 'coiffeur', 'rind', 'coalition', 'neck' 'leather', 'heart').[2]

C can be made soft, and become the *s*-sound in front of *a*, *o*, or *u* by the simple addition of *une cédille*: *garçon*, *façade* ('boy', 'façade'). Take the word *macon*, for instance. With a *cédille*, it becomes *un maçon*, 'a mason', and the *c* is pronounced like the *s* in 'mason'. But *Macon*, the name of the town and of the celebrated wine, having no *cédille*, has a *k*-sound. The *c* is naturally soft, without need of a *cédille*, when it occurs in front of *e*, *i*, or *y*: *celte*, *cible*, *cynique* ('Celtic', 'target', 'cynical').

The letter *g*—Like *c*, *g* is hard (the *g* of 'guess' in English) before *a*, *o*, or *u*: *garde*, *gorge*, *guttural*, *gaine*, *goinfre*, *goût*, *guide* ('guard', 'throat', 'guttural', 'girdle', 'guzzler', 'taste', 'guide'). It is soft—pronounced like the *s* in English 'pleasure' or 'leisure'—before *e* or *i*, or *y*: *genou*, *gifle*, *gynécologie* ('knee', 'slap', 'gynæcology'). *G* is never pronounced like the English soft *g* or the English *j*, as in 'George', 'gesture', 'John', 'judge'. The combination *gn*, as in *ignorer*, *guignol* is generally pronounced like *ny* in front of a vowel; that is, like the Spanish *ñ*. But in words of Greek origin, like *agnostique*, you pronounce hard *g* and *n*.

The letter *j* is never pronounced like *j* in the English 'judge', but like the French soft *g* (the *s* in English 'pleasure'): *Jean*, *juge*, *jauge* ('John', 'judge', 'gauge').

The combination *ch* is pronounced like the English *sh*,

[2]In English you have two means of arriving at the *k* sound: hard *c*, or *k* itself. In French the number of words beginning with *k* is drastically limited; and those that do exist usually imitate a foreign word starting with hard *c*—*Komintern*, *Krach* —or a foreign word that is virtually international: *kaki*. The *k* sound in French is also arrived at by *qu* in such words as *quartier*, *antiquité* where the *u* is silent, never given the value of *w* as it is in English 'quarter', 'antiquity'.

as in *chute*; or, in some words of Greek origin, like *k*: *psychiatre*.

And by the way, in words such as *psychiatre*, *psaume* ('psychiatrist', 'psalm') the *p* is pronounced as well as the *s*. Similarly, in *pneumatique*, you pronounce both the *p* and the *n*.

Initial *d* and initial *t* form one of the subtler indices which reveal whether a speaker is French, or a foreigner speaking good French. The difference is that in English, you attack these initial consonants, whereas in French you slide up to them. 'Tea' is palatal and explosive; *le thé* is dental and softer. Similarly, initial *p* is softer in French.

Miscellaneous Notes

Possession—It is worth reminding yourself that the possessive pronoun and adjective agree in number and in gender with the thing possessed, and not, as is the case in English, with the possessor. In English, you say 'his beard'; in French, *sa barbe*, or *la sienne* ('his'), since the word for 'beard' is feminine in French. Or again, 'her handbag' becomes *son sac à main*, and *le sien* ('hers'). The plural in either case is expressed by *ses*: *sa clé, ses clés* ('his *or* her key', 'his *or* her keys'); *son pied, ses pieds* ('his *or* her foot', 'his *or* her feet'). In other words, the possessive pronoun or adjective tells you only about the thing(s) possessed; you need the entire context in order to know who possesses the thing in question.

For the sake of euphony, you will say *son (mon, ton) aventure*, although the word is feminine, simply to avoid the head-on collision of two vowels which would occur if you said *sa aventure, ma eau, ta oreille*.

A word on *les adjectifs substantivés*—In English we find adjectives made into COLLECTIVE nouns only when they denote animate things: 'the rich', 'the poor', 'the guilty', 'the wounded'. In French, however, this technique is used in the singular and for inanimate things too: *le coupable, l'intéressé, le blessé, le bleu*. Notice that when translating such transformed adjectives into English, you have to use an adjective plus a (pro)noun: 'the guilty one', 'the interested party' (or, 'the person concerned'), 'the wounded man', 'the blue one' (or, 'the greenhorn'!, or 'the bruise'!). Further and very common examples are: *Je ferai le nécessaire*: 'I shall take the necessary steps'; and *Il a fait son possible* (or, *l'impossible*): 'He did all he could, all that was humanly possible'. *La pauvre!*, 'Poor girl!'

Adjectives—Many of the more colloquial and vivid adjectives are present participles. For instance: *agaçant*, 'annoying' or 'irritating'; *crevant*, 'deadly tiring' or 'killing' ('funny'); *embêtant*, 'irksome' or 'boring'; *empoisonnant* is similar to *embêtant* but is stronger, meaning 'a dreadful nuisance'; *enquiquinant* is similar to *empoisonnant*; *épatant*, 'marvellous' (a bit out-dated now and replaced by *formidable* etc.); *époustouflant*, like *étonnant*, means 'astonishing'; *exigeant*, 'demanding'; *tordant*, although its literal meaning is 'twisting', is extended to mean 'killingly funny'.

There are, however, numerous examples to prove that this is not necessarily so. 'Boring', for instance, is not *ennuyant*, as you might expect, but *ennuyeux*.

Certain other adjectives may surprise you. In some cases, the corresponding expression in English is stronger, or rarer, or is used differently, or is longer.

fatal—'mortal', 'deadly'; but also and especially, 'fated', 'predestined'
formidable—'stunning', 'smashing', 'tremendous'
inadmissible—'unacceptable', 'not to be stood for'
inouï—'unheard of', 'unbelievable'
insupportable—'unbearable'
mortel—'mortal', 'fatal' (wound); but also, 'deadly boring'
terrible—'terrible', *terrifiant*; but also a compliment: 'stunning', 'forceful', 'with lots of personality', 'a wow'

For more adjectives (and other words) which may catch you off balance, see FALSE FRIENDS at the end of the book.

Some adverbs, too, may need cautious handling. *Drôlement*, for instance. It does indeed mean 'funnily', 'drolly'; but again, 'awfully', 'terribly': *C'est drôlement loin*. 'It's really awfully far away'.

Or again, *rudement* and *méchamment*: 'rudely', 'nastily', but also, 'awfully'. *L'examen était méchamment dur*. 'The exam was terribly tough'.

Suffixes and prefixes all, of course, require careful attention. For example, suffixes such as *-ard*, *-aille(r)* and *-ouille(r)* instantly transform a perfectly sober word into a much more colloquial one, often near slang, and/ or with a derogatory tinge. *Un chauffeur*, 'driver'; *un chauffard*, 'reckless driver'. *Une pantoufle*, 'slipper'; *un pantouflard*, 'a stay-at-home'. *Un moteur*, 'motor'; *un motard*, 'motorcycle policeman'. *Une veine*, 'luck'; *un veinard*, 'lucky chap'. *Tripoter*, 'to finger', 'tinker *or* tamper with'; *tripatouiller*, 'to do this exaggeratedly'.

The suffix *-oter* diminishes the quality of the verb: *vivre*, 'to live'; *vivoter*, 'to live skimpily', 'to struggle along'. *Dormir*, 'to sleep'; *dormoter*, 'to snooze fitfully'.

So do *-acher* and *-icher*, in a more mocking way. *Tomber amoureux de*, 'to fall in love with'; *s'amouracher de*, 'to be infatuated with'.

The superlative *-issime* is easy to overdo: *riche*, rich; *richissime*, ultra rich.

The prefix *archi-* acts the same way, as a prefix, and is (or was) much affected by students.

The principal negative prefixes are *non-* and *im-* or *in-* (*im-* before *b* or *p*, as *imbuvable*, *impensable*: 'undrinkable' or 'unbearable','unthinkable'; *in-* elsewhere, as *incohérent*, *indécent*, *injuste*: 'incoherent', 'indecent', 'unjust'). The negative prefix *un-*, so common in English, is not found in French.

French-English

A

abordable. This means 'approachable', 'within reach', and applies particularly to prices. *Les fraises sont inabordables en cette saison.* 'Strawberries are sky high at this time of year.'

Aborder means 'to approach', a shore or a person, and here *abordable* would mean 'approachable', 'amiable in aspect'. *Certains de nos voisins sont peu abordables.* 'Some of our neighbours are not very friendly.' You are of course familiar with *d'abord*, 'first of all'; and with *de prime abord*, 'at first glance'. And whereas *par-dessus bord* does mean 'overboard', 'All aboard!' must be translated by *Messieurs, Dames, en voiture!*[1]

abruti. A very common adjective, often taken as a noun, from the verb *abrutir*, meaning 'to daze' or 'make stupid'. The adjective has a distinctly pejorative tinge when applied to someone else—*Espèce d'abruti!* 'Blockhead!' 'Big dunce!'—but you can apply it in all innocence to yourself: *Au bout de dix heures de travail d'une traite, je suis totalement abruti.* 'After working ten hours at a stretch, I'm in a real fog, I feel washed out.' The work itself could be called *abrutissant*.

accord (m). Roughly, any sort of agreement or harmony, from cultural to grammatical. *D'accord*, perhaps less desirable than *entendu* or *c'est entendu*, is the commonest way of saying, 'all right', 'OK'. *Je suis d'accord avec lui.* 'I agree with him.' *v.* also CORDE.

affaire (f). 'A bargain.' *Faire une (bonne) affaire*, 'to make (get) a bargain'. *Faire une mauvaise affaire*, 'to make a bad bargain'.

'An affair', 'a matter': *Il m'a longuement entretenu de toute l'affaire.* 'He spoke to me at length about the whole matter.'

You will recall that in the plural, *affaires* means '(big) business', as in, *un homme d'affaires*, a businessman'.—*Comment vont les affaires?—Plutôt bien.* 'How's business?—Pretty good.' An *affairiste* is an 'unscrupulous businessman'. *Les affaires* can also be one's 'belongings' (*v.* JUSTE): *Ranger ses affaires*, 'to put one's things away'.

The meaning of *s'affairer* (*autour de quelque chose* or *de quelqu'un*) goes off on a slight tangent: 'to bustle about'.

---

[1]Strictly speaking, the stationmaster (*le chef de gare*) should say '*Mesdames, Mesdemoiselles, Messieurs*', but in practice, hardly anyone but lecturers, or announcers on the radio, will be so formal.

The English, 'affair', or 'love-affair', is translated by *liaison* (f). *Une affaire de cœur* is simply 'a matter of the heart'.

afficher. A transitive verb, meaning 'to post notices' (*une affiche*). *Défense d'Afficher Loi du 29 Juillet 1881* ('Billposting forbidden by the law of 29 July 1881') is still to be found in big black letters on countless walls in Paris. *Une affiche*, 'a poster'.

Afficher, in a more *familier* usage, means 'to flaunt', 'show off': *Elle n'hésite pas à s'afficher partout avec ce type-là.* 'She is quite shameless about going everywhere with that fellow.' *Rester à l'affiche* is, where a film or play is concerned, 'to continue running (playing, showing)'.

affranchir. First of all, 'to free', 'to liberate'. *La question de l'affranchissement des esclaves fut à la base du conflit.* 'The issue of emancipation for the slaves was one of the root causes of the war.' More frequently it means 'to pay postage' on a letter or package. *Une carte pour l'Italie est affranchie à un franc dix.* 'A post card to Italy needs a 1F10 stamp.'

S'affranchir sur quelque chose or *être affranchi sur quelque chose*, is a slangy way of saying, *se mettre (être) au courant*: 'to be up to date'. It follows that *affranchir quelqu'un sur quelque chose*, means 'to bring someone up to date on something'.

agrandir. 'To enlarge'. *Un agrandissement* is any sort of enlargement. This is the word you need when you bring in negatives to the photographer's to have them blown up: *Je voudrais trois agrandissements de chaque négatif, 18 sur 24.* 'Will you please make three enlargements of each negative, 7 by 10 inches.'

En faisant reculer cette cloison j'ai pu agrandir mon salon. 'By having this partition moved back, I was able to make my living-room bigger.'

agréer. Not really 'to agree' (v. ACCORD) but 'to approve', 'grant', 'accept'. *Agréer une demande*, 'to grant a request' or 'act favourably upon an application'. *Agrément* (m) therefore is either 'consent' or, more often, 'pleasure' (*un jardin d'agrément*, 'pleasure garden'), but rarely 'agreement'.

ah bon. One of the most versatile little phrases in the language. Your voice plays on it as on an instrument, making it mean 'Oh really?' or 'Oh well in that case . . .', or 'Why didn't you say so in the first place?' Surprise, disbelief, understanding, consent (grudging or otherwise).

aïe! 'Ow!' 'Ouch!' 'That hurts!'

aimant (m). 'A magnet.' And the verb is either *aimanter* or *magnétiser*. *Magnétiser* (or, *hypnotiser*) *quelqu'un* means, 'to hypnotize someone'.

air (m). *Avoir l'air* can be a useful way of avoiding *sembler*, *paraître*. 'He looked tired.' *Il avait l'air fatigué.* 'She would seem to be wealthy.' *Elle a l'air d'être riche.*

aller. *Allez, allons, va!* As you can see, we want to stress the exclamatory uses of this verb, which, just like 'go' in English, lends itself to a whole list of expressions. Depending on the tone of voice, *allez!* can mean encouragement or derision: 'come on!' or else, 'go on!', 'come off it!' and so on. *Allons allons, soyons raisonnables:* 'Come on now, let's not overdo it!'—or any number of translations, depending on the context. *Va!*, especially, may be said to equate with 'there!' when it comes at the end of a sentence: *Ah, ne te fâche pas, va!*, or *Bon, fais ce que tu voudras, va!* The tone here is conciliatory or soothing.

aller (m). When buying a travel ticket, you specify *un aller-retour*, which is 'a return ticket' (US: 'round trip') or, *un aller simple*, 'a single (or one-way) ticket'.

ampoule (f). A word which you'll find in several contexts. *Une ampoule au talon* is 'a blister on your heel'. But when the doctor prescribes *une ampoule matin et soir* for stomach trouble, you are to drink 'a tube-full of liquid medicine twice a day'. The transparent glass *ampoule* is an exceedingly common way of packaging medicines in France, and you have to be careful not to saw off the two ends of it into the glass from which you're going to drink it! There are *ampoules injectables* (for injections or rectal use) as well as *ampoules buvables*. And of course there is the *ampoule électrique*, the 'electric light bulb'. If you're looking for a 'standard (US: floor) lamp', stand and all, you mean *un lampadaire*; 'a chandelier' is *un lustre*. Be careful: *un chandelier* in French means·'a branched candlestick'; a plain one is *un bougeoir*. *Une lampe* is 'a table-lamp'; *une lampe de poche* or *lampe électrique*, 'an electric torch' (US: 'flashlight'). And 'a wall-lamp' or 'sconce' is *une applique*. Conveniently enough, 'a candelabra' is *un candélabre*.

amuse-gueule (m). Usually used in the plural, *amuse-gueules*: the various salty or savoury things that accompany cocktails. A perfectly acceptable term, though *gueule* (f) by itself is a vulgar term for 'face'.

anglo-saxon. Loosely extended to mean 'English-speaking', as in *les pays anglo-saxons*.

animateur, -trice. Person in charge of leading or livening up a discussion or activity, particularly in a *village de vacances* or *un centre de loisirs*, or *dans un jeu télévisé*, a 'TV quiz show'.

anticipation (f). Often used synonymously with *la science-fiction: un roman d'anticipation*.

antiquité (f). In the singular, the word means 'ancient times', 'classical times', 'antiquity'. *Il se prend pour un héros de l'antiquité.* 'He thinks he's one of the epic heroes of ancient Greece.' In the plural, it means 'antiques', and you will see *antiquités* or *objets anciens* written above antique dealers' shops. The dealer himself is *l'antiquaire*.

appareil (m). Literally any apparatus, any machine. *On vient d'inventer un appareil génial pour les plongées en grande profondeur.* 'They've just invented an ingenious machine for the purpose of deep-sea diving.' Most often, this will mean 'the telephone': *Attention, tu as laissé l'appareil décroché.* 'Be careful, you left the phone off the hook.' (*v.* the chapter on THE TELEPHONE.)

Or again, it may mean 'a camera': *un appareil photo.* Be careful of the word *caméra* (f): it means only a 'motion picture camera' and so could be something of a *Faux Ami* for you.

appel (m). From *appeler*, of course, 'to call' or 'name'. Particular note should be taken of *appel téléphonique*, meaning 'a call' especially from the point of view of the person being called, or in official language, as when you telephone from the post office. *Communication* (f) would be the term more likely used by the person calling.

Faire appel à (la bonté de quelqu'un) is 'to appeal to', 'to call upon'. *Lancer un appel* is 'to launch an appeal', in the sense of a campaign. The English 'to appeal' can have as many different translations as there are contexts: *plaire, séduire, tenter, attirer, être attachant,* even *dire.* 'Let's not go to see that film, it doesn't appeal to me.' *Ce film-là ne me dit rien, n'allons pas le voir.* 'The little puppy looked at me so appealingly I just had to buy him.' *Le petit chiot avait un regard si attachant que ça a été plus fort que moi: je l'ai acheté.*

And of course there is *appellation contrôlée*, or 'registered trade-name', essential to the vocabulary of all wine *connaisseurs.*

appoint (m). *Faire l'appoint*, 'to have the exact change'. A notice in the bus will read: *Vous êtes priés de faire l'appoint.* 'Please get the right change ready.'

appointements (m. pl.). Another but less common term for *salaire* (m). *Ses appointements ne sont pas très élevés mais il a aussi des avantages en nature.* 'His pay isn't much but he also has some compensations in kind.' *Le salaire* is 'salary'; if you mean 'wages', then you say *gages* (m. pl.), which has the general meaning of 'hire', as well: *un tueur à gages*, 'a hired gunman'. *Honoraires* (m. pl.) are 'non-regular payments *or* fees'; what you pay *l'avocat, le dentiste, le docteur, le conférencier, le traducteur*, and so on. Also, in speaking of medical care, you can simply say, *je paie tant la visite* (either your visits to the practitioner's office or his visits *à domicile*) or *tant les soins*. A payment on a car or anything else bought *à crédit* is *un versement.* 'The deposit' which you leave in the beginning is called *les arrhes* (q.v.). *Pour mon nouveau poste de télévision, j'ai versé 300 francs d'arrhes, et le solde en 4 versements trimestriels.* 'I paid 300 francs down on my new TV set and the rest in 4 quarterly instalments.'

Soldes (m. pl.) is the term for 'clearance sales', while *solde* (f) means 'military pay'.

après-ski (m. pl.). *Les après-ski*, in spite of their name, are sometimes worn in town by children or teenagers, especially since *les sports* *d'hiver* (q.v.) have become so popular. They are simply ankle-high or knee-high boots made of real or imitation fur, nylon, etc.

arête (f). 'A fish bone'; never called *un os*, which is the bone of anything but fish.

armements (m. pl.). 'Weapons', 'arms'. *La course aux armements*, 'arms race'. *Négociations SALT,* 'SALT talks'.

armoire (f) **à glace.** Since this means 'a wardrobe', you may be puzzled the first time you hear a man described as *une véritable armoire à glace*: yet this is a very common way of saying that the person is very big and strong, square built.

arranger. 'To arrange', of course, but much more often 'to fix', 'patch up', 'improve', 'decorate', 'repair'. *Son studio est gentiment arrangé.* 'His (one-room) flat is fixed up handsomely.' *Laissez donc, je vais arranger ça.* 'Never mind, I'll take care of that.'

Special note should be taken of *arrangeant(e)* and *arrangement* (m). The adjective is akin to *serviable* (*v.* SERVIR) and means the opposite of 'fussy' or 'unco-operative', that is, 'accommodating', 'helpful'. *Il s'est montré vraiment trés arrangeant.* 'He proved really most co-operative.' And while *un arrangement* can be a musical one, done by *un arrangeur*, very often it is an understanding between two parties, and the expression, *un arrangement à l'amiable* is quite common—thank goodness: it means 'a civilized settlement of a dispute, without going to court'. *L'autre conducteur a consenti à un arrangement à l'amiable.*

arrêté (m). *Un arrêté préfectoral, ministériel*, etc. is 'a decree', for which another and less surprising word is, roughly speaking, *un décret* or *un décret-loi*.

arrhes (f. pl.). This is the deposit which you pay down (*verser des arrhes*) on something you are buying on short- or long-term credit; the sum yet to be paid is *le solde*. But the deposit you pay on a bottle is *la consigne* (q.v.).

arriver. 'To arrive', 'to come', of course, in the literal sense. But when *quelque chose arrive à quelqu'un*, the meaning is 'to happen'. 'A funny thing happened to me on the way to the office' would be, *il m'est arrivé un drôle de truc* (or, *quelque chose de bizarre*) *en allant au bureau. Malgré son grand âge, il lui arrive encore de faire cinq km à pied.* 'Old as he is, none the less he sometimes walks five kilometres.'

Qu'est-ce qui vous arrive? may often mean *qu'avez-vous?*: 'what's happened?' 'what's the matter?'

'To manage' may be another meaning, as in *Je n'arrive pas à fermer les volets.* 'I can't manage to get the shutters closed.'

When someone rings your doorbell, you say '(I'm) coming'. The Frenchman, however, does not say *je viens*, but: *j'arrive.* Most especially, the garçon at the *café, terrasse*, or *restaurant* where you have seated yourself will call *j'arrive!* from somewhere in the depths of the establishment to assure you that your presence has not gone unnoticed.

Un arriviste is *un ambitieux*, often unscrupulous and always unabashed about his determination to make his way up the social ladder; the science is *l'arrivisme*.

Arrivée (f) at the railway station or the airport means simply 'Arrivals', as opposed to *Départ* (m), 'Departures'.

Un arrivage is 'a delivery' of vegetables, fruit, or fish.

arrondir. 'To round out *or* off'. *Je te dois 99F30, on va arrondir à 100F.*

Il donne des petits cours pour arrondir son mois. 'He gives private lessons to eke out his income.'

Arrondir les angles, 'to be conciliatory', 'avoid arguments', 'have a softening influence'.

arroser. 'To water', as plants, with *un arrosoir* ('watering can'). A more colloquial meaning is, literally, 'to wine'!—'to celebrate with a good bottle'. *Mais c'est une nouvelle merveilleuse! Ça s'arrose!* 'That's splendid news! We must celebrate!'

Un café arrosé is a coffee into which you have poured some cognac or calvados.

And to distribute tips lavishly, give hand-outs, is also *arroser*.

article (m). Any 'article', grammatical, journalistic, or other. But you should be careful of the special and restrictive meaning of *articles de Paris*, written over shops selling small luxury items which represent the traditional French 'chic' and elegance, *les petits riens* which can transform a staid suit or a dull dress; hence, gloves, lace, perfumes, scarves and so on.

And when you hear that someone is *à l'article de la mort* you should know that he is 'at death's doorstep'.

Faire l'article pour quelque chose is a faintly pejorative expression, implying a certain amount of *boniment* (q.v.) and meaning 'to give a high-pressure sales talk for the thing (*or* person) in question', 'to vaunt' its qualities. *Mais oui, mon vieux, inutile de me faire l'article pour ton tourne-vis perfectionné, je le connais déjà.* 'It's all right old man, I know all about your perfected screwdriver, you don't have to convince me.'

artisanat (m). The work done by *un artisan*, the self-employed individual craftsman; or the class of such craftsmen. *L'artisanat se perd*, as people often moan today: 'individual craftsmanship is harder and harder to find'.

asparagus (m). If you ask for *asparagus* at the greengrocer's (*le marchand de primeurs* or *le marchand des quatre saisons*), you may receive a strange look and be sent next door to *le fleuriste*, because this is the word for the 'ferns' (actually, 'asparagus leaves') which accompany a bouquet. If you want simple greenery with your *tulipes*, you ask for *un peu de feuillage*. And if you really want 'asparagus', the vegetable, then it's *asperges* (f. pl.) you're looking for (note the plural in French).

Asperger means 'to sprinkle' or 'splash'.

assez. A word that bears looking at from more than one angle. It means 'enough': *il y en a assez*, 'there's enough of it'. *Il gagne assez.* 'He earns enough.' But it also means 'fairly' or 'rather' and *il gagne assez bien*, 'he earns a fair amount (rather well)', does not necessarily mean the same as *il gagne assez*.

In the sense of 'somewhat' *assez* can be replaced by *plutôt*: *elle est plutôt jolie*. If you're talking about quality or preference, then you must replace *assez* by *plutôt*: *Elle est plutôt jolie que laide.* 'She's more pretty than not.' *Je préfère rester à la maison plutôt que (de) sortir avec lui.* 'I'd rather stay at home than go out with him.'

En avoir assez de quelque chose is, literally, 'to have enough of something', 'to be fed up with it'. *En avoir marre* is an inelegant but common way of saying the same thing.

astuce (f). The dictionary meaning is limited to 'craft', 'ruse'. But in actual daily use, the meaning is extended to 'the tricky thing to do', 'the way out', 'the solution'. *Une simple astuce suffit pour résoudre ce problème.* 'All you need, to solve this problem, is to know a simple trick.'—*Je n'y arrive pas.*—*Question d'astuce!* 'I can't do it.'—'Find the gimmick!'

Une astuce is also a 'play on words'; one type is *le calembour*, 'pun'. *Astucieux*, meaning 'clever' or 'inventive', can be applied to things or to persons. *C'est très astucieux, cette chaise qui se replie.* 'That folding chair is ingenious.' *Ma couturière est vraiment astucieuse: elle a de ces trouvailles même pour mes vieilles robes démodées!* 'My dressmaker is so clever: she has such marvellous ideas even for my old dresses that have gone out of fashion!'

attenant. 'Adjoining', 'communicating', as two rooms or houses.

attirer. 'To attract', i.e. 'to draw', without necessarily being attractive (*v.* ATTRAYANT). *Il a attiré mon attention sur cette vieille maison fort attrayante.* 'He drew my attention to that very attractive old house.' *Ce tissu attire la poussière.* 'This cloth attracts dust.'

attrayant. 'Attractive'; rarely found in the form of the archaic infinitive, *attraire*, which can also be avoided by the use of the noun, *attrait* (m). *La montagne a un attrait irrésistible pour moi.* 'The mountains have an irresistible attraction for me.' 'To attract attention' requires *attirer* (q.v.). Today *attrayant* is sometimes replaced by *attractif*, an example of Franglais (see section on same).

auberge (f). 'An inn' or 'hostel' (a youth hostel is *une auberge de jeunesse*, or *AJ*); also, a name much affected by restaurants which deliberately set out to be quaint or old-fashioned. More likely than not, they will call themselves *l'Auberge du Cheval Blanc* or *du Coq d'Or*.

You might pay particular attention to *pas encore sorti de*

l'auberge, a colloquial expression which, surprisingly enough, means 'not yet out of hot water', 'still in trouble'. *Avec un pneu crevé, ils ne sont pas encore sortis de l'auberge.* 'They're in a real fix with that flat tyre.'

au-delà. 'Beyond'; the opposite is *en-deçà*. *L'au-delà* is 'the beyond', hence, 'the next life' and contrasts with *ici-bas*, 'here below', hence, 'this life on earth'.

au diable. Used by itself, this gives the idea of excessive distance. *Vous n'allez pas jusque là pour lui rendre son livre? C'est au diable (vauvert).* 'You're not going all the way there just to give him back his book! It's at the end of the earth.'

Aller au diable is something else again. *Si ce type t'embête encore, tu n'as qu'à lui dire d'aller au diable.* 'If that fellow bothers you again, just tell him to go to the devil.'

And *faire quelque chose à la diable*, 'to do something carelessly, any old way'.

auditeur, -trice. Listener, member of (radio) audience, *l'auditoire* (m). (The television equivalent is *téléspectateur, -trice*.) *Ecouteur* (m) will not do in this context, as *les écouteurs* are 'earphones', used for listening to one's *chaîne* (f) *haute-fidélité* (or, *chaîne hi-fi*).

aussi. You are familiar with the meaning of 'too', 'also'. But for that reason, you may sometimes be tripped up by a different meaning, appearing at the start of a sentence or phrase and usually requiring an inverted verb-subject order afterwards: 'therefore', 'in accordance' (with what has just preceded). *Sa famille s'en va, aussi doit-il la suivre.* 'Since his family is going away, he (accordingly) has to follow them.'

autrement. 'Otherwise', '(or) else', when used with a verb. *Fais vite, autrement je terminerai avant toi.* 'Hurry up, or else I'll finish before you do.' *Autrement dit*, 'in other words'.

'Much more', or 'very', when used with an adjective, to express a comparison. *Cet examen était autrement plus difficile que le premier.* 'This exam was much tougher than the first.'

avec. Colloquially, the prepositions *avec* and *sans* are used in an adjectival or adverbial sense. During the Second World War, *les jours avec et les jours sans* referred to the days with or without meat, sugar, and so on. *Ayant acheté un nouveau blouson, il est venu avec.* 'He'd got a new jacket and brought it along.'

avenant (m). Most commonly heard in the expression, *et tout à l'avenant*: 'and so on', 'in the same way', 'similarly'. *Ces gens-là aiment le faux partout, des bustes 'anciens', guéridons 'Louis XV', et tout à l'avenant.* 'People like that go in for fake this and imitation that everywhere, "antique" busts, little "Louis XV" tables, and so on, straight down the line.'

Ajouter un avenant is 'to add a clause *or* a rider to a contract'.

avoir (m). *Un avoir* is a sum with which you are credited.
   Se faire avoir (or, *se faire rouler*) is a sad little phrase: 'to be taken in' or 'for a ride', 'to be had'. It follows of course that *avoir quelqu'un* means 'to get the better of someone', 'to take him for a ride'; and you can use it in teasing: *ah, je vous ai eu, hein?* 'You see, I fooled you, didn't I?'

avortement (m). 'Abortion'. *Se faire avorter*, 'to have (get) an abortion'. The official term is *interruption* (f) *volontaire de grossesse (IVG)*. *Avortement spontané* is the medical term for *une fausse couche*: 'miscarriage'.

B

bagage (m). Two things which you can never notice too often about this word are: the spelling, and the fact that it is generally used in the plural, *les bagages*, when given the tangible sense of suitcases, trunks and what not. If you want it to mean 'mental equipment', one's 'stock of knowledge', then you revert to the singular. *Il faut que je fasse passer mes bagages à la douane.* 'I have to put my luggage through customs.' *Dans ce domaine-là il a un bagage considérable.* 'He's very knowledgeable in that field.'

baiser. Careful; this verb can be very crude. Until the nineteenth century, it meant 'to kiss', and it still does, when followed by a noun as a direct object: *il lui a baisé le front, les mains, les lèvres*, 'he kissed her on the forehead, the hands, the lips', or in the phrase, *il lui a fait le baise-main*, 'he kissed her hand'. But *il l'a baisée* is the equivalent of using a four-letter word in English to express, 'he made love to her'. If you simply mean 'he kissed her', you say, *il l'a embrassée*.

bande (f) **dessinée.** 'Strip cartoon (US: cartoon strip)' or 'comic strip', abbreviated *BD*. 'A comic book' is *un illustré*. 'A cartoon film', *dessin* (m) *animé*.

banaliser. A recent verb, meaning 'to make something commonplace (banal)'. *Banaliser l'avortement. Banaliser l'évasion, les voyages à l'étranger. Une voiture de police banalisée*, 'an unmarked police car'.

banlieue (f). 'The suburbs'; and you may distinguish between *la proche banlieue*, 'the nearer or immediate suburbs', and *la grande banlieue*, 'the outlying ones'. *Un banlieusard* is the suburbanite who commutes via *le train de banlieue. J'habite en banlieue.* 'I live in the suburbs.'

baratin or **barattin** (m). Like *boniment* (q.v.), quite *familier*, but minus the implication of making an effort to sell. It means 'hot air', 'loose, inconsequential talk', 'a spiel'. *Quand il s'agit de baratiner, il n'a pas son égal.* 'When it comes to giving you a long spiel, there's nobody like him.'

barrage (m). 'A road block.' *Sur la route de Senlis, nous avons été retardés par un barrage de gendarmerie.* 'We were delayed on our way to Senlis by a road block the police had set up.' Another way of expressing the same thing is to say *la route était barrée.*

Or again, 'a dam'. *Le nouveau barrage a créé un fort joli lac.* 'The new dam has created a very pretty lake.'

bassin (m). With **bassine** (f), this word seems to form one of those pairs which people have trouble keeping straightened out, like *la paillasse* ('straw mattress' or 'draining-board of a sink') and *le paillasson* ('doormat'). *Un bassin* is *une pièce d'eau*: 'a pool' or 'pond'; the humble *bassine* is *une cuvette*, or 'wash-basin'.

bémol (m). 'Flat', not in the sense of a lodging, but in music. 'A sharp' is *un dièse*. The English musical scale is, in French, Do Ré Mi Fa Sol La Si Do (C D E F G A B C). *Majeur* and *mineur* are certainly obvious, except in so far as *majeur* also means 'of legal age' (18 in France), and as *mineur* may signify 'under legal age' or, when a masculine noun, 'a miner'.

bénéfice (m). 'Benefit', but also, just as often, 'profit'. A word which learners of French seem reluctant to use: perhaps it looks or sounds too feminine. Something of a *Faux Ami*.

bêtise (f). Any mother of very young children is bound to use this word at least once a day: *Tu ne fais que des bêtises!* 'You're always getting into trouble, doing something you shouldn't'.' But adults can say it just as well of themselves or other adults: *J'ai fait une bêtise* could often be translated, 'I could kick myself!' In which case you may find *des Bêtises de Cambrai* soothing—rather sharp mints.

bibelot (m). Any small (decorative) object, trinket, gew-gaw, usually useless, sometimes antique (*bibelots anciens*), and collected or given as a present. The word takes on a slightly derisive tinge when used by someone who doesn't go in for such things.

Bic (m). 'A ball-point pen'. A trade name which has become identified with the article itself whatever its make, just as in the case of *un Kodak* and *un Frigidaire*. *Stylo* (m) *à bille* is the generic name.

billet (m). 'A note'; 'a bank note'; and the normal word for a 'travel *or* theatre ticket'. *Un ticket* does exist, but applies only to municipal bus or Paris Métro tickets, and to meal tickets at student restaurants. 'Traffic ticket', *contravention* (f).

billion (m). No longer means what 'billion' still means in the United States, i.e. 'a thousand millions'; this is expressed by *milliard* (m). No, since 1948 *un billion* has meant, as in the U.K., 'a million millions': 1,000,000,000,000. *Un billion* is more commonly called *mille milliards*.

blague (f). 'A joke'; a more colloquial term than *une plaisanterie*, and usually a less verbal sort of joke. *Blague à part* (or, to be still more *familier*, *blague dans le coin*), means 'no kidding', 'no joke', 'seriously'. *Sans blague!* would be your answer to someone else's startling statement.

Pipe smokers should know that *une blague à tabac* is 'a tobacco pouch'.

bleu (m). 'A black and blue mark' or 'bruise'; or again, 'a workman's overalls' (*v.* COMBINAISON), *un bleu de travail*.

Also, 'blue cheese': *le bleu d'Auvergne*, *le bleu des Causses*.

'To feel *or* be blue', or 'to have the blues', is *avoir le cafard* or *être cafardeux*, *avoir la déprime*.

But the blues in jazz are never called *les cafards!*, nor *les bleus*: simply, *les blues* (pronounced blooze).

Speaking of colours, there is a whole palette of expressions, such as:

être gris: *être saoul*, 'to be drunk', 'half-seas over'.
être marron: *se faire avoir*, 'to be taken in'.
un avocat marron: 'a dishonest lawyer'.
un jaune: 'a strike-breaker'.
le maillot jaune: 'the leading cyclist in the Tour de France'.
le gros rouge (*qui tache*): 'ordinary cheap wine'.
se mettre au vert: *se reposer à la campagne*, 'to relax in the country'.
être blanc comme un linge: 'to be white as a sheet'.
(*v.* also COULEURS).

blouson noir (m). The French equivalent of the 'juvenile delinquent' and he is named after his black leather jacket. An extension of this, *le blouson doré*, refers to a *fils à papa*, or 'rich spoiled boy', who goes to the bad.

bobo. The baby word for 'hurt', 'pain'. *Où as-tu bobo?* 'Where does it hurt you?' *Mais non, n'aie pas peur, ça ne fait pas bobo.* 'Don't be afraid, it doesn't hurt.' (Even adults may sometimes say *il n'y a pas de bobo*, a very informal substitute for *il n'y a pas de mal*: 'there's no harm done, nothing serious'.)

There is of course an infinity of baby words built on the same double-syllable principle. *Lolo, le lait*; *nounou, la nurse* or *la gouvernante*; *nounours, l'ours en peluche*, 'teddy-bear'; *dodo, le sommeil*. *Fais un gros dodo*, 'sleep tight'.

boisson (f). The general word for 'beverage', 'drink'. If you want a drink (of something alcoholic, especially), you had best say, *je voudrais un verre de . . .* or, if you're really up on your Franglais, *un drink*. On the menu, *boisson en plus* (or, *en sus*) warns you that your beverage is not included in the price of the meal. Once you have ordered your main dish, *le garçon* or *la serveuse* will ask, *Et comme boisson s'il vous plaît?* 'And what will you have to drink?'

The choice will be between wine and mineral water, or possibly beer; you must not expect a request for coffee or tea *with* the meal to be heard with equanimity. . . . In other contexts, *la boisson* and *boire* can, just like 'drink' in English, refer specifically to alcohol. *Il boit un peu trop*, 'he drinks a bit too much'. *Quand je l'ai vu hier soir, il était pris de boisson.* 'When I saw him last night, he was drunk.' *Etre porté sur la boisson*, 'to be given to drink'.

boîte (f). Any sort of box, from *boîte de conserve*, 'tin of food', to *boîte aux lettres. Mettre une lettre à la boîte*, 'to post a letter', 'put it in the pillarbox' (US: 'mailbox'), as distinct from *mettre une lettre à la poste*, 'to take a letter to the post office'.

Une grosse boîte is a familiar term for *une grosse maison*, 'a big *or* important business firm'.

But *une boîte (de nuit)* is 'a night club'.

La boîte à ordures is the individual dust-bin or garbage-pail which you empty into the collective *poubelle* (f) or *vide-ordures* (m) of your building each evening. The dustman or trash collector is *l'éboueur*.

Mettre quelqu'un en boîte, 'to hoax someone', 'pull his leg'.

boniment (m). 'Hot air' or 'propaganda', a lot of jabber signifying nothing or including a good deal of exaggeration. *Bonimenter* is the verb (*v.* also ARTICLE). *Faire du boniment* can mean specifically 'to give a lot of sales talk', 'to push something'.

bonneterie (f). You find almost everything (for women) but bonnets in a *bonneterie*: stockings (*des bas*), and panty-hose or tights (*collants*); the extension to *gaines, jupons* and *soutiens-gorge* ('girdles', 'half-slips' and 'bras') and *lingerie* in general is easy, and may go so far as *maillots de bain, pantalons, corsages, 'pulls', chemises de nuit, robes de chambre* ('swimsuits', 'slacks', 'blouses', 'sweaters *or* jumpers', 'nightgowns', 'bathrobes' or 'dressing-gowns') and—as near as you'll get to a bonnet— *foulards*.

boom (m). Used in financial circles to mean a 'boom'; while in student circles *une boom* or *boum* or *une surboom* or *surboum* means 'a dance', 'a soirée'; it is along the same lines as *une surprise partie* or *surprise party* [*sic*]. An evening of dancing and drinking, usually at someone's house.

bouger. You know that this means 'to move', 'to budge'. But when you buy a table-cloth, for instance, you are wise to ask, *Est-ce qu'elle bougera au lavage?* 'Will it shrink in the wash?' a more colloquial term than *rétrécir*.

Avoir la bougeotte is a different matter: 'to be restless'. Rather *familier*.

bougie (f). The ordinary candle, more ordinary (*grossière*) than *une chandelle*, which is longer and thinner. Neither word suits the taper used in the church, which is *un cierge*.

When the garage mechanic tells you that you have *une bougie qui est morte*, he is referring to a spark(ing-) plug! (*v.* the chapter on CARS.)

Une vente à la bougie is, like *une vente aux enchères*, 'an auction sale'. The 'Going—Going—Gone' may be expressed by the successive extinguishing of three candles placed in front of the auctioneer, *le commissaire-priseur*.

bougnat (m). A feature of the French urban landscape that is fast disappearing: neighbourhood retailer of coal, butane gas, and wood. Usually a den of a shop with *un comptoir* which makes it something of a *bistro* (or *bistrot*) as well, and you will see *café-bois-charbons* written over the door. Legend had it that every other *Auvergnat* who came to settle in Paris became *un bougnat*.

bouquet (m). 'A bouquet' or 'clump' of trees as well as flowers. Also familiar to wine lovers, as the 'aroma of wine'.

C'est le bouquet! 'That's the end!' 'That's torn it!' See also, in the same vein, COMBLE, COMMODE, COMPLET.

bourratif. Definitely colloquial, and meaning 'filling', as applied to a dish or course. *Les spaghetti sont très bourratifs.* 'Spaghetti is very filling.'

By the way, when at table your hostess urges you to take another helping, don't try to build an analogy on *bourratif* and say, *merci, je suis bourré(e)*. But above all, you must never say, *je suis plein(e)*, since *être pleine* applies only to animals and means, 'to be big with young'. There are several polite unaffected ways of saying, 'no, thank you'. *Merci, c'est délicieux mais je n'ai plus faim*; or, *merci, je me suis déjà bien servi*; or simply, *non merci*. You may also run across, *je ne peux plus*, but this is reserved for occasions when you know your *convives*, your 'fellow guests', really very well.

bout (m). One of those little words which lends itself to a dozen expressions. Let us recall particularly: *je suis à bout, je n'en peux plus*, 'I'm all done in, exhausted'.

Ça fait un petit bout d'ici. 'It's a fair distance from here.' *Nous avons fait un petit bout de chemin ensemble.* 'We travelled a little way together.'

If you want to say 'at the end of the room', *à la fin* will never do; you need, *au bout de la pièce*, or *dans le fond*.

Un bout of something is 'a bit', 'a scrap'. *Il n'a pas pu nous proposer mieux qu'un petit bout du gigot de la veille.* 'He had nothing more to offer than a scrap of yesterday's leg of lamb.' *Elle a mangé du bout des lèvres.* 'She just nibbled.'

But *un petit bout de chou* belongs in a non-culinary context; this corresponds to 'little lamb', 'sweetie pie', i.e. 'a baby'.

A bout de bras, 'at arm's length'.

Joindre les deux bouts, 'to make both ends meet'.

boutique (f). 'Shop'; as distinct from *un magasin*, which is bigger, and *le grand magasin*, which is a 'department store'. *Parler boutique*, 'to talk shop'. The shopkeeper is *le boutiquier*.

box (m). Not 'a box' (*v.* BOÎTE), but that much-sought-after convenience, especially in Paris: 'a garage', 'a private and covered parking place', often bought or rented with one's flat. The plural is *boxes*.

La boxe, despite its gender, is the masculine sport of boxing; 'a boxer' is *un boxeur*.

brancher. 'To plug in' an electrical appliance. *Débrancher* is 'to unplug'. *La prise* and *le fil* are, respectively, 'the plug' and 'the wire'. 'A fuse' is *un plomb*, q.v. (*v.* also AMPOULE).

A branch of a large store is *une succursale*, sometimes abbreviated on awnings, stationery, etc. as *Succ.*

bribes (f. pl.). Always used in the plural. Something of a false friend, perhaps, since it means 'scraps', 'odd leftovers' (of food, cloth, even conversation overheard), and has nothing to do with the English word 'bribe' which is *un pot-de-vin*.

bricole (f). Any thing or affair of minimal importance. *Bricoler* means 'to potter *or* mess about', 'to do-it-yourself', 'make something' or 'put something together'. *Un bricoleur* is the person addicted to doing-it-himself, *le bricolage*.

brin (m). A word that lends itself to many figurative uses. You have not only *un brin d'herbe*, 'a blade of grass'; but *un brin de conversation* (or, *de causette*), 'a chat'; and *un brin de bon sens*, usually used in the negative: *elle n'a pas un brin de bon sens*, 'she hasn't a scrap of common sense'. *Un beau brin de fille*, 'a fine strapping girl'.

brosser. 'To brush', of course. But *brosser un tableau* has the strictly figurative idea of sketching the general outline of a situation. *Notre conférencier d'aujourd'hui va vous brosser un tableau de la conjoncture actuelle.* 'Today's lecturer will outline the present situation *or* state of affairs for you.'

bureau (m). Collectively, the 'officers of a committee', organization, etc. Also, 'a desk'. Also, 'an office', except that of a notary (*une étude*), and that of a doctor, dentist, or barrister (US: lawyer), *un cabinet*. Among the more common office items are:

agrafe (f): 'staple'.
agrafeuse (f): 'stapler'.
Bic (m) (registered trade name): 'ball-point pen'.
bloc (m) (*sténo*): '(shorthand) tablet *or* pad (of paper)'.
buvard (m): 'blotter'; *papier buvard* (m): 'blotting-paper'.
cahier (m): 'notebook'.
calendrier (m): 'calendar'.
cartouche (f) *d'encre*: 'ink cartridge'.
chemise (f): 'Manila *or* plastic folder'.
ciseaux (m. pl.): 'scissors'.
classeur (m): 'filing cabinet'.
clavier (m): 'keyboard' (of typewriter).
comptabilité (f): 'accounting department'.

comptable (m): 'accountant'.
corbeille à papiers (f): 'waste-paper basket'.
coupe-papier (m): 'letter-opener', 'paper-cutter'.
courrier (m): 'post', 'mail'.
craie (f): 'chalk'.
crayon (m): 'pencil'.
crayon (m) *gras*: 'crayon'.
dictaphone (m) (registered trade name): 'dictaphone'; *dicter*: 'to dictate'.
dossier (m): 'file' (documents).
double (m): '(carbon) copy'.
élastique (m): 'rubber-band'.
encre (f): 'ink'.
enveloppe (f): 'envelope'.
facture (f): 'bill', 'invoice'.
feutre (m) or *stylo feutre*: 'felt marker'.
fiche (f); 'index card'.
fichier (m): 'card index'.
gomme (f): 'eraser'.
machine à écrire (f): 'typewriter'; *taper*: 'to type'.
papier collant (m): see *Scotch*.
photocopie (f): 'photocopy'; *photocopieuse* (f), the machine itself.
punaise (f): 'drawing-pin' (US: 'thumbtack').
registre (m): 'register', 'record book'.
règle (f): 'ruler'.
Scotch (m): 'Scotch tape' or 'Sellotape' (registered trade names).
standard (m): 'telephone switchboard'.
  standardiste (f): 'operator'.
stylo (m): 'pen'.
  stylo à bille (m): 'ball-point pen'; *v.* BIC.
tampon (m); 'rubber stamp'.
telex (m): 'telex'.
timbre (m): 'postage stamp'.
touche (f): 'key' (of typewriter).
trombone (m): 'paper clip'.

(*v.* also DACTYLO; PAPIER; and the chapter on THE TELEPHONE.)

C

ça. The contraction of *cela*, as you know. But you must also remember that *ça* is far more 'spoken', so that when you are writing, especially a formal report or essay, or even a letter to someone you don't know well, *cela* is definitely called for.

cabinets (m. pl.). A polite word for 'the lavatory' or 'rest room'. *Où sont les cabinets?* (*v.* also LAVABO).

In the singular, *cabinet* does mean, among other things, a 'ministerial Cabinet'. *Un conseil de cabinet*, or, more frequently, *un conseil des ministres*, 'a Cabinet meeting'. And *cabinet* is the word for a 'law office' or 'doctor's office' (*v.* BUREAU).

cachet (m). Like *un comprimé* , this means 'pill' or 'tablet' (of aspirin, etc.). Nowadays, *une pilule* has come to mean almost exclusively *la pilule anticonceptionnelle*, 'contraceptive pill' (*v.* CONTRA-CEPTION). *Elle prend la pilule.* Nonetheless the old phrase *avaler la pilule*, 'to swallow (bitter) medicine', still holds good.

Since *un cachet* is also 'seal' or 'imprint', *le cachet de la poste* is the 'postmark' on a letter. The rules of a contest may stipulate that *le cachet de la poste fera foi*: 'the postmark will be conclusive in determining the first entry'.

Or again, this is a word you want to remember when called upon to pay a compliment to something even if it is not really attractive: *Ah oui, ce fauteuil a un certain cachet, indiscutablement.* 'Oh dear, yes, that armchair certainly is distinctive (chic, charming, etc.).'

cadre (m). What *l'encadreur* will put around your paintings, mirrors, and so on. But *un cadre* is not only 'a frame': it is also a person who forms part of the higher or administrative personnel of a firm. *Son filleul fait maintenant partie des cadres.* 'His godson's on the managerial staff now.' *La formation des cadres* means 'the training of employees (or of students in special schools) for executive posts'.

ça fait . . . A very common way of saying, 'that looks . . .' or 'that gives a . . . impression'. *Ça fait beau, ça fait mieux, ça fait jeune*: 'that looks nice', 'that looks better', 'that's youthful looking'. *Ça fait moche*, 'that looks awful'. *Ça fait combien?* is a very colloquial way of asking, 'How much does that cost?'

cake (m). A special sort of *Faux Ami*, bred by Franglais: 'fruit cake' only. Any other sort of cake is *un gâteau* or *une pâtisserie*.

calé. This past participle is commonly used as an adjective to indicate that someone is '*très fort,*' 'very well qualified' or 'well up on something'. *Elle est très calée en mathématiques.* 'She's very strong in maths.'

camper. 'To camp out'; also called, *faire du camping* (*v.* the chapter on FRANGLAIS). *Camper un personnage* is a very handy phrase for the student called upon to criticize a work of literature and is fondly used by book reviewers. It means 'to make a given character three-dimensional, believable'.

car (m). A troublesome *Faux Ami*. Not 'a car' at all, which is *une voiture*, but 'an interurban *or* touring coach' (US: 'bus'). 'A city bus' is *un (auto)bus*.

caractère (m). Very frequently used to describe someone's temperament or nature. *La tradition veut que toute belle-mère ait mauvais caractère.* 'Tradition has it that all mothers-in-law are sour-tempered, *or* mean.' *Il a beau avoir bon caractère, il y a une limite à tout.* 'Good-natured as he is, there is a limit.' *Elle a un caractère assez égal.* 'She is even-tempered.' You will often find *être de bonne (mauvaise) composition* instead of *avoir bon (mauvais) caractère.*

Avoir du caractère, or *faire preuve de caractère*, 'to have character'.

'A character' ('He's a real character!') is *un original*; 'a fictional character' is *un personnage.*

caravane (f). Coming into use more and more, at the expense of *roulotte* (f), to mean 'a caravan' (US: 'trailer'), or house on wheels pulled by a car. *La roulotte* by now means a 'gipsy caravan' first of all, if not exclusively.

carie (f). 'A cavity', in the dental sense. 'A filling' is *un plombage*. If you're unlucky it may become necessary to *arracher la dent*, a vigorous way of saying, 'to pull the tooth'. While the operation goes on, you will be seated in *le fauteuil du dentiste*, since 'the dentist's chair' is an armchair in French (and in fact).

carré. An adjective that has nothing to do with the expression 'square', meaning 'not with the trend', or as the younger French generation would have it, *'pas dans le vent'*. No, it means 'straightforward', 'frank', 'blunt'. *Carrément* is 'frankly', 'without beating about the bush'. *Mais demande-lui donc carrément une augmentation.* 'But just ask him straight out for a rise.' *Il est carré en affaires.* 'He is plain-dealing, straightforward in business.'

cartouche (f). Not only any sort of 'cartridge' (as in your fountain pen, for instance), but 'a carton of cigarettes'. You should be warned, however, that cigarettes are not generally sold by cartons in France.

cas (m). Again, the basis of a multitude of expressions. One which may not appear in the dictionary is *un cas* when speaking of someone: 'He's a real case, really singular *or* special'. *Ah celui-là, c'est un cas.*

And *un en-cas* is 'a snack', 'a stop-gap', or 'packed lunch', *en cas* (or, *dans le cas*) *où vous en auriez besoin.*

casserole (f). 'A cooking pot *or* pan', and not what it has come to mean by extension in English: 'a one-dish meal', which would be *un plat.*

catch (m). A fine old Franglais word, meaning 'wrestling'. *Un catcheur* is, logically, 'a wrestler'.

'The catch' or 'clasp' of a necklace, coffer, and so on is *un fermoir.*

ça va (allait, ira, irait). An indispensable but dangerous catch-all, as it is tempting to make use of it ten times more often than one should, at the expense of more precise vocabulary. When you greet someone whom you've already met and know rather well, you say *Comment ça va?* or simply, *Ça va?*, and the someone replies, *Ça va, et vous? (et toi?)*, or *Ça va comme ci comme ça*, or *Ça ne va pas très fort*, etc. *Ça va?*, then, can mean 'How are you?' 'How are things?' 'Is it all right?' and the answer, *Ça va (bien)*, means, 'OK, fine, everything's all right'. *Je me sens fatigué mais ça ira mieux demain.* 'I feel tired, but I'll be all right tomorrow.'

Again, *ça va* may often be used in pairs: *Bon bon, ça va ça va.* 'All right, all right, that's enough'; or 'OK, I've got the idea'.

ça y est (était, sera, serait). Another Jack-of-all-trades sort of expression; heard again and again, in any context, and often used to announce an action beginning or completed, quite like 'there!', or 'got it!', 'I did it', 'there they go', 'that's that'. *Ils craignaient que leur fils ne réussisse pas son bachot, mais ça y est.* 'They were afraid their son wouldn't pass his Baccalauréat, but he got it all right.' *Venez voir le feu d'artifice—ça y est, ils ont commencé.* 'Come quick and see the fireworks—there, now they've started.'

As a question, *ça y est?* can just as easily take on any shade of meaning: 'Have you got it?' 'Is it over?'

You can easily see the laconic, vague, often unsatisfying quality of this expression, and why you should be careful of overdoing it.

cellule (f). 'A cell', in any sense—blood, prison, monastery. But you may need to take special note of another meaning: 'the light meter' of your camera.

centrale (f) **nucléaire**. 'Nuclear power plant'. *Force* (f) *nucléaire*, 'nuclear power'.

ce que. There is surely no need to remind you of all the grammar which attaches to *ce que*. But one very common use of *ce que* which often does not appear in the grammar books is the exclamatory: *Ce qu'il peut être bête!* 'Incredible how stupid he can be!' *Ce que ce film m'a plu!* 'Oh, I loved that film!' *Ce qu'ils ont dû s'ennuyer!* 'How bored they must have been!' As you will have realized already, *ce que* used in this way is simply an abridged form of *Qu'est-ce que*, or a substitute for *comme . . . Comme il est grand! Ce qu'il est grand!*

c'est-à-dire. 'That is to say'; and as you would expect, it is used (and abused) as often as are 'that is', or 'I mean' in English. Or again, it's a ready-made question formula, just like 'meaning?' or 'that is?', but in this capacity it is likely to sound as ill-bred or abrupt as its English counterparts.

chagrin (m). This may well mean general 'sadness' or 'tearfulness' and apply as well to a child who bursts into tears as to an adult: *Le pauvre petit, il a un gros chagrin*. The verb, *chagriner* or *être chagriné*, is not so commonly used.

chahuter. Roughly, 'to rag', 'to heckle', or 'deliberately to interrupt' (a speaker) with boisterous or disorderly behaviour. *Dans la classe de sciences naturelles, on ne chahute jamais.* 'In the natural sciences class (or classroom; *v.* CLASSE), there is never any problem of discipline.' *Le candidat a été pas mal chahuté pendant son discours.* 'The candidate was the object of quite a lot of heckling during his speech.'

chambre (f). 'A room'; almost exclusively 'a bedroom' although the full name for it is *une chambre à coucher*. *Une chambrée* is 'a military barracks'; *un dortoir,* 'dormitory'. *Cité* (f) *dortoir,* 'dormitory (town)', whose inhabitants all commute to work elsewhere during the day and come back to it only at night, to sleep.

Chambrer is 'to warm (red) wine'—theoretically, 'to room temperature', *à la température ambiante.*

chameau (m). When someone is disagreeable, quarrelsome, mean, you call him or her, *vieux chameau, va!*—literally, 'nasty old camel'—and immediately you feel better. This is standard form for speaking disrespectfully of a mother-in-law: *mon chameau de belle-mère.* Or you may find *la vache!* as soothing as *chameau!* (*v.* the chapter on FAMILIAR, OR INFORMAL, FRENCH).

There are of course a number of expressions using animals. You might note that *un âne* is 'a dunce', 'an imbecile'; and *une ânerie,* 'a stupid thing to do'. *Avoir un chat dans la gorge* translates, 'to have a frog in your throat', and *avoir la puce à l'oreille* is 'to smell a rat'. *Il ne faut pas prendre les enfants du bon Dieu pour des canards sauvages,* 'it's a mistake to treat people like a bunch of fools'. *Il fait un froid de canard,* 'it's freezing cold'.

champignon (m). The noble 'mushroom'. Beware, when you buy mushrooms in the market, of the way in which the price is indicated: not per *kilogramme* (2.2 pounds), as with most fruit and vegetables, but by 250 *gr.* or *la demi-livre,* and occasionally even by 100 *gr.*

Le champignon is also, colloquially, 'the accelerator' in the car; *écraser le champignon,* 'to step hard on the accelerator' (US: 'the gas').

chance (f). A classic *Faux Ami,* as it does not mean 'chance', but 'luck'. If you say *j'ai eu la chance de le rencontrer,* you are saying 'I was lucky enough to meet him'; whereas perhaps you meant 'I had a chance to meet him': *j'ai eu l'occasion de le rencontrer* (*v.* OCCASION).

Pas de chance! 'Bad luck!'
La malchance, 'bad luck'.
Bonne chance! 'Good luck!'

chandelle (f). 'A candle', generally slenderer and more elegant than *une bougie* (q.v.). Where you might use the latter in an emergency, when the fuses blow (*v.* PLOMB), a *chandelle* is what you want when you dress up the dinner table for a *dîner aux chandelles.*

Devoir une fière chandelle à quelqu'un means 'to have real cause to be grateful'. *Il vous doit une fière chandelle.* 'He owes you an awful lot.'

Voir trente-six chandelles, 'to be knocked unconscious'. *En tombant elle a dû se cogner contre la poignée, elle a vu trente-six chandelles.* 'She must have struck the doorhandle as she fell; she was knocked out.'

chanter. A verb that is straightforward enough, you say: it means 'to sing'. And so it does; but *faire chanter* is 'to blackmail'; *le chantage* is 'blackmail' itself; and the person responsible, 'the blackmailer', is *le maître chanteur*—a term which has no feminine form. . . . When *quelque chose chante à quelqu'un*, then 'something appeals to, *or* tempts, someone'. *Aller au concert cet après-midi? oui, ça me chante.* 'Yes, I feel like going to a concert this afternoon.' This is distinctly a colloquial use of the verb, and you will want to be careful not to overuse or to write it.

chargé. Literally, 'loaded'. In current use, it means therefore 'busy', 'occupied', 'full'. *Que personne ne me dérange, j'ai une matinée très chargée.* 'I don't want anyone to bother me, I've got a very busy morning ahead of me.' *Etre chargé de* is 'to be in charge of *or* responsible for' something, and not 'charged with' (a crime, misdemeanour). That calls for *accusé de*.

To translate 'he is loaded (with money)', you say *il est bourré de fric* (*v.* the chapter on FAMILIAR, OR INFORMAL, FRENCH).

chemise (f). 'A man's shirt', although the word is feminine; whereas a woman's blouse, particularly of the button-down-the-front variety, is a masculine word, *un chemisier*. (*Le chemisier* is also 'the shirtmaker'.) A blouse of a less man-tailored sort is likely to be *un corsage*. A nightgown is *une chemise de nuit*, and may be accompanied by *un peignoir*, *un déshabillé*, or *une robe de chambre*. (The latter term applies as well to a man's as to a woman's bathrobe or dressing-gown.) *Etre en bras de chemise*, or *en manches de chemise*, 'to be in shirtsleeves'.

Une chemise can also be 'a (Manila) folder', for filing or protecting papers (*v.* BUREAU).

If it's 'an undershirt' you want, then you mean *un maillot de corps* (or *un T-shirt*).

And you need to be careful about *une blouse* (pronounced 'blues'), which nowadays has rarely anything to do with a woman's blouse. It means 'a smock', for artist, housewife, or nursery-school child (and may then also be called *un tablier*), or a doctor's or nurse's white coat. You are right, of course, in protesting that *un tablier* is also 'an apron', of the kitchen or hostess variety.

chercher. *Chercher* has more than its grammar book meaning of 'to look for', 'to seek'. It can be used for: 'to pick up' or 'to collect', in quite the same way as *prendre*. *Ils viendront demain chercher le tapis pour le nettoyer.* 'The cleaners are coming to pick up the rug tomorrow.' *Il faut que j'aille à l'autre bout de Paris chercher ma* *voiture neuve.* 'I have to go all the way over to the other side of Paris to pick up my new car.'

Il ne faut pas chercher à comprendre is one of those marvellous *phrases toutes faites.* Literally, 'you must not seek to understand', which is decidely too oracular: 'there's no explanation, no rhyme or reason'; or 'it's beyond me', or 'just accept (the situation) as it is'.

Vous l'avez cherché is like *c'est bien fait pour vous:* 'you asked for it', 'it's your own fault', 'it serves you right'.

And again, there is the *chercher* which can mean 'cost up to': *Si vous voulez une bonne reproduction de ce tableau, attention, cela peut aller chercher jusque dans les 3000 francs.* 'If you want a good reproduction of this painting, be forewarned: it can go as high as 3,000 francs.' *Un chercheur* is 'a researcher', of either sex.

cheveux (m. pl.). 'Hair', in general. *Il s'est fait couper les cheveux en brosse.* 'He's got a crewcut.' *La chevelure* is 'the head of hair': *Ce qui fait la beauté de cette fille, c'est sa chevelure abondante.* 'The stunning thing about that girl is her thick hair.' *Un cheveu* is 'a (strand of) hair', while *un poil* is 'an isolated hair or bristle'; *les poils d'une moustache* or *d'une barbe, les poils de sanglier d'une brosse, les poils d'une fourrure* or *d'une bête.* But: *Il perd ses cheveux,* 'he's going bald'. Baldness is *la calvitie;* the adjective is *chauve.* Your 'scalp' is *le cuir chevelu.* And when the wind blows your hair about, you are *échevelé,* 'dishevelled'. *Poilu,* as an adjective, is 'hirsute', 'hairy'. As a nickname, it refers to the French infantryman in World War I.

Poil figures in a couple of colloquial expressions. *Avoir un poil dans la main,* 'to be extremely lazy'. *Il n'a plus un poil d'accent en français.* 'He hasn't the least trace of accent any more in French.'

Another very informal phrase is, *arriver comme les cheveux sur la soupe:* 'to be very much out of place, unexpected, incongruous'.

Une explication tirée par les cheveux is 'a far-fetched explanation'. And surely there is no need to remind you that *couper les cheveux en quatre* is simply 'to split hairs'.

chômage (m). 'Unemployment'. *Etre au chômage,* 'to be unemployed, jobless'. *Un chômeur; une femme au chômage. Demandeur, -euse d'emploi,* 'jobhunter'. *Allocation* (f) *de chômage,* 'unemployment compensation'.

chiffon (m). The humble 'duster', or any scrap of cloth. *J'aurai juste le temps de donner un coup de chiffon.* 'I'll have just enough time to do some quick dusting.' *Chiffonner,* however, does not mean 'to dust' (*épousseter*), but 'to crumple' or 'wrinkle'; and also, figuratively, 'to vex' or 'annoy'. *Cette nouvelle le chiffonne.* 'This piece of news troubles him.' *Parler chiffons* is what women are said to do: get together and talk about clothes.

circulation (f). A word you can hear all too often, since everyone agrees that there is too much of it: 'road traffic'. *Circuler,* or *rouler, en voiture* means 'to go by car'. *L'agent de police,* exasperated, will shout: *Mais circulez plus vite, Monsieur, circulez plus vite!* Of course you may also apply circulation to blood: *la circulation sanguine.*

And although *trafiquer* and *un trafiquant* do exist, they are *Faux Amis*, since they have to do with 'trade' and 'dealings', usually illegal: *le trafic de la drogue*, 'narcotics trade'. Yet *le trafic routier* is a term which you may safely use for 'traffic on main roads'.

cirer. 'To wax' or 'polish' (parquet flooring, furniture, shoes). *La cire* is 'wax', such as candles are made of, whereas *le cirage* is shoe- (or other) polish. *Etre dans le cirage*, 'to be in a fog'.

ciseau (m). 'A chisel.' If it's 'scissors' you want, then you must say, *les ciseaux* or *une paire de ciseaux.*

claque (f). A word some parents use often: *Veux-tu une paire de claques?* 'If you don't behave I'll slap you.' *Une gifle* is a less colloquial term for 'slap'.

If the play you've gone to see is *un four*, 'a flop', the only people likely to be applauding are *la claque*, those planted in the audience with the express purpose of clapping. *Rentrer claqué de son travail* is 'to come home dead tired from work'. *Prière de ne pas claquer la porte en sortant* is an injunction not to slam the door on your way out.

classe (f). In scholastic terms, either 'the class', i.e. 'the course', or 'the classroom' itself. In office terminology, *classer* means 'to file', in *un classeur* (*v.* BUREAU).

In general, *classe* and *classer* can be used as you would 'class' or 'rank' in English. 'The working class': *la classe ouvrière.* 'The governing *or* ruling class': *la classe dirigeante.* In military terms, *faire ses classes* is 'to go through training camp'.

clou (m). 'A nail', of the sort you drive into a wall. A finger-nail is *un ongle*; a toe-nail, *un ongle de doigt de pied.*

The *clou de la soirée* or *du spectacle* is 'the star attraction', the act which steals the limelight.

Mettre quelque chose au clou is 'to pawn it', to leave it with *un prêteur sur gages* (*v.* MONT-DE-PIÉTÉ).

coincer. 'To catch', 'trap', 'wedge', 'put in a tight corner'. Very commonly heard, in both literal and figurative use. *L'ascenseur est coincé entre deux étages.* 'The lift is stuck between two floors.' *J'ai deux rendez-vous pour 10h, me voilà coincé!* 'I've got two 10 o'clock appointments: I'm stuck!'

combinaison (f). A dictionary will tell you that this is 'a pair of overalls', such as a garage mechanic wears. But women especially need to know that this is 'a slip', the feminine undergarment. The word *slip* (m) does exist—but usually means men's 'underpants' (US: briefs *or* undershorts); *une culotte* is for a woman. 'A half-slip' or 'petticoat' is *un jupon.*

Combinaison also means 'a scheme' or 'plot'; a more *familier* (and sometimes pejorative) term is *la combine*, which is at the basis of *le Système D* (*v*. DÉBROUILLER).

comble (m). Included here to remind you of *c'est le comble!* and similar sarcastic expressions with *bouquet, complet, commode* (q.v.): 'That's just fine!'

comédien (m). A reminder that *un(e) comédien(ne)* means 'an actor' ('actress') and does not by any means necessarily imply a comic actor, or what English calls 'a comedian'. The primary meaning of *La Comédie Française* is simply 'The French Theatre' (*v*. the chapter on ENTERTAINMENT).

Jouer la comédie is 'to act in a play' or 'to try to take somebody in'. *Avec moi, elle ne joue jamais la comédie*. 'She never tries to put anything over on me.'

Faire une comédie is 'to make a fuss', 'to put on an act (of protest)'. *L'enfant a fait toute une comédie pour aller se coucher*. 'The child put up a big fuss about going to bed.'

'A comedy' is either *une comédie* or *une pièce comique*; 'a tragedy', *une tragédie* or *une pièce tragique*.

Le dramaturge is the 'dramatist' or 'playwright'.

comment. Another of those omnipresent and all-purpose words. First of all, as a question, meaning *Je n'ai pas compris*, but less polite by far than *Je vous demande pardon?* or *Je m'excuse?* 'Sorry?' 'I beg your pardon?'

And then of course, meaning 'how?' *Comment a-t-il fait son compte pour arriver si tard?* 'How did he manage to get there so late?' *Et comment!* 'And how!'

Beware of the all-too-lazy *comment dirai-je?* or simply, *comment dire?* or *comment dit-on?* 'how shall I say?' 'what do you call it?' *Lors de la représentation, j'ai ressenti, comment dirai-je, un sentiment, comment dire, d'angoisse, enfin, comment dit-on, d'inquiétude,* 'During the performance I felt, what shall I say, a feeling of, well, anxiety, I mean uneasiness, what do you call it?'

Comment!, in a vehemently exclamatory tone, can mean, 'well, of all the nerve!' or 'what on earth!' or any other vigorous expression of indignation. *Comment! tu t'es permis de l'inviter sans me prévenir!* 'Well, of all the . . . You took it on yourself to invite him without informing me!' *Ça alors!* expresses the same feeling, more familiarly.

The English verb 'to comment' is *commenter*, or *faire un commentaire* or *une remarque*.

commode. Certainly one of the more common adjectives, meaning 'handy', 'convenient', 'readily feasible'. *Cet instrument est très commode pour dénoyauter les olives*. 'That's a very handy gadget for stoning (US: pitting) olives.'

Ce n'est pas commode pour aller chez lui. 'It's not very easy to get to his place.' *Elle n'est pas commode*. 'She's not easy to get along with.'

Often used sarcastically to mean just the opposite of convenient:

Alors ça par exemple! C'est commode! 'Well now that's just fine (the end, all I needed, too much).' In this connexion, *v.* also BOUQUET, COMBLE, COMPLET.

complet. Applies to any public place, institution (such as a children's camp) or conveyance (such as a bus) which is full. At a concert hall, this is the equivalent of 'Sold Out' or 'Standing Room Only'—except that French theatres and auditoriums rarely if ever sell standing room.

Un complet or *un complet veston* is commonly called *un costume*: 'a man's suit'.

Also: *C'est complet!* 'It's the last straw.'

compteur (m). 'The meter': *compteur à gaz, compteur électrique.* When you rent a flat or a room, you do well to ask whether *le gaz et l'électricité* (and even *l'eau*) *sont compris dans le prix*, included in the price, or whether they are *en plus*: in which case they will often be calculated *sur la base du compteur individuel*, in your lodgings.

concours (m). 'A competition' or 'a competitive examination'. *Il a été reçu premier au concours d'entrée à Sciences Po.* 'He got the top score on the competitive entry exam for (the *Ecole des*) *Sciences Politiques*.' *Pour être Agrégé, il faut réussir le concours de l'Agrégation, alors que le Doctorat est une question de thèse.* 'To receive the title of *Agrégé*, you have to pass the competitive exam called the *Agrégation*, whereas to get your doctorate, you write a thesis.'

Le concours also signifies *l'aide, l'assistance. Notre émission a été réalisée avec le concours d'Untel*: 'Our programme was produced with the collaboration of So-and-So.' *Prêter son concours à une vente de charité* might be translated, 'to help organize a charity bazaar'.

conditionnel (m). A verb in the conditional tense may require a second reading, since this tense is often used with the force of '*paraît-il*': 'it would seem that', 'he is said to have . . .' *Les forces du sud auraient détruit trois ponts.* 'The southern army is said to have knocked out three bridges.' *Il ne serait pas rentré chez lui depuis dimanche.* 'Apparently he hasn't been home since Sunday.'

A special instance of this special use of the conditional is the verb, *savoir*: it may take on the meaning of *pouvoir. On ne saurait trop vous conseiller cette solution.* 'We (can) very strongly recommend that solution (to the problem).'

conduire. 'To drive (a car)', 'to lead', 'guide', 'direct'. *A gauche du salon est un long couloir conduisant vers les chambres.* 'To the left of the living-room is a long corridor leading to the bedrooms.' *Attendez l'ouvreuse, elle vous conduira à vos places.* 'Wait for the usherette, who will show you to your seats.'

But look again at some of the pitfalls awaiting the speaker whose native tongue is English: *Un conducteur* is 'a driver' (of a car), but this is not the word you want for 'an orchestra conductor', who is *un chef d'orchestre*. His function is, *diriger l'orchestre*. If you are talking about a musical group other than an orchestra—*un ensemble vocal ou instrumental*—then you had better say that it is *dirigé par Untel*, or that it is *placé sous la direction d'Untel*.

Similarly, the conductor of a train, bus, or tram cannot be called *le conducteur* but, *le receveur*. 'The driver's licence' is *le permis de conduire* (*v.* the chapter on CARS).

confection (f). Nothing to do with confectionery or sweets; for this you need *la confiserie*, which is at once the shop selling sweets, the making of them, and the sweet itself.

La confection is the making of clothes and hence, 'ready-made clothes' themselves, also called *le prêt-à-porter*; as distinct from *les vêtements sur mesure*, 'clothing made to measure'. But *c'est elle qui a confectionné* or *fait sa robe de mariée*. 'She made her own wedding-dress (US: gown).'

congé (m). The meaning of *congé* that most people are interested in is that of holidays; *les congés payés* is the minimum four-week annual holiday period that the law requires every employer to pay his workers. *Un congé de maladie* is 'sick leave'; *un congé de maternité*, 'maternity (US: pregnancy) leave'. 'Military leave' is generally *une permission*; *v.* also FERMETURE ANNUELLE.

Two troublesome expressions because of their resemblance are: *prendre congé de quelqu'un*, and *donner congé à quelqu'un*. The first, like *quitter*, means 'to take leave of someone'; while the second, like *congédier*, is 'to dismiss (sack) someone'.

congélateur (m). 'The freezing compartment' of a refrigerator, or 'a freezer' by itself; also often called *un freezer . . . Un réfrigérateur* may also be styled *un frigidaire*, which is a trade name. Frozen foods are *les surgelés*.

conjoncture (f). Economic or political situation, set of circumstances. *La conjoncture est bonne, mauvaise, favorable*, etc.

conserver. 'To preserve.' *Elle est bien conservée pour son âge.* 'She appears young (is well preserved) for her age.' *Les conserves* are 'tinned (US: canned) goods'; *en conserve* means 'preserved', when speaking of food.

Le conservateur d'un musée is 'the curator of a museum'; he may also be *conservateur* (adj.) in the political sense: 'conservative'. If he is a she, she is *Madame la conservatrice* (sometimes even *Madame le conservateur*) and she may be *conservatrice* (adj.) in her opinions.

consigne (f). At *la gare*, this is the '(left-) luggage office (US: cloak- *or* check-room)'. And if you buy a bottle at the wine merchant's or the grocer's (*le marchand de vin(s)* or *l'épicier*), you may well pay a *consigne*, a 'deposit' on the bottle. If not, the bottle may be marked *verre perdu*, since there is no return on your payments. The deposit you put down when you rent a car is *une caution*.

If you are called upon to *prendre les consignes* of a particular job, you are to take over from the post's present occupant and go through a prior period of instruction or familiarization.

For a pupil (*un élève*), *être consigné* means 'to be told to stay after school' or 'to come to school on Saturday afternoon'; at any rate, 'to be punished' (*v.* PROFESSEUR).

consommation (f). The drink you order in a café or night club.

constater. 'To notice', 'remark', 'observe'. *Mais, cher monsieur, je ne vous accuse point, je constate, voilà tout.* 'But, my good man, I'm not accusing you, I'm merely stating.' *On a pu constater une diminution du nombre de spectateurs dans les salles obscures.* 'A drop in attendance at the cinema has been observed.' The noun is *la constatation.*

contestataire (m. and f.). A person who challenges an order or the established order or pattern. A word in common use since *les événements de mai '68 à Paris.*

contraception (f). 'Contraception'. *Les moyens contraceptifs*, 'contraceptive devices'; the most common are *la pilule* (pill), *le stérilet* ('IUD'), *le diaphragme* ('diaphragm'), *la méthode Ogino. Le contrôle des naissances*, 'birth control'. *Centre de planning familial*, 'family planning centre'.

contre-cœur, à. Whereas an Englishman may do something 'unwillingly' or 'against his will', a Frenchman acts against his heart: *à contre-cœur*; or again, *le cœur n'y est* (*était*, etc.) *pas.*

coordonnées (f. pl.). *Donner ses coordonnées* is to give one's name, address, telephone number, etc., to someone for future reference. *Je vais noter vos coordonnées* is very often heard.

corde (f). Not 'a musical chord', which is *un accord*, but 'twine', and so on. But if you want to talk about 'electric cord *or* wire', you need the word *fil* (*électrique*) (m). And if *quelque chose n'est pas dans les cordes de quelqu'un* the person is not very well qualified to do something. *Les maths ne sont pas dans ses cordes.*

correct. Something of a *Faux Ami*; for although it can mean 'correct' in the sense of 'exact' or 'accurate' or 'right', it equates more often with 'polite', 'decent', 'well-bred', 'proper'. The opposite is *incorrect. Ils l'ont licencié le mois dernier, mais ils ont été corrects* (*l'ont fait correctement*). 'They gave him the sack last month, but they were decent about it.' *Elle est d'une correction exemplaire.* 'Her conduct (*or* breeding) is irreproachable.' 'To correct' may be expressed by *corriger* or *reprendre.*

cosmonaute (m). An astronaut; the feminine form is *une femme cosmonaute. Un vaisseau spatial* is a space ship, *une fusée* is a rocket. *Une mission spatiale*, space mission. *Le compte à rebours*, count-down. To land on the moon is *atterrir sur la lune* or *alunir; alunissage* (m) is the noun. The splashdown which completes the mission is *l'amerrissage* (m); the verb is *amerrir* (*v.* also ESPACE).

cote (f). A recent use of this word is 'popularity' or 'rating' in opinion polls. *La cote de Monsieur Machin, analysée à travers les derniers sondages, semblerait être en baisse.* 'The latest surveys seem to indicate that Mr. So-and-so's popularity is waning.' Note that there is no circumflex, as there is on *la côte* ('coast', 'rib', 'slope') and *le côté* ('side').

couleurs, marchand de (m). He is sometimes hard to distinguish from *le quincaillier* and, to complicate things further, he may, or used to, be called *le droguiste* and his shop *la droguerie*. Let's make a very rough distinction: *la boutique du marchand de couleurs* is traditionally a woman's haven, with anything from *toile cirée* ('oilcloth'), paints, soap, frying-pans and toilet-paper to disposable nappies (US: diapers), all plastic and metal gadgets for the home, shampoos, and Christmas tree ornaments. But *la quincaillerie* has an unmistakably masculine atmosphere, being limited strictly to tools, screws, nuts, bolts and nails, and catering not only to the Sunday *bricoleur* but also to the professional carpenter, mason, and others.

coup (m). Certainly one of the master keys to any number of linguistic doors which otherwise remain closed to you in French. The dictionary gives you columns of expressions with *coup*; you simply have to learn off the great majority of them and be able to use them in context, since out of context they can be catastrophic. Think of what the countless uses made of 'get', with or without its postpositions, mean to a foreigner learning English, and you have the idea.

Here are several expressions which you may want to consider more closely:

coup d'œil: *Ça se voit au premier coup d'œil.* 'It is evident at a glance.' *Jeter un coup d'œil sur*: 'to give a quick look at'.

coup de foudre: Most often used to mean 'love at first sight'.

coup de main: 'A hand', 'helping hand'. *Peux-tu venir me donner un coup de main pour tapisser mon salon?* 'Can you come over to give me a hand in papering my living room?'

coup de fil: 'A telephone call'. *Il n'y a qu'à nous donner un coup de fil.* 'All you have to do is give us a ring (ring us up).'

sur le coup: 'At first', 'at the time'. *Sur le coup je ne me suis pas rendu compte de ce qui s'était passé.* 'At the time, I scarcely realized what had happened.'

coup d'air: 'Draught', 'chill'. Also, *coup de soleil*, 'sunstroke' or 'sunburn'. Both used with *attraper un*. *Il a mal à l'œil; il a dû attraper un coup d'air.* 'One of his eyes hurts; he must have caught a chill.' *Elle a attrapé un méchant coup de soleil.* 'She's got severe sunburn.'

coup de fusil: Not only 'a gunshot', but 'an unexpectedly high restaurant *or* hotel bill'.

coup de tête: 'An impulse'; *agir sur un coup de tête*, 'to act impulsively'.

à chaque coup, à tous les coups: 'Every time'. Synonymous with *à chaque fois*.

donner un coup de balai, peigne, klaxon, fer, and so on and on:

'to sweep', 'comb', 'honk the horn', 'iron', etc. Literally, 'to give a touch *or* blow of the instrument in question'. An astonishingly common construction, replacing *balayer*, *peigner*, *klaxonner*, *repasser*. . . .

coupable (m). The guilty person; or, as an adjective, 'guilty'. But you may stumble over the noun, 'guilt', which is *la culpabilité*.

coupe-papier (m). 'Letter-opener' (*v.* BUREAU). This is as good a time as any to look at the formation of such words, which we may call the compounds of function. This one would be translated literally 'cut-paper'. When you compare it with the English 'paper-cutter' (or 'letter-opener'), you notice first of all the inversion in the order of noun and verb, and then the fact that the verb (*coupe*) is actually another noun in English: 'cutter'. The rule of verb-plus-object in French is a consistent and useful one. Look at all of the *coupe*-words; *presse-papiers* ('paper-weight'); *serre-livres* ('book-ends'); and especially the long list of words formed with *porte-* (q.v.).

crédit (m). In the singular, this is 'financial *or* moral credit'. *Acheter à crédit*, 'to buy on credit'. *User de son crédit auprès de quelqu'un*, 'to use one's influence on someone'. The plural means 'funds'. *La ville a été obligée d'abandonner ses projets pour le nouveau stade, faute de crédits*. 'The city has been forced to drop its plans for a new stadium, for lack of government allocations (funds).'

crème (m). Yes, masculine, when you mean 'coffee and cream', 'white coffee', ordered at *un café* or *une terrasse*. *Un express* is ordinary 'black coffee'; and *un filtre*, 'drip-coffee'.

crever. This is the word you need when your car begins to bump along suspiciously: *Je crois que j'ai un pneu crevé*. 'I think I've got a flat tyre.' 'The puncture' itself is *une crevaison (v.* the chapter on CARS).

If you yourself are *crevé*, you are not 'wounded' but simply 'dead tired'. This is not a very elegant expression but is certainly current enough; similarly, *crever* in the sense of 'to die'.

crise (f). This word may seem to you to crop up everywhere at once, even where English would use 'attack' or 'problem', instead of 'crisis'. *Il se trouve devant une très grave crise de conscience*. 'He is confronted with a most serious moral problem.' *A la suite de la crise ministérielle la femme du ministre a fait une crise de nerfs et lui a eu une crise cardiaque*. 'After the governmental crisis, the minister's wife went into hysterics and he himself had a heart-attack.' *La crise pétrolière*, 'the oil crisis (US: crunch)'.

croiser. Here is an alternative to *rencontrer* when you want to say that you ran into someone. *J'ai croisé sa sœur l'autre soir*. 'I bumped into his sister the other evening.' It can also mean 'to pass someone' (with or without seeing him) who is going in the opposite direction. *J'ai dû le croiser en venant*. 'I must have gone past him on my way here.'

crudités (f. pl.). One of the most blunder-engendering of *Faux Amis*. Nothing to do with the crudeness of a person, but among the first items on a menu: 'an assortment of raw vegetables'. *Cru* means 'raw', and does also mean 'crude' or 'coarse' when applied to someone's language, to a film, etc.

cuivres (m. pl.). 'The brass' in an orchestra. 'The woodwinds' are *les bois*; 'wind instruments' in general are *les instruments à vent*. The other categories of instruments are those *à cordes* and those *de percussion*.

curé (m). Strictly speaking, *le curé* is not 'the curate' but 'the vicar'; and *le vicaire* is not 'the vicar' but 'the curate'.

cure (f). 'A cure', 'a treatment', as at a spa or watering-place. But the verb, 'to cure' is *guérir*; and 'a cure' in the sense of a recovery is *une guérison. Un guérisseur* is 'a healer'.

cure-dent (m). Not a cure for aching teeth, but the humble 'toothpick', which serves to *se curer les dents*, 'to clean (by picking) one's teeth'.

D

dactylo (f). A feminine word, though it looks masculine; for *une dactylo* is 'a typist'; and 'a shorthand-typist/secretary' *une sténo-dactylo*, since *la sténographie* means 'shorthand' or 'stenography'. *Prendre (en sténo) sous la dictée*, 'to take (shorthand) from dictation'. *Une thèse doit être dactylographiée*. 'A thesis must be typed.' But the machine itself, 'the typewriter', is *la machine à écrire*, and using it is *taper à la machine. La frappe*, however, is the fact of typing something. *J'ai donné le texte à la frappe*, 'I've sent the text off to be typed.'

d'après. When it means 'according to', this word is used just like *selon*. *D'après lui, c'est la plus belle ville de France*. 'According to him, it's the loveliest city in France.' *D'après la pendule, il est plus tôt que je ne pensais*. 'According to the clock, it's earlier than I thought.'

It can also be used where *selon* cannot, to mean 'adapted from' or 'based on', also expressed by *adapté de* or *tiré de. Un grand film d'après le célèbre roman de Zola*, 'an important film based on Zola's famous novel'.

débordé(e), être. Very common expression: 'to have too much work', 'to be swamped'.

débrayer. Means both 'to let out the clutch' of a motorcar and, in speaking of a workman, 'to go on strike, down tools'. The noun in either case is *débrayage* (m).

débrouiller, se. Beyond the shadow of a doubt, the first word you should learn in French, since without it, you cannot understand the French and their outlook on life. *Se débrouiller* and the justly famous *Système D* (*le système de la débrouillardise*) express a whole concept, essentially individualistic, which is only very feebly translated by 'to manage', 'to get along', 'to muddle through', 'to make out for oneself'. If you call someone *très débrouillard(e)*, you are paying him one of the highest compliments that the list of French adjectives allows for: it means a compound of *astucieux*, *énergique*, *indépendant*, and *volontaire*, not to mention *imaginatif*, in short, resourceful.

—*Mais Monsieur le Directeur, il n'est pas possible de terminer les préparatifs si vite.*—*Je ne veux pas le savoir, débrouillez-vous pour que ce soit fait aujourd'hui en huit.* 'But, sir, it's impossible to get everything ready so fast.'—'That's not my problem, just be sure it is done a week from today.' *Le pauvre garçon ne gagne pas lourd mais il se débrouille quand même.* 'The poor chap doesn't earn much, but he manages all the same.'

débutant. *Un(e) débutant(e)* is 'a beginner' in general, in any field; the meaning is not limited to that of the young woman making her entry into society, 'the deb', as in English. The same goes, of course, for *débuter* and *faire ses débuts*.

dégivrer. 'To defrost', as a refrigerator. *Le dégivrage* is 'the defrosting', whereas *un dégel* is 'a thaw' (in the weather or the political climate).

dégriffé. With the famous designer's label (*la griffe*) removed. *Soldes de dégriffés*, clothes with their labels removed on sale at reduced prices.

dégustation (f). 'A tasting *or* sampling of food'; often written over *cafés* and *terrasses*. The verb is *déguster*, although the general verb for 'to taste' is *goûter*.

déjà. This is pretty clearcut: the adverb meaning 'already'. But you had better learn by heart: *C'est déjà ça! C'est toujours ça* (*de gagné* or *de pris*) is a nearly identical twin.—*Le plombier ne viendra pas avant vendredi, mais il a promis de venir tout au début de la matinée.*— *Eh bien, c'est déjà ça!* 'The plumber won't come till Friday, but he's promised to come first thing in the morning.—Well, that's something, anyhow!'

As you can see, the idea is one of being resigned to a bad situation and grateful for what help, or money, you can get.

demander, se. Should you wonder how to say 'I wonder', here you are: *je me demande*. 'A wonder', however, is *un miracle* or *une merveille*; and 'Alice in Wonderland' is known as *Alice au Pays des Merveilles*.

démarrer. The verb for starting the car and, very frequently, for starting anything in general. This general sense, although by no means *incorrect*, is inelegant and distinctly *familier*. *Le démarreur* is 'the starter' in the car. *La manivelle* is 'the crank'; for those grim moments *quand le démarreur ne fonctionne pas* (*v.* the chapter on CARS).

    J'ai beaucoup de travail mais je n'arrive pas à démarrer. 'I have loads of work, but I can't seem to get going on it.'

demi (m). 'A beer', as you order it in a café. *Un demi-panaché*, 'beer and *limonade*' (q.v.)—a 'lemonade shandy'.

dépanner. To repair what has broken down; *la panne* is 'the breakdown'. *Tomber en panne*, 'to break down'; *être en panne*, 'to be out of order' (*v.* the chapter on CARS).

    A further, very common, meaning is, 'to help someone out temporarily', and usually, materially. *Je n'ai plus de sucre, auriez-vous la gentillesse de me dépanner?* 'I've no more sugar, would you be kind enough to let me have some?' *Puisqu'il ne pouvait pas se payer une chambre à l'hôtel, je l'ai dépanné.* 'Since he couldn't pay for a hotel room, I gave him a bed at my place.'

dépayser. Literally, 'to make (someone) feel as though he were in another country'. In fact, the feeling of *dépaysement* (m) can come with the move from one house or neighbourhood to another, or even from one atmosphere or décor to another. *De la salle Louis XIII, nous sommes ensuite passés dans une salle fin dix-neuvième: quel dépaysement!* 'On leaving the gallery in Louis XIII style, we entered a late nineteenth-century room: what a change!, *or* all the difference in the world!' *Avec ce changement d'école, mon fils se sent un peu dépaysé.* 'My son has changed schools and feels a bit out of place.' *Que de gens cherchent à se dépayser en lisant!* 'How many people try to find new horizons by reading!'

dépister. A verb to be careful of, since it can have contrary meanings. Most commonly, perhaps, it means 'to track down': *dépister les sources du cancer*, 'to track down (find out) the causes of cancer'. But the same verb can also mean 'to throw off the scent'.

déposer. This is the word you want when you leave something with the *concierge*—a practice which is still widespread and often very convenient. *Je ne peux pas passer prendre le paquet, ayez la gentillesse de le déposer chez ma concierge.* 'I can't come over to pick up the parcel; please be so good as to leave it with the porter.'

    Il a déposé ses bagages à la gare. 'He's left his bags at the station.'

    Déposer quelqu'un is 'to drop someone off' (at his home, at the corner, etc.). *Je peux vous déposer?* But be careful: *déposer un roi* is 'to bring down (dethrone) a king'!

dépression (f). This is not the word you really want for 'an economic depression' such as that of the 1930's: here, *une récession* is called for, or *une crise économique* or *financière*, or *le Krach*, 'the crash'. While we are on depressing subjects, however, note that *une dépression nerveuse* is 'a nervous breakdown'. If you are feeling only momentarily 'depressed', you are *déprimé*. Something that is 'depressing' is *déprimant*.

déranger. The past particle can mean 'mad', or 'deranged' as in English. But you'll need this verb many more times a day to mean: 'to bother', 'to put out' or 'impose upon'. It is often used in the negative, as an expression of polite concern. *Je ne vous dérange pas?* 'I hope I'm not interrupting anything?' *Chut, il ne faut pas déranger ton père, il travaille.* 'Hush, don't bother your father, he's working.' Also, 'to go to the trouble of coming': *il s'est dérangé spécialement pour vous voir.* 'He took the trouble of coming just to see you.'

dérouiller. Distinctly colloquial for 'to beat' or 'thrash'; *une dérouillée* is 'a thrashing'. The strict sense is 'to remove rust'; hence, 'to polish', even figuratively.

desservir. A word worth noticing because from one meaning to another, the prefix *de(s)-*, usually a privative in French as in English, can lose all its weight. *Desservir une table* is 'to unserve (hence clear) the table'; *desservir quelqu'un*, 'to do someone a disservice'.

    But *desservir* in the context in which you are most likely to encounter it, that of public transport, does not mean the opposite of *servir* at all. *Ce quartier est bien desservi par l'autobus.* 'This district has a good bus service.' *Les arrêts desservis entre 8h15 et 23h30 sont les suivants.* 'The places at which the bus stops between 8.15 a.m. and 11.30 p.m. are the following.'

diapositive (f). 'A colour slide' or 'transparency'. Also called *un diapositif*, or simply *un(e) diapo*.

Dieu. You will find traces of divinity everywhere you go in France, 'the eldest daughter of the Church'. In family names, like *Dieudonné*; in place names, like *Villedieu-les-Poêles*; and in the name of every other *rue* and *place*, where the saints are rivalled only by *le Général Leclerc, Gambetta, Clemenceau, la Résistance, la Libération, le Général de Gaulle* and, since 1963 of course, *le Président Kennedy*. When it comes to first names, however, you will note that *Jésus* is never given, as it is so commonly in Spanish. Nor are 'the gods' at the theatre called '*les dieux*' but rather, *le paradis* or *le poulailler*.

    There is nothing blasphemous about *Mon Dieu!*: 'Oh dear', 'dear me!' and so on, in the same quite innocent vein. *Bon sang!* and especially *Bon Dieu!* are a good deal stronger, however, whereas *Ciel!* sounds a bit too much eighteenth century. The name of the baker at the corner of our street is quite simply *Dieu*—which is a neat reminder that in France, *le restaurant* and *l'Eglise, le chef saucier* and *le prêtre, la table* and *l'autel* have always been close rivals.

difficilement. A very common adverb, as proven by the number of

French people who, when learning English, insist on inventing 'difficultly' in place of 'with difficulty', or 'not easily'.

diplôme (m). This is more than the piece of paper or parchment on which it is written that you have graduated from such and such an institution: it is the degree itself. *Pour trouver un poste intéressant, il faut avoir un certain nombre de diplômes.* 'To find a promising job, you have to have several degrees.'

To graduate from *or* to be a graduate of the Sorbonne is *être diplômé de la Sorbonne.*

direction (f). The first thing to notice here is that, as a general rule, to ask directions is not *demander des directions,* but *demander des indications* or *demander la route. Pardon Monsieur, voulez-vous m'indiquer la route pour Malmaison?* 'Excuse me, sir, would you please give me directions for Malmaison?' And 'a good sense of direction' is *un bon sens de l'orientation.*

In a car, *la direction* is 'the steering' (*v.* the chapter on CARS).

And although you may not think of it the first time around, in French you rarely 'conduct' an orchestra (*v.* CONDUIRE); you 'direct' it. *L'orchestre est placé sous la direction de . . .* or, *l'orchestre sera dirigé par . . .* 'The orchestra is (will be) conducted by . . .'

'Directions for use' (or for opening a tin, etc.) is *le mode d'emploi.* With a capital *D, la Direction* becomes the upper echelons of the administration. *Votre demande a été transmise à la Direction.* 'Your request (*or* application) has been sent on up to the proper authorities.'

discuter. A verb that needs to be looked at along with *disputer,* which is liable to be the stronger of the two. *Discuter* can mean simply 'to discuss', 'to talk (over)', without going so far as to argue; whereas *disputer* immediately implies at least a heated discussion. The same distinction may be made between *une discussion* and *une dispute. Disputer quelque chose* is 'to contest it' or 'to contend for it', from *un prix* to *un match* to *un objet vendu aux enchères.*

All doubt disappears with *se disputer:* 'to have a falling out', a real difference or quarrel over something. *Quand je pense que nous nous sommes disputés pour si peu de chose!* 'I can't believe we actually argued over something so unimportant!'

distraire, se. You might not guess that this verb is used as frequently as *s'amuser* to mean 'to have fun', 'to relax'. *Arrête-toi donc de travailler, il faut bien se distraire un peu!* 'Leave off work, you've got to have some fun.' *Une distraction* is 'an amusement', 'fun'— or else 'absent-mindedness' or the fact of 'being distracted'. *Il est très distrait,* 'he's very absent-minded'.

divorcer. You need to pay particular attention to the intransitive construction that this verb requires: *divorcer d'avec* (or, *avec*) *Untel* is the only way to say 'to divorce someone'. You may prefer to get around this form by saying, for instance, *ils sont divorcés depuis six mois* or again, *ils ont divorcé* . . ., or, *le divorce a été prononcé* (or *obtenu*) *il y a* . . .

dixième (m). The most common sort of chance you can buy in the weekly *Loterie Nationale*: a ticket which entitles you to one-tenth of the full stakes if your number comes up. Of course it costs only one-tenth of what a full *billet* does. In either case, you can buy your *billet* in a *tabac* (q.v.) or from any of the street-corner booths in which a man (often disabled) or sometimes a woman (usually knitting) sits patiently all day for the express purpose of selling *des billets de la Loterie*. *Tirage Mercredi* or *Tirage Ce Soir* tells you that the drawing is to be on Wednesday (or tonight). *Gros Lot de 100.000 francs*, 'big stakes *or* first prize of 100,000 francs' (*nouveaux francs*, of course; *v.* also FRANC). *Le Loto* is a more recent and highly popular form of lottery; the cards to be filled in are sold in certain *tabacs*.

donner. One of those verbs which play so active and varying a part in daily speech. You might pay especial attention to expressions in which *donner* replaces 'make' in English. *L'air de la mer donne faim.* 'The salt air makes you hungry.' And the same goes for 'to make (someone feel) hot, cold, *or* sleepy'.

Ce n'est pas donné—a phrase which crops up frequently in these inflationary days—means 'it's not cheap'; in other words, 'it's expensive'.

Ne rien donner, in regard to an attempt or a manœuvre, can be translated as 'being of no avail', 'not leading anywhere'. *On a voulu le raisonner, mais cela n'a rien donné.* 'They tried to reason with him, but got nowhere.' *Donner quelque chose* means, then, 'to lead somewhere', 'give some result'. *Qu'est-ce que ça donne?* 'What's the result?'

Donner raison à quelqu'un means 'to side with someone', 'to consider that he is right'. *Le patron a donné raison à mon collègue plutôt qu'à moi, alors, me voilà dehors!* 'The boss decided my colleague, and not I, was right: so here I am, out of a job!' And *donner tort*, as you would expect, is 'to blame someone', or 'to side against him'.

Donner le change à quelqu'un is one of those elusive phrases which do not lend themselves to pithy, accurate translations. You might say 'to hoodwink someone'.

Watch out for the distinction, apparently troublesome, between *donner du mal*: 'to be difficult', 'give trouble', and *se donner du mal*: 'to go to a lot of trouble'. *Ce travail* (or, *cet enfant*) *me donne du mal.* 'This job (*or* this child) is difficult, troublesome for me.' *Il se donne du mal pour son travail* (*son enfant*). 'He goes to a lot of trouble for his job (his child).'

dont. A bit of grammar that does not come naturally to all French children, as they—and even some adults—sometimes replace it by *que*: *C'est celui que je t'ai parlé*, instead of *C'est celui dont je t'ai* parlé. One recent song about a girl went: . . . *celle que je suis avec, celle que je suis le mec.* . . .

dossier (m). 'A file of records *or* information' on someone or something. ('A nail-file' is *une lime à ongles*.) Also, 'the back of a chair', which you cannot call simply '*le dos*'.

double (m). 'Carbon copy' or 'duplicate'. The idea extends to resemblance between persons: *Chaque personne a son double* (or *son sosie*) *quelque part dans le monde*. 'Everyone has a double somewhere in the world.'

    Une voie à double sens is 'a two-way street', as opposed to *une voie à sens unique* ('one-way street') or *à sens interdit* ('no entry').

    Doubler is 'to overtake *or* pass another car'. *Interdit de doubler en virage*. 'No overtaking on corners (no passing allowed in a curve)' (*v*. the chapter on CARS).

    Doubler is also, 'to line'; and when you buy a skirt or a suit, you look to see whether it is *entièrement doublé*, and to check on the quality of *la doublure*, 'the lining'. *Une enveloppe doublée*, 'a lined envelope'.

    Une doublure is also 'the stand-in' or 'understudy' of a cinema star; *se faire doubler*, 'to use a double'. *Doubler*, in cinematic terms, also means, 'to dub in sound': *la version doublée*, as opposed to *la version originale*. 'The dubbing' itself is *le doublage*.

    Faire double emploi, 'to be redundant *or* superfluous'.

    The opposite of *double*, in certain contexts where English may require 'single', may be *simple* (*v*. also ALLER). *Les prix ont augmenté du simple au double*. 'Prices have doubled.'

dragée (f). 'A sugar-coated almond.' Great quantities of them are distributed on the occasion of *un baptême* or *une communion*.

dresser. An unmistakable *Faux Ami*, since it has nothing to do with getting dressed, which is *s'habiller*; nor with dressing someone else, which is *habiller*; nor with 'a dress', *une robe*, nor yet with apparel in general, *les vêtements*. And still less with 'a chest of drawers' (US: 'dresser'), which is *une commode*. The meaning which you most need to remember is that of 'setting up, i.e. establishing, *or* drawing up a document'. *Le Président nous a dressé le bilan des activités de la Bourse en 1979*. 'The Chairman summarized the activities of the Stock Exchange in 1979' (*v*. also BROSSER).

    Or again, 'to train': *dresser un chien*. *Le dressage* is 'the training'. Nothing to do with 'the dressing' of a salad, which is *l'assaisonnement*.

droit (m). 'A right', or 'the right' of a moral sort. Although 'to be right' is *avoir raison* (and 'to be wrong', *avoir tort*), 'to be in the right *or* within your rights' (in an automobile accident, especially) is *être dans son droit*, just as 'to be in the wrong' is *être dans son tort*. *Le droit* is also 'the law', 'legal science'. *La Faculté de Droit* is 'law school'; *un étudiant en droit*, 'a law student'. *La loi* means 'the law' in the sense of a ruling, 'a bill (*un projet de loi*) passed into law'. *Un hors-la-loi*, 'an outlaw'.

'Right' as opposed to 'left' is, of course, *la droite*, as opposed to *la gauche. Prenez le premier virage à gauche et vous verrez la Mairie sur la droite* (or, *à droite*). 'Take the first turning to the left and you'll see the Town Hall on the right.' *La droite* and *la gauche* are also the political 'right' and 'left'.

E

échapper. This verb can serve not only where you would instinctively use 'escape' in English—*s'échapper de prison*—but as often where the situation calls for 'let slip', 'overlook', 'elude', 'be beyond (one)'. *Le vase m'a échappé des mains*. 'The vase slipped out of my hands.' *J'avoue que le sens de son astuce m'a totalement échappé.* 'I must admit that the meaning of his witticism (sally, joke) was beyond me, *or* escaped me, altogether.' *Il a laissé échapper un gros mot en pleine réunion.* 'Right in the middle of the meeting he let slip a swear word.'

A number of French words take on a special meaning when it comes to automobiles, scooters, or anything motorized: and *le pot d'échappement* is 'the exhaust pipe'.

You may be wondering what separates *s'évader* from (*s'*)*échapper*. When you really mean 'an escape', as from prison, the two are pretty nearly interchangeable. A certain film was titled *La Grande Evasion*; another, however, was called, *Un Condamné à Mort S'est Echappé*. Yet the meaning, obviously, is the same in both cases. But as soon as you want any of the figurative meanings given above, *évader* will not do at all.

échéance (f). 'The due date', or 'maturity *or* expiration date' of a bill, a bond, a lease *or* a permit. But *à brève échéance* (like, *à court terme*) and *à longue échéance* (and *à long terme*) have a more common and extended meaning: 'in the short run', and 'in the long run'. The latter can also be expressed simply by *à la longue. Echéance* comes from *échoir*, 'to lapse', 'fall due', etc., not from *échouer*, whose noun is *échec* (m), 'failure'.

écho (m). *A voir des échos de quelque chose*, 'to know about something through hearsay'.— *Est-ce que c'est un bon film?—Je ne sais pas, je n'en ai pas eu d'échos.*

écologie (f). 'The ecology movement.' *Les écologistes ont exprimé leurs revendications*. 'The environmentalists voiced their demands.'

écouteur (m). 'The ear-piece' of the telephone receiver. French telephones often come equipped with a second *écouteur* on a separate wire.

EDF (f). *L'Electricité de France*, the state utility monopoly. Its Siamese twin is the GDF (m), *Gaz de France*.

éducation (f). One of those subtle global terms, rather like 'breeding' in English, a compound of tact, politeness, delicacy. And so, more often than not, a *Faux Ami*, since 'education' in the English sense is *l'instruction* (f). *La façon dont 'untel' s'est comporté témoigne d'un manque total d'éducation.* 'The way So-and-So behaved shows a total lack of manners.' None the less, *le Ministère de l'Education Nationale* does mean the Ministry of Education. 'He is very well educated', *Il a beaucoup d'instruction* or *Il a fait beaucoup d'études* (or *des études très poussées*).

électrophone (m). 'A record player' functioning independently of a radio (*un poste de radio*); whereas *le tourne-disques* has to be hooked with the radio. *Un pick-up* and *une table de lecture* are other terms for *un tourne-disques*. 'The turntable' is *le plateau*.

élever. The critical expressions here are *bien élevé* and *mal élevé*: 'well-bred *or* -behaved', and 'ill-bred *or* -behaved'. *Cette fille est très sympathique, et bien élevée surtout.* 'That's a very nice girl and, above all, she's polite.' *Ce garçon a beau avoir une grande fortune, il est si déplaisant, si mal élevé!* 'That fellow may be as rich as Crœsus, still he's so disagreeable and so rude!'

Elysée (m). *L'Elysée* or, more properly, *le palais de l'Elysée*, is the equivalent of the American White House: the residence of the *Président de la République. L'Hôtel Matignon* is like No. 10 Downing Street in England, since it is where the *Premier Ministre* lives. *Le Quai d'Orsay* designates *le Ministère des Affaires Etrangères*, the Foreign Office.

L'Hémicycle (m) is the hall in which the *députés* hold their debates, at the *Chambre des Deputés* (*le Palais Bourbon*). The other half of *la législature* is *le Sénat*; *les Sénateurs* sit at the *Palais du Luxembourg*.

embarrasser. Although you may use this verb to mean 'to embarrass', you had better use *gêner* instead. *Je suis très gêné, je suis confus*, 'I'm most embarrassed'. (*Je suis gêné* can also mean 'I'm temporarily hard up for cash'.) For 'embarrassing', *délicat* or *gênant* is called for. *C'est très gênant (délicat) de lui demander directement.* 'It's very embarrassing to ask him outright.'

Save *embarrasser* for 'to encumber', 'to place an obstacle'; *les colis embarrassants*, or *encombrants, ne sont pas admis dans les autobus. Un embarras* is an obstacle or difficulty. *Etre dans l'embarras*, 'to be in difficulties'. *Avoir l'embarras du choix*, 'to have far more than one needs to choose from'.

embouteillage (m). The all-too-often needed word for 'traffic jam'. *Si tu avais vu l'embouteillage ce soir à l'heure de pointe!* 'You should have seen the traffic jam (bottleneck) during the rush hour this evening.'

Embouteillage does not nor ever will mean any other sort of jam: neither the sort you eat, which is *la confiture*, nor the sort you get into—'a tight spot' or a 'a fix'. For the latter there is, as you would expect, a plenitude of expressions: *avoir des ennuis* or, in terms more *familier*, *avoir des pépins*, *être dans le pétrin* (literally, the apparatus for kneading dough), *être dans de beaux draps* (sarcastic).

émotion (f). As it is most often used in English, emotion usually equates with 'sentiment' or 'feeling'. In French, the word extends easily to 'excitement' in general. *Que d'émotion(s)!* 'Such excitement!' *Mon fils nous a donné des émotions hier soir: il avait disparu pendant deux heures!* 'My son really gave us a scare last night: he disappeared for two hours!'

Emouvoir, however, is not the same as *exciter*. *Emouvoir* is 'to move' or 'touch', also 'to upset'. *C'était un spectacle des plus émouvants.* 'It was a most moving sight.' *Un(e) émotif (-ve)* is a person who is very sensitive, readily stirred. *Il faut s'y prendre très doucement avec lui, c'est un grand émotif.* 'With him you have to go about things very carefully; he's so easily upset.'

emprunt (m). 'A loan.' In the *bureau de poste*, you often see signs advertising the *emprunt SNCF*, or 'government railway bond issue'; *l'emprunt EDF*, or 'nationalized electricity bond issue', and so on. The verb, *emprunter*, does not mean 'to lend', which is *prêter*, but 'to borrow'; and *un prêt* also means 'a loan'. *Il m'a consenti un prêt de 15.000 frs.* 'He has granted me a loan of 15,000 francs.' *Il aurait emprunté à Balzac cet art du portrait.* 'His mastery of character description is said to have been modelled on Balzac's'—and notice the construction of the verb: *emprunter à*, 'to borrow from'.

Emprunter can also mean 'to make use of', 'avail oneself of'; and again you can see government posters, *Empruntez les transports publics*: 'Avail yourself of public transport'. The verb here is transitive. *Emprunter l'escalier mécanique*, 'to take the escalator'.

en. A pretty straightforward item of grammar, you say, and so it is. But by making it precede various verbs, you can change their meaning as radically as you can with postpositions in English. For instance: *En venir là* (or, *à cela*), 'to sink that low', 'to come to that'. *Je n'aurais jamais pensé qu'il en serait venu là.* 'I'd never have thought he would come to that.'

En être là, 'to be at . . .' as in, *Où en êtes-vous?* 'Where are you at?' ('How far have you got?'). *Voilà où nous en sommes.* 'Here is as far as we've got.' *A propos de votre demande de permis, dites-moi ce qu'il en est.* 'Tell me what's happened to your application for a licence.'

S'en prendre à quelqu'un, 'to turn against someone', 'hold something against him', or 'to take it out on him'.

S'en faire, 'to worry'. *Ne vous en faites pas.* 'Don't worry (about it).'

encore. The first thing to notice is that the word is not used as a noun in

French the way it is, in a sort of reverse Franglais, by English-speaking people at the end of a concert or recital. Where you may shout 'Encore!', the Frenchman shouts *Bis! Le soliste a eu quinze rappels.* 'The soloist was called back fifteen times.'

. . . *Et encore!* is worth your attention. In a tone of anger or indignation, it means, like *mais encore!*, 'so what?' 'what of it?' But uttered with a philosophical sigh, it signifies 'and even so, that may not be the case'; 'and even then'; and so on. *Madame, le travail de votre fils est tout juste acceptable, et encore . . .* 'Madam, your son's schoolwork is barely sufficient, and even at that . . .'

enfin. The chief meaning of this adverb is certainly clearcut: 'finally'. But as it is used in daily speech, it can be elusive. Often it rectifies or qualifies what has just been said. *Oh je le déteste! Enfin, je ne l'aime guère.* 'I hate him! I mean, I don't like him at all.' *Il répète toujours la même chose . . . enfin, très souvent.* 'He's forever saying the same thing . . . well, very often anyhow.'

Or again, you may be arguing (amiably) with someone and, exasperated, you cry *mais enfin!*, meaning, 'oh, for heaven's sake!', or 'now look here!' or whatever you tend to say under such circumstances. *Mais enfin! où voulez-vous en venir?* 'But what on earth are you trying to get at?' (For another meaning of *en venir, v.* EN.)

ennuyer. 'To bore'. Also, 'to bother *or* embarrass', as in *Ça m'ennuie* (*C'est très ennuyeux) de lui demander de me rendre ce service* (or *Je suis très ennuyé, je n'aime pas lui demander . . .* etc.). 'I feel very awkward (embarrassed) about asking him to do me this favour.' *Je suis ennuyé,* as you can see, is not at all the same as *Je m'ennuie,* 'I'm bored'.

en plus. Literally, 'in addition'; as opposed to *compris,* 'included'. *Menu à 30F: hors d'œuvre, plat de viande, dessert; boisson en plus* (or *en sus). Service 15% non compris.* 'Tip or service charge 15% extra.' *Les prix indiqués dans ce catalogue sont hors taxe; TVA en plus.* 'The prices quoted in this catalogue do not include tax; add on VAT.'

en principe. Impossible to get through the day without making use of this most exasperating, most elastic of expressions. Of course it means: 'as a rule', 'in theory'; but no words can convey the infinite scepticism that accompanies it, the shrug of the shoulder, the lift of the eyebrow. The implication of complicity may be very strong. *En principe elle vient dîner chez nous ce soir; mais tu la connais, je dis bien—en principe.* 'She's supposed to have dinner with us tonight but you know what she's like: she's *supposed* to come.'

entendre parler. When someone asks you pointblank, *avez-vous lu ce livre?* and you want to say 'no, but I've heard of it', then this is the expression to fall back on: *non, mais j'en ai entendu parler. On n'entend parler que de cet homme politique en ce moment.* 'You hear of no one but that politician these days.'

Entendu, meaning 'all right', 'it's agreed', is generally preferable to *d'accord*, which corresponds to 'OK'. *D'acc* is really too limp to be anything more than slangy. *OK* (pronounced as in English) has been adopted by a number of (mostly younger) French people.

S'entend is not to be confused with *sous-entendu*. The first is quite like *bien entendu, bien sûr*: 'of course', 'it goes without saying'; it stresses an already apparent meaning. But *un sous-entendu* points to 'an implied *or* hidden meaning'. *Son style devient obscur à force de sous-entendus*. 'His style is quite obscure, you have to read so much between the lines.'

entorse (f). If you are so unfortunate as to sprain your ankle, this is the word that applies: *j'ai une entorse à la cheville*. Figuratively, a minor departure from the law or from the truth calls for the same expression: *Son action est une entorse au règlement*. 'His action is a slight deviation from the law.'

Entrez! When someone knocks at the door, this is the expression you need. You cannot use *avancez!*, although an analogy with the Italian may be tempting.

épreuve (f) **de force**. 'Showdown.'

espace (m). The first thing to notice is the masculine gender, since *race* and *place* might lead you to suppose that *espace* too was feminine. Next, the difference between *l'espace* and *la place*. *Espace* is simply less tangible, let us say, or less earthly: *l'exploration de l'espace*, 'exploration of (inter-planetary) space'. 'Space ship', *engin spatial*. Words or objects which are *espacés* are those arranged with intervals between them. *Ses visites se sont espacées*. 'His visits became more and more infrequent.' City planners talk about *les espaces verts*, 'open areas' or 'green spaces'.

La place means 'room' or 'seat'; *Cette place est-elle libre, s'il vous plaît?* 'Is this seat free?' (in the train, cinema, etc.). The Mad Hatter and his friends, had they spoken French, would have cried, *Plus de place, plus de place!* 'No room, no room!' In the plural, *plus de places* means 'no more seats'.

Louer une place is 'to buy a ticket' for a play or concert.

And of course *une place* is also 'a public square'.

essentiel (m). 'The important thing', 'the main thing' (which you may first be tempted to translate literally *la chose importante*). *L'essentiel c'est de réussir à le voir aujourd'hui*. 'The main thing is to get to see him today.' *Le tout* and *le principal* are also used in this way.

étanche. The word for 'watertight'; *l'étanchéité* (f) is the noun. Not to be confused with *imperméable*, 'waterproof', and *imperméabilité* (f), the corresponding noun. *Un imperméable* is 'a raincoat' or 'mac'. When you take it to be cleaned you may need to specify whether you want it merely *nettoyé*, 'cleaned', or *ré-imperméabilisé*, 'waterproofed', as well.

étrennes (f. pl.). New Year's gifts; now an old-fashioned notion, superseded by the giving of Christmas presents. Today *étrennes* are almost exclusively a way of remembering—around December 31 (*la Saint-Sylvestre*) or January 1, and with an appropriate sum of money—the people who have served you throughout the year: the *concierge* and *le facteur* ('postman') are the most obvious examples. Even if you move into your new flat on New Year's Eve, you will do well to give *des étrennes* to your new *concierge*, and of course you must not forget the old one when you move out (*v.* also POURBOIRE).

Etrenner quelque chose is 'to use something (especially clothing) for the first time'.

euphorisant (m). A 'stimulant' or 'upper', a medicine or drug that makes you float, feel high.

évident. *C'est évident*, 'It's obvious'. But *ce n'est pas évident* is not exactly the opposite: 'that may be no easy matter'. *Il faudrait qu'il se trouve demain pas plus tard qu'à 9 heures à Avignon. Ce n'est pas évident.*

évolué(e) Another of those terms of social judgement (*v.* also ÉLEVER), so handy and so critical, which might not occur to you immediately. You can apply it (*a*) to a whole people, as you can the verb in English and in which case you would translate by 'very civilized', 'advanced', 'refined', but probably not by 'evolved'. Or (*b*) to an individual or individuals, in which case 'enlightened' or 'refined' is perhaps the best translation.

examen (m). The ordinary 'examination', as distinct from *un concours* (q.v.). *Passer un examen* is the standard way of saying, 'to sit for an exam' (US: 'to take an exam'). But 'to pass an exam'—to come out of it successfully—must be translated *réussir un examen* or, *être reçu à un examen*. If the case is unfortunately the opposite, then you have a handful of expressions from which to choose: *échouer à l'examen* or, more commonly, *être recalé*; or in terms still more authentically *estudiantins*, *louper* or *rater son examen* or *être collé*. 'The examiner', except in the case of a medical exam, is *l'examinateur*; note the extra syllable.

expérience (f). A notorious traitor of a word: not only 'experience', as in English, but also 'experiment'. You cannot wish the word '*un expériment*' into existence, although you do have *expérimental*, and *expérimentateur* (another case of the extra syllable). And to compound the confusion, the word for 'experienced' is *expérimenté*. This is not so complicated as it sounds, but it does take some getting used to.

When you want to talk about, for instance, your experiences in Russia, you can say *ce qui m'est arrivé* or *ce que j'ai vu en Russie*.

Tenter une expérience is either 'to do an experiment' or 'to attempt something', 'to give it a go'.

expertise (f). A troublesome word, as it does not mean what its identical twin means in English—i.e. 'proficiency', 'knowledge'. It refers to the estimate or judgement (of the extent of damage caused by some accident, for instance) made by *un expert*. The verb is *expertiser*.

exprès. *Faire quelque chose exprès* is the most common way of saying 'to do something deliberately, *or* on purpose'. And of course you can replace *faire* with any other appropriate verb: *elle est venue exprès, il a plongé exprès, je m'en vais exprès*, etc.

extensible. 'Stretchable', or 'stretch' (when speaking of cloth).

extra. Not 'extra' or 'additional', which is *en plus, en surnombre, de trop*, or *supplémentaire*, but instead 'extraordinary', 'exceptionally good'. A bit *familier*. The butcher will often mark *rosbif* [sic] *extra*: 'top quality roastbeef'.

F

façon (f). 'Fashion' in the sense of 'way' or 'manner', or of 'craftsmanship'. But 'clothing fashion' is *la mode. D'une façon comme d'une autre*: literally, 'anyhow', 'at any rate'. *A sa façon*, 'in his (her) own way', can be used as a back-handed compliment. *Il était très aimable—enfin, à sa façon (v.* also: SANS FAÇON).

faire-part (m). An announcement of a birth, death, or marriage; 'to announce something' is *faire part de quelque chose. Il m'a fait part de ses projets de mariage*. 'He told me of his plans for getting married.'

fait. Or, *bien fait*: said of a cheese that is ripe. *Mûr* applies to ripe fruit, vegetables and even, figuratively, to people, but will not do for cheeses. Familiarly, *être (re)fait* is like *se faire avoir*: 'to be had', 'to be duped'.

falloir. This being an impersonal verb, you will hear it most often in the form of *il faut. (Il vous faut travailler davantage*; or, *il faut que vous travailliez davantage*: 'You have to, *or* must, work more'.) But that is no reason for confusing it with *fauter*, which is a different matter altogether: 'to sin' (as used by a priest in confession), 'to be seduced'.

Il faut ce qu'il faut is one of those marvellously concise, untranslatable expressions: 'It takes what it takes'. Said on an occasion requiring a big celebration, as when a proud papa distributes dozens of cigars at the birth of his first child.

farces et attrapes (f. pl.). The whole range of practical jokes, tricks, hoaxes, gadgets to fool people. *La farce* is also 'a (culinary) stuffing'; and the verb, *farcir*, applies only to stuffing. 'To play a practical joke' is *faire (or jouer) une farce (à quelqu'un)*.

farfelu. Means 'bizarre', 'whimsical', 'fanciful', 'exaggerated'. Although this word and its corresponding noun, *le farfelutisme*, are said to have been coined by André Malraux, many dictionaries took a long time about accepting them. *J'ai rencontré un camarade que j'avais perdu de vue: toujours aussi farfelu.* 'I ran into an old friend I'd lost track of: just as light-headed and wacky as ever.'

faubourg (m). Although *la banlieue* denotes suburbs in general, *faubourg* still retains its meaning of 'an outlying and humble neighbourhood of working-class population'. An apparently contradictory connotation of aristocracy attaches to the old *Faubourg St. Germain* which, like the present *rue du Faubourg St. Honoré*, is now not only within the gates of Paris, but right in the centre and one of the most sought-after quarters.

faux frais (m. pl.). These are incidentals, the items which you are prone to forget in making out your budget—*les taxis, les pourboires, les fleurs pour votre hôtesse, les timbres-poste, et le reste!*

férié. *Un jour férié* is 'a holiday', as opposed to *un jour ouvrable*, or 'working day' when shops, banks, and the like are open. *Le lundi de la Pentecôte est un jour férié.* 'Whit Monday *or* the Monday after Whitsun is a holiday.'

ferme (f). 'A farm'; but whereas in English you live 'on a farm', in French you live 'in' it: *dans la ferme*, or *à la ferme*.

As an adjective, *ferme* has, among others, a meaning which may not appear in the dictionary: *Il fut condamné à trois ans de prison ferme.* 'He was sentenced to three years' imprisonment.' As opposed to: *Il fut condamné à trois ans de prison avec sursis.* 'He was given a three-year suspended sentence.'

The word for a 'firm' or 'business' is not *ferme* but *firme* (f), though by far the commoner term for it is *une société (anonyme)*.

fermeture annuelle (f). A fact of commercial life which has attained the proportions of a national phenomenon: virtually every *boutique* or *magasin* (except *les grands magasins*, or 'department stores') and many restaurants and theatres will close for the month of August. Beginning usually in mid-June an announcement of the dates of its *fermeture* is tacked to every shop-door or chalked on the windows. For the few Parisians who remain in Paris during this singular month, there is the joy of being able to drive and park their cars with relative ease, countered by the problem of finding *une boulangerie, une crémerie, une boucherie, une blanchisserie,* even *un tabac* open in the neighbourhood. The government is making vigorous efforts to persuade people to stagger their holidays (v. CONGÉ) over the period from June to September, particularly since *la rentrée*—'the re-opening of schools'—does not come much before the middle of September. But August remains the height of the season *au bord de la mer*—and of the tourist season in Paris.

fermeture éclair (f). 'A zipper'. A registered trade name (*v.* BIC).

fermeture pression (f). 'A snap fastener', for clothing.

fête (f). 'Holiday', in general (although 'to go on holiday' is *partir en vacances*). But *les fêtes*, or *la période des fêtes*, refers almost exclusively to the Christmas-and-New-Year's season. *Sa fête* is 'one's saint's day' or 'name-day'; *son anniversaire*, 'one's birthday'. *Fêter son anniversaire*, 'to celebrate one's birthday'.

feu (m). Doubtless you already know that when you want to ask for a light for your cigarette, you cannot request *une lumière, une flamme*, nor anything but *du feu: avez-vous du feu? Une allumette* of course is 'a match'; *un briquet*, 'a cigarette lighter'; *un cendrier*, 'an ashtray'; *un porte-cigarettes*, 'a cigarette case' (*v.* PORTE-).

Faire du feu is 'to light a fire' or 'to heat' one's house. *Le temps est si doux que je n'ai pas fait de feu.* 'The weather is so mild that I haven't turned on the heat in my house' (*v.* INCENDIE).

Mettre le feu, however, is 'to set fire to' something. *Attention où tu poses ton fer à repasser, tu vas mettre le feu.* 'Be careful where you put your iron, you'll set the house on fire.'

Les feux are 'traffic lights'. *Le feu vient de passer au vert.* 'The light has just turned green' (*v.* the chapter on CARS).

feutre (m). 'A felt-tip pen.'

figuratif. If you're talking about art, this is the translation of 'figurative'. But 'a figurative meaning' is *un sens figuré*—as opposed to 'literal meaning', *le sens propre*—and 'figuratively' is *au sens figuré*. 'A figure of speech', however, is *une façon de parler*. *Façon de parler* said as a sort of afterthought, means 'as it were', or 'so to speak'.

figurer, se. A much more common means than you might imagine of expressing: 'to know', 'to imagine'. *Figurez-vous que je l'ai vu hier.* 'Did you know that I saw him yesterday?'

filer. 'To run' or 'ladder', when it comes to stockings. And 'to disappear rapidly' when it comes to persons, time, or money. *Filer à l'anglaise* is 'to take French leave'.

fille (f). The thing to steel yourself to from the beginning is that there seems to be no age limit for calling a female *une fille*; and that the term in itself need have neither infantile nor dubious connotations (although *aller voir les filles* does distinctly mean 'to go to a brothel'). A woman of 75 may well call her contemporary *une fille: c'est une brave fille*. Clearly there is no disrespect implied here; but for a woman of 20 to call the same person *une fille*: unthinkable. Since the line is so hard to draw, it all being a matter of context and *milieu*, you will do well to say *une femme, une jeune femme, une femme d'un certain âge* (roughly, 'middle-aged'), or *une dame* for an older respected woman, at least until you are certain whom you're talking about and to whom. For a female of your own age or less, there is no problem (*v.* also GARÇON).

Une vieille fille is 'an old maid', although politeness would call for *une femme célibataire*.

Une amie, or *une petite amie*, 'girl friend'.

Le nom de jeune fille, 'maiden name'.

flacon (m). 'A small bottle' or 'flask', particularly for medicines and perfume. You would never say *une bouteille* in speaking of either of those items, any more than you would speak of '*un flacon*' *de vin*. *Une carafe*, 'a decanter'.

flambée (f) **des prix**. A forceful journalistic term for the effects of inflation.

flotter. A colloquial way of saying *pleuvoir*, just as *la flotte* can replace *la pluie*, but as a general rule you will do better to use the more classic terms. *Il n'est pas tombé de la dernière pluie* means 'he was not born yesterday'.

In monetary terms, since fixed rates of exchange were abandoned in 1973, *le flottement des monnaies*, 'the floating of the various currencies', has been a term of key importance. 'Exchange rate': *taux* (m) or *cours* (m) *du change* or *des changes*. *Une monnaie forte* (*faible*), 'a strong (weak) currency'.

foncièrement. 'Basically', 'profoundly'; and more widely used than you might expect, judging from the rather restricted sound of *foncier*, 'landed', as in *crédit foncier*. *Il faut se méfier de cet homme, il cache bien son jeu mais il est foncièrement méchant.* 'Beware of that man, he's thoroughly bad but he knows how to cover it up.'

fond (m). *Au fond* is a handy little phrase corresponding to 'come to think of it', or 'when you come right down to it', or 'at bottom'. *Un fond* is 'a background' (as in painting) and *au fond de la salle* is 'at the back of the room'. *Le fond de la mer*, 'the seabed' or 'ocean bed'.

force (f) **de frappe**. 'Striking power.'

forcément. A more commonly used adverb than you might think, for 'necessarily'. *Vous qui êtes français, vous connaissez tous les fromages—Pas forcément!* 'Since you are French, you must be familiar with every sort of cheese.' 'Not necessarily!' Similarly, *c'est forcé* is very often employed to mean 'it's unavoidable', 'it's necessarily so', and *ce n'est pas forcé* to mean the contrary (*v.* also OBLIGATOIRE).

forme (f). *Etre en forme* is a most convenient expression for 'to be in good shape, feeling well'. *Allez donc au théâtre sans moi, je ne me sens pas très en forme.* 'Go on to the theatre without me; I'm not really feeling up to snuff.' *Elle est en pleine forme.* 'She's just fine.' 'A form', in the sense of a standard or official document, is *un formulaire—le formulaire de demande de la carte de séjour*, 'the application form for a residence permit'—or simply, *une feuille. Il faut remplir les feuilles d'impôts pour la fin février.* 'Tax-forms must be filled out by the end of February.'

four (m). Not only 'oven', but 'a failure' or 'flop' as well. In the latter meaning it cannot be applied to persons, however: only to plays, music, books, any sort of performance or entertainment.

fourneau (m). 'A furnace', as you would expect; but also 'a stove' or 'cooker'. 'A furnace' is also termed *une chaudière*, especially when placed in your own flat for individual central heating. 'A stove' is more commonly called *une cuisinière* (*électrique* or *à gaz*), a word which in turn can also mean 'a cook'. Which is why many a Frenchman, translating literally, may call your cook 'a cooker'.
'The bowl' of a pipe is *le fourneau*; 'the stem' is *le tuyau*.

franc (m) The terms *nouveau franc* and *ancien franc* (or *centime*) still crop up often, even though the official conversion from old to new francs was achieved back in 1959, by moving the decimal point (actually in French a comma, *la virgule*) two places to the left. People born since then obviously have no trouble discussing even very large sums—e.g. the price of a flat in Paris—or the price of shoes in the official way (1.000.000F or 400F); older people may tend to stick to *anciens francs* (100.000.000 or 40.000). Even news announcers will sometimes say, *Lors du hold-up commis ce matin, les malfaiteurs ont réussi à s'enfuir avec la somme de trois cent mille francs, c'est-à-dire, 30 millions de nos centimes actuels.* Of course, when buying something—a car, for instance—you write out your cheque in the official way: *trente-quatre mille sept cent soixante-cinq francs et 99 centimes* (34.765,99).
Etre franc (*-che*), 'to be frank'.
Avoir son franc-parler, 'to be outspoken', 'not to mince one's words'.

frapper. A verb that crops up in a handful of everyday contexts. *Entrez sans frapper* on an office door enjoins you to 'enter without knocking'. *Tiens! on frappe*: 'I say, there's someone at the door.' 'I hear someone knocking': *J'entends frapper.*
Frapper also has the more forceful meaning 'to strike'. First of all, physically: *il a frappé le cambrioleur.* 'He struck the burglar.' *Ce qui m'a surtout frappé, c'est la propreté de son intérieur.* 'I was especially struck by the spotlessness of his home.' *Il y a une ressemblance frappante entre l'oncle et le neveu.* 'There is a strik-ing resemblance between uncle and nephew.' *On va frapper une nouvelle pièce de 10 francs.* 'They're going to mint a new 10 franc coin.'
Frapper le vin (*blanc*), 'to chill (white) wine'.

froid (m). As a noun, *le froid* does mean 'the cold'—in terms either of weather or of refrigeration. But 'a cold', the sneeze and cough variety, is *un rhume*, and 'to have a cold' is *être enrhumé*; 'to have a bad cold', *être très enrhumé* or *avoir un gros rhume*. Whereas 'to catch a cold' is *attraper un rhume,* 'to catch cold' is *attraper* or *prendre froid.*

froisser. 'To crumple' or 'wrinkle'; and 'to ruffle' in a figurative way: 'to offend', which you can also express by *offenser,* of course. 'To hurt *or* wound (someone's feelings)' is *blesser,* which may also mean, 'to inflict a physical wound'. *Mais ne te froisse pas! je te dis ce que je pense, voilà tout!* 'Don't get your back up! I'm just telling you what I think.'

Un tissu infroissable (or, indéformable) is '*an* uncrushable (US: wrinkleproof) cloth'.

fugue (f). *Faire une fugue,* 'to run away from home'; *un enfant fugueur.*

fumiste. An elusive adjective (or noun). *Un fumiste* has an inclination to laziness and day-dreaming, and doesn't take his work seriously. A close cousin of *un farceur* and *un plaisantin,* as in *un joyeux fumiste.*

If you have a fireplace, you will require the services of a professional *fumiste,* who is a very serious person indeed; his business is *la fumisterie,* 'the repairing of stoves and chimneys'. *Un ramoneur* is the man who cleans them, 'a sweep'.

fusionner. This is the verb you want in talking of a merger between two companies (*sociétés*; *v.* S.A.). 'The merger' itself is *la fusion.*

G

gâchis (m). A strong, and common, word for an opportunity-wasting mess caused by bungling or ineptness.

Messiness as such is *fatras* (m), *désordre* (m), *pagaille* (f).

gaffe (f). 'A boat-hook', certainly; but far more frequently, 'a social blunder', like *une bévue* or *un faux pas. Il a fait une gaffe énorme.* 'He made a terrific blunder.' *Faire gaffe,* without the indefinite article, is a very colloquial phrase: 'to be careful', 'to pay attention'. *Alors, faites gaffe à la différence entre ces deux expressions!*

galette (f). On 6 January, or Twelfth Night, it is the custom to '*tirer les rois*': you buy a round flat flaky cake, *la galette (fourrée aux amandes,* or not), with which the *boulangerie* will usually furnish a gilt-paper crown. The person who finds the little plastic king (still called *la fève* because initially the custom was to insert a bean in the cake) in his portion of *galette* is the king (or queen), and has the right to choose his queen (or her king). This is a very pleasant little ceremony, reserved for the family or close friends.

In slang, *la galette,* like *le fric,* means 'money', 'dough'.

gant de toilette (m). Also called, *une main de toilette*. 'A wash-cloth' which instead of being a flat square, is sewn up to form an oblong glove. It is made of *tissu éponge* ('towelling *or* terry-cloth'), just like 'a bath towel' (*une serviette éponge*).

garage (m). On certain little-frequented and excessively narrow roads in Provence, the word will indicate a modest lay-by at the edge where you can pull off to let a car go by in the opposite direction. Otherwise, however, the word means, as in English, 'a repair shop' or 'a closed space for parking your car' (*v.* BOX). Notice that you put your car *au garage*, and not *dans le' garage*.

garce (f). One of the nastier epithets applicable to the female of the species: 'a bitch', no less. So beware, and for heaven's sake don't think that it means 'a tomboy'! 'A tomboy' is simply *un garçon manqué* or (rarely) *une garçonne*.

garçon (m). The same remark as for *fille* (q.v.): no apparent age limit. *C'est un brave garçon.* 'He's a fine chap (nice fellow).' Again, to be on the safe side in speaking, you will do well to say *un homme*, *un jeune homme*, *un homme d'un certain âge* or more respectfully, *un monsieur*. The maid, when you come home and ask her for messages, will say, not *un garçon*, but *un monsieur a téléphoné*.

By analogy with *une vieille fille*, *un vieux garçon* is 'a bachelor', especially a confirmed one; again, a more courteous term is *un célibataire*. *Enterrer sa vie de garçon*, 'to have a last fling with the boys before marrying'.

And no matter what his age, 'the waiter' in a restaurant or at *une terrasse* is *le garçon*; to summon him you call *Garçon!*, and not *Monsieur*.

Un garçon de courses is 'an errand boy', otherwise called *un coursier* (just like a horse—in more poetical terms).

gare (f). This is one of the two sorts of *gare*, as you are probably aware: the 'station' or 'terminal' sort. *L'aérogare* is 'the air terminal' (*des Invalides* in Paris), as distinct from *l'aéroport*, 'the airport' (*Orly* or *Roissy-Charles de Gaulle* in Paris).

The other sort of *gare*, being exclamatory, has no gender. *Gare à vous!* 'Beware!' 'Watch out!' or, in a threatening way, 'I warn you!' *Ma belle-mère est arrivée hier sans crier gare.* 'My mother-in-law arrived yesterday without any warning.'

garer, se. 'To park one's car.' But the fact of parking is *le stationnement*; *stationnement interdit*, 'no parking'.

gars (m). The dictionary will tell you that this means 'a young fellow'; but the implication if you call someone *un gars* is distinctly one of a superior speaking to (or of) an inferior or, just possibly, one of great familiarity among equals. *Allez les gars!* could be rendered 'come on, boys!' 'let's go, gang!' or some such phrase. The pronunciation calls for a barely audible *r* and a totally inaudible *s*; otherwise you'll find yourself saying *garce* (q.v.).

gâteau (m). 'Cake'—except fruit cake (v. CAKE). *Un gâteau sec*, like *un biscuit*, is 'a sweet biscuit' (US: 'cookie'), while *un gâteau salé* is 'a cheese *or* cocktail biscuit (US: cracker)'.

Un papa (or, *une maman*) *gâteau* is 'a doting parent'; the verb, *gâter*, is 'to spoil'. *Un enfant gâté*, 'a spoiled child'.

A near-slang expression is, *c'est du gâteau*: 'it's as easy as pie', 'it's like falling off a log', 'it's a walk-away'.

gendre (m). 'Son-in-law.' Used alternatively with *beau-fils* (m). Not to be confused with *genre* (m), q.v.

genre (m). 'Gender', 'sort', 'manner', 'type', hence, 'style' as well. *Ça m'étonne de lui, ce n'est pas son genre*. 'I'm surprised at him, that's not at all like him.' *C'est ce qu'on fait de mieux dans le genre*. 'It's the best thing of its type that you can find.'

Un genre de, or *une sorte de*, may be used and over-used in as meaningless a way as 'a kind of' or 'a sort of' in English.

gens (m. and f. pl.). Lest we forget the classic confusion between *gens* and *peuple*: *les gens* means 'people'; and *le peuple*, 'a people' in the anthropological or political sense. *Les peuples de ce continent*, 'the peoples of this continent'. *Les gens de ce quartier*, 'the people in this neighbourhood'. *En appeler au peuple* is a way of saying 'to bring a question before the voters in a referendum', 'to appeal (*or* go) to the people'.

The singular of *gens* is *la gent* (both pronounced like the masculine name *Jean*), from the Latin *gens*, nomin., and *gentem*, accus. *La gent* carries a literary meaning, tinged with irony as in La Fontaine: *la gent marécageuse*, 'frogs'; or *la gent épicière*, 'grocers'. The archaic adjective *gent(e)* meant 'well-born': *gente dame*, 'gentlewoman'.

goûter (m). Written just like the verb from which it comes, 'to taste'. It approximates to the English custom of afternoon tea, being a snack taken in the late afternoon and specifically, in the case of school-children, at about 4 or 4.30, when the schools finish. Which is why it is often called *un quatre heures*. At this time there will be a rush to the nearest *boulangerie* or *pâtisserie*, to buy *un petit pain au chocolat* (a soft roll with chocolate tucked inside), *un croissant*, *un chausson aux pommes*, or simply bread.

It is amazing the number of people, and not only children either, you can see walking about *à l'heure du déjeuner*, *du goûter*, or *du dîner*, nibbling away at one end of the *baguette* (v. PAIN) they've just bought for the approaching meal. So if you send someone out to buy bread, you will do well to order one bigger than you really need, to allow for its shrinkage on the way home!

A quick, light meal at any time of day is *un casse-croûte*.

Goûter is not to be confused with *goutter*, 'to drip'; *une goutte* is 'a drop'.

graisse (f). *La graisse* or *la matière grasse* or *le corps gras* is 'the fat' or 'grease' used in or resulting from cooking, whereas *le gras* is the fatty part of the meat; *le maigre* is the lean.

La graisse can also be any sort of grease, such as that used on machinery; and *le graissage* is the lubrication done on a car.

Cheese or cream marked *60% MG* (*matières grasses*) has a fat content of 60%. To indicate, on the contrary, that they have a low fat content or none at all, yogurts and certain cheeses will be marked *maigre*. *Faire maigre* is 'to abstain from eating meat', as on fast days; *faire gras* is of course not so much to eat fat as 'to eat meat'.

Finally where you may call a dish *gras*—'fatty' or 'heavy'— beware of calling it *graisseux*, which means downright 'greasy'! And if you ask *le pharmacien* for 'cough syrup', he's likely to ask whether you have *une toux sèche* or *une toux grasse*—'a dry *or* a throaty cough'.

grève (f). 'A labour strike'; *la grève générale*—no difficulty in understanding this, surely; the difficulty lies in putting up with it, as it affects all public transport and utilities. *Faire la grève* is 'to go out on strike'; (*être*) *en grève*, '(to be) on strike'. And 'the striker' is *le gréviste*.

La grève in the sense of 'shore' is used for the most part in poetry, rather like 'strand'. It is often applied to that part of the Norman coast nearest to *le Mont St. Michel*.

Etre grevé d'impôts is something else again: 'to be burdened with taxes', so that *être dégrevé d'impôts* is a far more pleasant expression: 'to be given some tax relief'.

griller. 'To grill' or 'toast'—and 'to overheat', 'to use up by overheating', as in *griller le moteur*, *griller la résistance* (*électrique*). *Le pain grillé*, made in *un grille-pain*, is 'toast'; but it is often considered chic to talk of *des toasts*, rounds of pre-toasted bread. *Griller un feu rouge* is 'to go through a red light'.

grognon. From *grogner*, 'to growl' or 'snarl'; and said of someone, especially a child, who is grumpy or cranky.

gros mot (m). Not a 'big word', but a 'bad word', or 'swear word' (*juron*, m).

gros plan (m). A 'close-up' in photography. *Dans cette scène on voit le héros en gros plan*.

grossir. 'To gain, *or* put on, weight.' You can also say, *prendre du poids*. 'To lose, *or* take off, weight': *maigrir*. *Actuellement elle suit un régime rigoureux pour maigrir*. 'Now she's following a strict slimming diet.'

H

habile. 'Skilful', 'able'. You can apply this to something abstract —*un habile jeu de mots*, 'a clever (*or* agile) play on words'—as well as to material circumstances. *Elle est très habile de ses dix doigts.* 'She is really clever with her hands.'

habillé. Not only 'dressed', but also 'dressy'. *Moi à ta place, ma chère, je prendrais ce manteau-là, il est infiniment plus habillé.* 'If I were you, my dear, I'd buy that coat, it's much the more dressy.' *Un déshabillé* is 'a negligee'. You need to be careful, by the way, about using the adjective *négligé*; it is not necessarily derogatory. *Elle reçut son amie en négligé.* 'She was casually dressed when her friend came in.' But: *On le remarqua au négligé de sa tenue.* 'He stood out by the carelessness of his appearance.'

hausse (f). The contrary of *la baisse*, in financial and commercial matters. *Les loyers sont en hausse.* 'Rents are going up.' *La hausse des prix*, 'the rise in prices'. *Baisse importante sur le veau*, at the butcher's: 'a big reduction in the price of veal'.
  Hausser les épaules, 'to shrug one's shoulders'. 'The shrug' itself, however, is not *la hausse* but *le haussement d'épaules*.

hexagone (m). With a capital H, this designates continental France (because of its readily discernible six-sided shape), without either Corsica or any of the *DOM* (*Départements d'Outre-Mer*) or *TOM* (*Territoires d'Outre-Mer*). *On estime que cette année environ 60% des Français resteront dans l'Hexagone durant la période des congés annuels.*

histoire (f). Another of those words the correct and frequent use of which marks the genuine speaker of French. You know that it means 'history': *l'histoire des pays d'Europe centrale*; and 'story' or 'tale': *une histoire pour enfants. Il raconte des histoires drôles comme personne.* 'He tells funny stories better than anyone else.'
  But you will also find it meaning 'cock and bull story', 'fuss', 'trouble', 'matter', 'business'. *Ce n'est pas la première fois qu'il a des histoires avec la police.* 'It's not the first time he's had a run-in with the police.' *Ne me racontez pas d'histoires.* 'Don't hand me a lot of guff (give me a lot of bull)' (*v.* also BARATIN). *Toute cette histoire me retourne.* 'The whole business upsets me.' *Ils m'en ont fait des histoires avant de m'accorder ce certificat!* 'They made such a fuss before giving me this reference!'

hôtel particulier (m). This cannot be translated as 'a private hotel', but as 'a town house'. Many of the finer and older ones in Paris, particularly in the Marais district, have been restored and are open to the public or used as museums, libraries, etc.; a number of others have been taken over by ministries, embassies, or schools.

housse (f). 'A slip-case' or 'cover', over car seats, armchairs, and the like, or mounted over a metal frame as a movable wardrobe. Or a protective soft bag to cover, for instance, *un aspirateur* ('vacuum cleaner'), as opposed to *un étui*, a small rigid case enclosing an easily portable object, as *un étui à lunettes*, or *un écrin*, 'a jewel-case'.

Une housse belongs to the relatively small number of words beginning with '*un h aspiré*'—so that you say *la housse*, and not '*l'housse*'. *La honte, les Halles, le héron, la hotte, la haine, la hauteur, la hausse, le haricot, la halte, le homard, le hasard, le hibou* and *la Haute Loire* are others in this select group.

I

ignorer. Used as often as a phrase which an English speaker finds more likely: *ne pas savoir*. *J'ignorais qu'* or *je ne savais pas qu' il était marié*: 'I didn't know he was married'. But 'to ignore someone', in the sense of a social slight, might better be translated *faire semblant de ne pas voir* (*entendre, écouter*) *quelqu'un*.

For 'an ignoramus', *ignare* is the term you want.

illuminé. Noun and adjective. The noun is loosely used to mean not only a visionary but also a demented person, *un fou*. So, it is definitely not the word that fits if you want to pay someone the compliment of calling him 'enlightened', which would be *éclairé*, or perhaps *évolué*. Similarly, *une lampe éclaire bien* ('a lamp gives good light'), or *une pièce est mal éclairée* ('a room is ill lit'). *Un monument* however is indeed *illuminé* ('a monument is flood-lit'). *L'illumination*, 'flood-lighting'.

illustré (m). 'Comic book'; *v.* BANDE DESSINÉE.

impayable. Nothing to do with finances, but 'priceless' in the sense of 'too funny', 'the end', as said of an anecdote.

important. An important, and rather tricky, adjective, for it means not only 'significant', but 'sizeable', 'impressive' as well. *Il importe de savoir lequel des deux rivaux a la fortune la plus importante* (*v.* IMPORTER). 'We must know which of the two rivals has the greater fortune.' *C'est l'immeuble le plus important qui ait été construit ici depuis vingt ans*. 'It is the biggest building that has been erected here in twenty years.'

importer. 'To import', first of all; and 'an importer', like 'an examiner', takes an extra syllable in French: *un importateur*.

'To be important', also—a verb which is lacking in English. *Il importe d'établir l'heure exacte à laquelle il est sorti*. 'The exact time at which he went out is of vital importance.'

A most important derivation of this verb is the handful of *n'importe* expressions: *n'importe qui, n'importe quand, n'importe où, n'importe comment* . . . 'No matter who (anyone), no matter when (any time), no matter where (anywhere), no matter how (anyhow, any way).'

impression (f). This is the noun of two different verbs: *imprimer*, 'to print'; and *impressionner*, 'to impress' or 'to be impressive'. You may read of a book that it is the first *réimpression* of a given work in some years; and inside the book you may find, *première impression, Janvier 1962; deuxième impression, Novembre 1972. Cet événement m'a grandement impressionné* (or, *m'a fait une grande impression*). 'That event made a big impression on me.' 'Impressive' is expressed by the participle, *impressionnant*—harder to remember than *imposant* for 'imposing', since in the latter case both are participles.

incendie (m). A word that looks as though it should be feminine. *Un incendie* is bigger than *un feu*; you could not call *un feu de bois*, or *un feu de camp, un incendie. Un incendie* is what the firemen (*les* [*sapeurs*] *pompiers*) are called out for. *Faire du feu* is 'to light a small fire', doing it deliberately, or 'to heat one's house'; *mettre le feu* means 'to set fire (to something), often inadvertently'; while *incendier* means 'deliberately to set (something big) on fire'; *v.* also FEU.

indicatif (m). The theme-song or music habitually used to announce or conclude a radio or television programme.

indiquer. The verb to remember when you want to ask directions (*v.* DIRECTION). *Voulez-vous m'indiquer le chemin* (or *la route*) *pour aller à Chartres? Indications* (f.pl.) is the corresponding noun.

Furthermore, 'to recommend'. On the bottle of *médicament* which you buy *chez le pharmacien*, you will read: *Indications: rhume, bronchite etc.* 'Recommended in cases of cold, bronchitis etc.' *Agir à son insu, ce n'est pas indiqué.* 'It is not advisable to act without his knowing of it.'

Contre-indiquer, sometimes encountered in a medical context, is 'to advise against'. *Les cas de contre-indication de ce traitement sont les suivants.* 'This treatment is not recommended in the following cases.'

infect. A very colloquial adjective, used to mean simply 'filthy', 'lousy', 'incredibly bad', but not 'infected', which is *infecté(e)*.

infirmer. *Infirmer une nouvelle* is, like *démentir*, to deny a reported piece of news; the opposite of *confirmer* or *corroborer*. The noun is *démenti* (m) or, more rarely, *infirmation*.

inférieur. Means both inferior (*Cet article est d'une qualité très inférieure*) and lower (*les membres inférieurs*, 'the lower limbs'). The *département* of *Seine Maritime* (including Le Havre) used to be called *Seine Inférieure* (a reference to the lower reaches of the

Seine)—until its inhabitants protested, and the name was officially changed.

influer sur. Another way of saying *influencer* (transitive), or *avoir de l'influence sur quelqu'un*: 'to (have) influence (upon) someone'. *Une personne influente* is 'an influential person'.

informatique (f). Covers the whole modern phenomenon of 'data-processing' and 'data-transmission'.

innocenter. Like *importer* (q.v.), a verb lacking in English, and meaning 'to acquit', 'to clear someone'.

inscrire, s'. 'To register', or 'to matriculate', particularly in a school or university. *Les frais d'inscription* are 'tuition costs'. Also, in general, 'to sign up' as a member or supporter of something.

instantané. 'Instantaneous'; or, when speaking of coffee and other products, 'instant'. *Un instantané* is 'a snap-shot'.

intéressé. This adjective expresses a meaning which English has preserved mostly in the negative: 'disinterested', i.e. 'unselfish', acting out of reasons other than egoism. *Intéressé*, then, is 'self-interested' or, as one dictionary puts it, 'not disinterested'; and similarly, *intéressant* may be applied to something which is, or is likely to be, 'profitable' or 'advantageous'.

As a noun, *l'intéressé(e)* is free of the pejorative air which may hang about the adjective, since it means simply 'the person involved *or* concerned'.

intérêt (m). Not only 'financial profit'—where it can be used in the plural (*On a rajouté les intérêts à mon livret de caisse d'épargne.* 'They've added the interest on to my savings account')—but any sort of 'advantage' or 'utility'. *Vous aurez intérêt à* (or, *C'est dans votre intérêt de*) *lui laisser toute liberté de jeter sa gourme.* 'You will do well to let him sow his wild oats.' *Je ne vois pas l'intérêt (de faire cela).* 'I don't see the point (in doing that).' One large store recently advertised new credit facilities in startling terms: *Une offre sans intérêt*—a deliberate play on both meanings of the word.

There is a nice distinction to be made. (*a*) *Ce livre n'est pas intéressant*: 'This is a dull book'. (*b*) *Ce livre est sans intérêt*: 'This book is worthless, of no value'. In the first instance, you stress the boring aspect of the book; in the second, the lack of profit derived from it.

interprète (m). Not only 'an interpreter', as in English, but often 'a singer', 'instrumentalist', 'actor', or other performing artist. The verb *interpréter* does not mean 'to interpret' as an interpreter does (*faire l'interprète*), but 'to comment', 'explain', 'sing', 'play', 'act', and so forth. *Cette chanson sera interprétée par . . .* Or, *l'interprète de cette sonate pour piano sera . . .* 'This song will be sung by . . .' Or, 'this piano sonata will be played by . . .' And of course, *l'interprétation* can mean 'rendition', 'singing', 'playing', 'acting'.

interroger, s'. Literally, 'to examine oneself'; 'to wonder', 'to engage in introspection', 'consider', 'reflect'. More formal than *se tâter*, which more clearly implies a hesitation between choices.

interrupteur (m). 'An electric light switch' (*v.* BRANCHER).

intoxication (f). One of the more memorable *Faux Amis*: it means 'poisoning' and not 'drunkenness', which is *l'ivresse* (f). *Intoxication alimentaire*, 'food poisoning'. Although you can call 'a poisoning' *un empoisonnement*, this word also means 'a terrific nuisance', 'a bother'. *Quel empoisonnement!* 'What a nuisance!' *Il n'a que des empoisonnements* (or, *des tracas*) *à son bureau.* 'He's been having nothing but trouble at the office.'

invraisemblable. Since in English you rarely go around saying 'verisimilar', you may be surprised at the frequency with which *c'est invraisemblable* is used in French, meaning 'unlikely' or, more affirmatively, 'surprising', 'astonishing'. *C'était invraisemblable le nombre de gens venus l'écouter.* 'An astonishing number of people turned out to hear him.' *Vraisemblablement* is a quite acceptable substitute for *probablement*.

issue (f). First of all, this is not the word for an 'issue' of a magazine, newspaper etc. *Un numéro* is the right term.
L'issue is, however, 'the outlet' or 'exit' of a place or, in a more intangible situation, 'the way out', 'the solution'. *C'est sans issue* can be said as well of a dead-end road or cul-de-sac (*une voie sans issue*) as of an apparently hopeless or insoluble affair. The corresponding verb is *sortir*, *émerger* (*de l'impasse*), as there is no verb '*issuer*'. If you want to say that an odour 'issues' from somewhere, *se dégager de* or *émaner de* is the appropriate expression, *se faire entendre*, for a noise issuing from somewhere. *Des voix se firent entendre de derrière la porte.* 'The sound of voices issued from behind the door.'

J

Javel, eau de. Chlorine bleach for clothes. Scouring powders will sometimes be marked *javellisant*.
Javel is also a Métro stop in Paris. *L'usine du quai de Javel* referred to the Citroën works, now largely transferred outside Paris.

jet (m). A use not often stressed in a dictionary: 'the first draft' (of a manuscript, project and the like) is *le premier jet*.
Un jet d'eau, 'an (artificial) fountain'.

jeton (m). 'The token' which you need for telephoning from *une cabine* *publique*. Its price varies depending on whether you call from *la poste*—'the post office'—or from *un café* or *un tabac*. Calling from a *tabac* (q.v.) is more expensive; you buy your *jeton* at the counter before going downstairs to the phone kiosk (booth). The more recent outdoor phone kiosks take coins, not tokens.

No *jetons* are used in the Paris public tranport system; instead you use *un* or *des ticket(s)* or *une carte orange* ('monthly pass').

jeunes, les (m.pl.). Frequently used in place of *la jeunesse*, to mean 'youth', 'the younger generation'. *Les jeunes de notre époque*, 'young people today'. Another of those *adjectifs substantivés*, like *le coupable* (q.v.). *Un terrain de jeu pour les jeunes* is 'a children's playground (*or* playing field)'.

Les vieux refers to 'old people', 'the older generation', and cannot, in this context, be replaced by *la vieillesse* (although you might expect an analogy with *la jeunesse*) but by *les vieillards*. A common but not very courteous way of referring to one's parents is *mes vieux*, or *les vieux*.

You might note that *les anciens* does not mean what *les vieux* means. *Les anciens* are 'the former members' of whatever it is: *une réunion des anciens du Lycée X*, 'a reunion (*or* meeting) of the former pupils of Lycée X'.

joindre. 'To reach *or* get in touch with someone': *joindre par téléphone*. *Où peut-on le joindre rapidement?* Not to be confused with *rejoindre*: 'to join', 'to catch up with'. *Ne nous attendez pas, nous vous rejoindrons là-bas*. 'Don't wait for us, we'll meet you there.' *Toucher* can also have the same meaning as *joindre*.

jouer. 'To act', 'to help' or 'influence'. *L'attitude de l'accusé a beaucoup joué en sa faveur*. 'The accused man's attitude greatly helped his case.'

juste. Surely you know that this means 'just', as opposed to 'unjust', *injuste*. But *juste* also means 'tight' (a dress), 'a near thing' (*J'ai eu mon train, mais c'était juste*), or 'barely sufficient' (*Il avait juste de quoi acheter le journal*); and sometimes, 'just' or 'only'. *Attendez-moi, je vais juste chercher mes affaires*. 'Wait for me, I'm just going to get my things.' 'A near thing' can also be expressed by *de justesse*: *nous sommes arrivés avant vous, mais de justesse*.

Justement! signifies, 'But that's just it!' 'That's just the point you were about to miss!' *Au juste* means 'exactly'. *Mais j'y pense, quand est-ce qu'il part, au juste?* 'But come to think of it, just when is he leaving exactly?'

L

lacune (f). Rarely used in any but a figurative sense for 'a gap', 'a void'. *Il y a d'importantes lacunes dans ses connaissances géographiques.* 'His knowledge of geography is very patchy (US: spotty).' And the standard expression *combler une lacune,* is 'to fill in the gap', 'supply the missing part', 'make up for a lack'.

The adjective 'patchy', 'spotty', 'faulty', is *lacuneux* or, more commonly, *lacunaire.*

langes (m.pl.). Not to be confused with *linge* (q.v.). *Des langes* are 'swaddling clothes', and the verb is *langer,* or *emmailloter.*

larme (f). A neat way of protesting that you want only very little—even less than *un doigt*—to drink: *Une larme seulement.* 'Just a drop, please.'

lavabo (m). 'A wash-stand' or 'bathroom sink'. And very often, a euphemism for 'the lavatory'. *Où sont les lavabos?* (or, *les toilettes* or *les cabinets*; or *les water,* pronounced waterre; or *les W.C.* or *V.C.,* pronounced as the letters are pronounced in the French alphabet). In a café, 'the lavatory' will most often be called *les toilettes* and be *au fond de la salle*—'in the back of the room'—or *au sous-sol,* 'downstairs'. In either case, it will be next to the telephone booth.

lèche-vitrines (m). 'Window-shopping'. *Le samedi matin elles aiment faire du lèche-vitrines.* 'They like to go window-shopping on Saturday morning.'

liaison (f). The word for '(love) affair'. *Une affaire* will never do here. Cf: Laclos, *Les Liaisons Dangereuses.*

'To be in touch with someone' is *être en liaison* (or, less militarily, *en contact*) *avec quelqu'un.*

You might note that it is possible to overdo the sort of liaison which you have been taught to do in speaking, as in *allez-y. Une fausse liaison* like, *'c'est mal-t'à-propos',* or *'c'est d'un joli zeffet'* is quite illegitimate, although it may seem to be called for, particularly when two vowels occur together. This sort of 'error' may come naturally and is quite forgivable, but it is really good only for laughs.

licencié. If you are *licencié,* either you have *une licence* (roughly, a B.A.), or you have been laid off, given the sack (*un licenciement*). *Toucher une forte indemnité de licenciement* is 'to get a large amount of severance pay'. *Un licenciement économique,* dismissal because of budgetary restrictions and not for lack of merit, entitling you to the highest percentage of compensation. If you resign, *vous démissionnez* or *vous donnez votre démission, la démission* being 'resignation'. This necessitates 'giving a month's notice': *donner un mois de préavis.* For another use of *préavis, v.*

the chapter on THE TELEPHONE; *v.* also CHÔMAGE.

In either case, *licencié* is not to be confused with *licencieux*, which means 'licentious'.

'To be licensed to' do or to sell something, *avoir une patente*.

ligne (f). *Les grandes lignes* indicates 'the outline', or 'the main points', of a situation or project. *Le patron n'a fait que donner les grandes lignes du projet, sans entrer dans les détails.* 'The boss only outlined the plan, without going into detail.'

At the railway station, however, *les grandes lignes* refers to 'the main-line *or* inter-city (US: interurban) trains', as opposed to *les trains de banlieue*, 'suburban trains'.

limonade (f). If on a hot, dry afternoon you order this at a *terrasse*, you may be disappointed when the *garçon* brings you, not 'lemonade', but 'lemon-flavoured soda water' (*eau pétillante*). What you probably meant was *un citron pressé:* lemon juice, sugar, and ordinary water (*eau plate*). Nor has *limonade* anything to do with limes, *citron* (m) *vert*, which you will be very lucky indeed to find, ever, at any French *terrasse*.

linge (m). Linen; *linge de corps*, 'personal linen', 'underclothes'; *linge de maison*, 'household linen'. The *blanchisserie* will often mark *linge au poids*, meaning washing done at so much per kg. and not per item.

La lingerie, you will remember, is not only women's underclothing (which is more properly *la lingerie fine*) but the linen trade as well, or even a linen room or closet.

La lessive is generally the washing you do yourself—*faire sa lessive*—as opposed to *donner son linge à laver*; and *la lessive* can also be the soapflakes or powder used in washing. *La lessiveuse*, the old-fashioned 'wash-tub'. *Machine* (f) *à laver*, 'washing machine'. *Sèche-linge* (m) or *séchoir* (m), 'dryer'; *machine séchante*, 'automatic dryer'.

Etre lessivé is a definitely *familier* way of saying 'to be worn out *or* dog-tired'.

logiciel (m). 'Computer software'; also called . . . *le software*!

lyophilisé. 'Freeze-dried', as coffee.

M

machin (m). A verbal crutch, corresponding to 'thingumabob', 'what-d'yacallit', 'what'shisname'. You can overdo it, of course, and even compound it by saying *chose-machin* (m) or *machin-chouette* (m), but often you'll find there's no getting around it. Definitely spoken, not written, French; an even more colloquial form is *bidule* (m) (*v.* also TRUC).

magnétophone (m). 'A tape recorder.' 'The tape' is *la bande magnétique*; 'to tape record' is *enregistrer sur bande magnétique*; 'tape recording' is *un enregistrement sur bande magnétique*. 'To erase', *effacer*.

maigre. 'Thin', 'meagre'. In speaking of a person, it is more tactful to say *mince*, or even *svelte*.

When it comes to cheese and yogurt, it denotes a low fat content (*v.* GRAISSE). Not to be confused with *écrémé*: literally 'decreamed', i.e. 'skimmed'.

maison (f). 'House' or 'home', of course. But you will often hear '*le home*', which today's Frenchman seems to feel more adequate than *la maison* or *le foyer* to express the idea of intimacy which attaches to the English 'home'. 'To go home': *rentrer à la maison, rentrer chez soi*.

Also, 'house' in the sense of 'a business firm'. But it will never do for a doctor's, dentist's or barrister's (lawyer's) office, which is *un cabinet*; nor for a notary's which is *une étude*. (When telephoning for an appointment or for information, you ask: *C'est le cabinet du Dr. Untel? C'est l'étude de Maître Machin?*) Nor for a hairdresser's, which is *un salon de coiffure*. In the case of any small one-man practice or business, the best thing to do when telephoning is to use the person's name only.

mal (m., or adv.). As in the case of *bien*, *bon*, and *mauvais*, one could go on for paragraphs of idiomatic expressions and clichés. The following items are basic:

Pas mal! or, *Pas si mal* (*que ça*)! The equivalent of 'not bad'; in other words, 'pretty good'. A common understated form of praise or appreciation. As in the English expression, the intonation is important.

Elle n'est pas mal du tout: 'She's quite pretty' (*v.* PAS MAL).

Il ne s'en est pas tiré si mal que ça, or more colloquially: *Il s'en est tiré pas si mal*. 'He got out of it (*or*, over it) pretty nicely.'

Il n'y a pas de mal is the polite response to someone's apology for having, let us say, stepped on your foot or woken you up by telephoning too early in the morning.

Avoir mal is 'to be in pain'; *avoir du mal* (*à faire quelque chose*) is 'to have trouble (doing something)'. *Se donner du mal*, 'to go to a lot of trouble'. *Faire mal*, 'to hurt (physically)'; *faire du mal*, 'to harm' (in the abstract). *Ça lui fait mal quand il marche*, 'it hurts him when he walks'. *Ça lui fait du mal de marcher*. 'Walking doesn't do him any good.' Beware of *mal au cœur*, which has nothing to do with 'heartache', being simple 'nausea'. *Mal au ventre* is ordinary 'stomach ache'.

malicieux. May be a *Faux Ami*, as it means 'mischievous'; *la malice* is 'mischief'.

For 'malicious' and 'malice', use *méchant* and *la méchanceté*.

manchette (f). 'Cuff'; 'a cuff-link' is *un bouton de manchette*.
Also, 'a big headline' in the newspaper; the general term for headline is *un titre*.

manifestation (f). 'A demonstration.' In talking, this can be shortened to *la manif*. The person taking part in one is *un(e) manifestant(e)*.

mannequin (m). 'A fashion model', if it's a living man or woman (but the word is always masculine), or else 'a dummy'. But be careful how you translate 'model' in any other context. 'A model train', for instance, is *un train miniature*. 'A scale model' of an architectural project is *une maquette* (q.v.). A 'model child' is, however, *un enfant modèle*.

manquer. You know that *manquer* means, roughly, 'to miss'—someone, a train, doing something, one's aim, and so on. You have certainly been warned that 'I miss you' turns out in French, 'you are missing to me'. But even experienced speakers *ne manquent pas de tomber dans les nombreux pièges tendus par le verbe, 'manquer'*. So let us just run through a handful of examples:
Elle m'a manqué: 'I missed her.'
Je lui ai manqué: 'She (he) missed me.'
J'ai manqué mon bus: 'I missed the bus.'
J'ai manqué de (j'ai failli) me faire écraser: 'I nearly got run over.'
Il manque quatre pages à la fin du Tome Premier: 'Four pages are missing from the end of Volume I.'
Il manque de respect. 'He is lacking in respect.'
C'est un manque (de tact etc.): 'it's a lack (of tact).'
Bien des choses à votre mère.—Je n'y manquerai pas. 'Give my regards to your mother.'—'I certainly shall.'
Il ne manquerait plus que ça! 'That would be the last straw!'
Un manque à gagner, 'a profit missed'.
C'est à ne pas manquer, 'It's a must.'
Manquer is sometimes used interchangeably with *rater* or *louper*, as in the example with the bus, above. *J'ai manqué (loupé, raté) mon dessin*: 'My drawing did not come out.' *Il s'est manqué.* 'His suicide attempt failed.'

maquette (f). 'A scale model' of a car, building, statue, etc., or 'layout' or 'design' for a book. The person who makes it is *le maquettiste*. Not to be confused with *la moquette*, 'wall-to-wall carpeting' (*v.* also MANNEQUIN).

marché (m). 'The market'; *un marché découvert*, 'an open-air market'. *Faire le marché*, 'to go marketing', with *un sac* (or *un panier*) *à provisions*, or *un caddy* (large bag on wheels), which has almost replaced the *filet* (m), 'string shopping-bag'.
Fruit and vegetables are sold mostly *au poids* ('according to weight'), specifically, *au kilo(gramme)*, 'so much per kilogramme'. Occasionally they are sold at so much *la pièce*, each one

separately, as with melons; or, 'per bunch', *la botte* (*de radis*, for example); or even *le tas*, 'the pile', of two or three heads of lettuce. 'A root or bunch of celery' is not *une botte* but *un pied de céleri*. 'A whole garlic' is *une tête d'ail*, and each of its cloves is *une gousse*. *Un marchand des quatre saisons* is 'an itinerant vendor', with a wagon instead of a stall.

Marchander is 'to bargain' to bring down the price; something which it is better not to try in the ordinary *marché*.

Marché Commun, 'the European Common Market'; *La Communauté Economique Européenne* (*CEE*), 'the European Economic Community' (EEC).

marcher. One of the words the English-speaking resident in France is likely to pick up most quickly and to delight most in using, in a sort of Frenchified English, *pour rire* ('just for laughs').

You might refresh your memory as to what the word does not generally mean. It does not often mean 'to march', which is more properly *défiler* or *marcher au pas*. Nor does it mean 'to market', which is *vendre*, *mettre en vente*; 'to do the marketing' is *faire le marché*, *faire ses courses*, *aller au marché*.

It is a way of saying 'to walk', like *aller à pied* or *faire* (*le trajet*) *à pied*. It is above all a way of saying, 'to run'—as a car; 'to function', 'to work' or 'succeed'—as any plan or scheme; or, in any of these senses, 'to go'. *La marche* is 'walking', or 'walk': *Le prochain village est à trois heures de marche d'ici.* 'The next village is three hours' walk from here.' *La marche à pied est le meilleur exercice.* 'Walking is the best exercise.' *Les chaussures de marche*, 'walking-shoes'. *Ma voiture marche mal*: 'My car doesn't run very well.' *Il croyait avoir des places gratuites, mais ça n'a pas marché.* 'He thought he'd have free seats, but it didn't work.'

More slangily, *marcher* means 'to fall for something', 'to be taken in'; and *faire marcher quelqu'un*, 'to fool someone', 'make a sucker of him'. *Il a marché comme un seul homme.* 'He swallowed it, hook, line and sinker.' *La marche arrière*, is 'reverse gear' in a car; 'to back up' or 'go into reverse' is *reculer, se mettre en marche arrière, faire marche arrière*.

Une marche is a step of a flight of stairs.

marée (f) **noire.** Literally, 'black tide'—the slick-polluted waters that wash up on shore when an oil tanker has spilled its cargo at sea.

Marianne. She is to republican France what Uncle Sam is to the United States, or John Bull to England. Appears on postage stamps, in every town hall, in political cartoons etc.

marier. Lest you forget, you have a transitive and a reflexive intransitive form, and they do not mean the same thing. *Marier quelqu'un* is 'to marry or pair someone off to someone else'; whereas *se marier avec quelqu'un* is the equivalent of the transitive verb, *épouser quelqu'un*: 'to marry someone'. *Un mariage* is both 'wedding' and 'marriage'. This ceremonial, or wedding, itself is also *la cérémonie* (*nuptiale*) or *les noces*. *La mariée* is of course 'the bride'; 'the groom' is *le marié*.

You can say that a mixture or a blend of two colours, two sorts of humour and so forth is *un mariage réussi. Epouser* can also mean 'to adhere strictly' (to an idea), or 'to fit tightly'; so conceivably you could say of a dress *qu'elle épouse les hanches et qu'elle est un heureux mariage de vert et de bleu!*

maroquinerie (f). The normal term for 'a leather-goods shop'—gloves, handbags, luggage. You may sometimes see it styled *une sellerie*, but you're not likely nowadays to find any saddles sold there. *Une bourrellerie*, however, if you can locate one, is still likely to live up to its name and sell not only harness but all sorts of leather straps.

marque (f). Among other things, 'brand-name', 'trade-mark' or 'make'. 'A mark' or 'grade', in the scholastic sense, is *une note. Image* (f) *de marque* is a recent phrase: the 'brand image', so to speak, of any prominent figure. *Il fait beaucoup de sport; c'est bon pour son image de marque.* 'He goes in for sport in a big way; it's good for his image.' *Soigner son image de marque*, 'to look after one's image.'

matériel (m) **d'informatique.** Computer hardware. Also called . . . *le hardware.*

mathématiques modernes (f.pl.). The 'new maths', introduced into the primary and secondary schools curriculum in about 1970. *La théorie des ensembles* is the set theory.

méridional. 'Southern', as *un accent méridional*, 'an accent of the south of France'. *Un méridional* is 'a southerner', 'a person from the Midi'. The contrary, *septentrional*, meaning 'northern', is used only for regions. 'A northerner' is *une personne du nord.*

mètre (m). Distance is counted in *kilomètres*, abbreviated *km*, roughly 3/5 of a mile. In buying *de l'essence* ('petrol'; US: 'gasoline') for your car, you calculate how many *litres* you use *au cent*, 'per hundred kilometres'. Rooms are measured in *mètres carrés*, 'square metres', abbreviated m^2. People too are measured in metres: *mon frère est assez grand, il mesure un mètre 83 (centimètres).* 'My brother is quite tall, about six feet.' 'A tape-measure' is *un mètre à ruban* (or, a *décamètre*, as the case may be). *Un mètre* may also be 'a ruler' one metre long, although a shorter or a longer ruler is *une règle.*

métropole (f). France itself, the mother country, as distinct from its colonies, in the old days, and from the present 'overseas territories' (*territoires d'outre-mer*) (*v*. HEXAGONE). *Revenir en métropole*, 'to come back to continental France and Corsica'.

mettre. One of those protean verbs that can mean any number of things, in addition to 'to put' and 'to place'. For instance, 'what shall I put on?' is simply *qu'est-ce que je vais (me) mettre?*, although 'to wear' the clothes, once you've put them on, is *porter.*

Se mettre à faire quelque chose is often a convenient substitute for *commencer*: *il s'est mis à bailler*, 'he began to yawn'. *S'y mettre* is, more specifically, 'to set about doing a given task', 'to buckle down to work'.

Mettre en état—'to restore' something, 'to get (it) into good *or* working condition'—is only one of a handful of expressions with *mettre en—*: *en marche*, *en cause*, *en scène*, *en page*, *en ordre*, *en musique*; and as you can see, here *mettre* must be translated in as many different ways: 'to start', 'to implicate', 'to direct (a play)', 'to lay out', 'to arrange', 'to set to music'.

In sports jargon, *mettre la gomme* is 'to step up speed'.

mettre en valeur. A phrase greatly in fashion, as applied to the development or improvement of a hitherto undeveloped or rundown neighbourhood or region, usually with the idea of attracting tourist trade or business. *Actuellement on parle beaucoup de mettre en valeur la Camargue.* 'There is much talk these days of developing the Camargue area.' The noun is *la mise en valeur*.

In other senses, *mettre quelque chose en valeur* is simply 'to set off *or* enhance something'. *Le vert de sa robe met en valeur ses yeux.* 'The green of her dress sets off her eyes.'

mielleux. May prove something of a *Faux Ami*, since it does not mean 'having a taste of honey', which is *miellé* or *ayant un goût de miel*. *Mielleux* is used figuratively, like 'honeyed' in English, to mean 'flattering', 'hypocritical'.

MLF (m). *Le Mouvement pour la Libération des Femmes*, the 'women's lib movement'.

moins. It might be useful to clarify a use of *à moins*: *Elle a eu si peu de veine qu'elle est très déprimée. On le serait à moins!* 'She's been so unlucky that she's very much depressed. Who wouldn't be?' In other words, used in this way, with a conditional tense and most often with *on*, *à moins* means 'who can blame him?' or 'it doesn't take that much to. . .'.

moisir. 'To rot' or 'grow mouldy'; and by extension, in speaking of a person, 'to stay somewhere too long'. *Ne moisissez pas dans cette place, vous y perdriez votre temps.* 'Don't hang on to that job too long, it's a waste of time.'

monde (m). In the expression, *tout le monde*, *monde* means neither 'earth' nor 'world', but a given 'population' or 'society'. So that to say, *nous avons du monde ce soir*, 'we have some people coming over this evening', follows naturally. Similarly, *il y avait un monde fou au bal*, 'there was a terrific crowd at the dance'. And *s'il y a trop de monde chez le boucher, ce n'est pas la peine d'attendre*—'if there's too long a queue at the butcher's, don't bother to wait'.

Used in another sort of phrase altogether, *un monde* can mean 'a big fuss': *l'incident est sans importance, mais il en fait tout un monde.* 'What happened is insignificant, but he's making a mountain out of a molehill.'

Mondain(e) means 'worldly', 'belonging to fashionable

society'; *la vie mondaine, un dîner mondain.* But *la (brigade) mondaine* designates policemen assigned to moral offences, drugs etc. *Un homme (une femme) du monde,* 'a society man (woman)'.

monnaie (f). A classic *Faux Ami,* as you undoubtedly know, but a slip of the tongue comes when you least expect it. *La monnaie* is 'change', 'small change', 'coins'; *l'argent* is 'money'. *Faire la monnaie d'un billet de 100,* 'to change (*or* get change for) a 100 franc note'.

Une monnaie is a currency; it can be *étrangère, de réserve, stable* ('foreign', 'reserve', 'stable'), etc.

If you want to say of someone, that he is 'monied', *monnayé* will not do: *riche, fortuné,* or even *argenté* is what you need. *Monnayer* means merely 'to capitalize on something' (an object, a title, etc.),'to trade something for money', but not in the sense of pawning it (*v.* MONT-DE-PIÉTÉ).

mont-de-piété (m). 'The pawnshop' now called *Crédit Municipal.* The old-fashioned individual 'pawnbroker' is *le prêteur sur gages. J'ai mis* (or, *engagé) ma montre au mont-de-piété.* 'I've pawned my watch.'

(In terms far more *familier,* you say, *J'ai mis ma montre au clou,* or *chez ma tante.*)

moudre. 'To grind.' One of those infinitives you rarely need but when you buy ground coffee, you need to know the past participle, *moulu.* (Nothing to do with *mouler,* 'to mould', whose past participle is pefectly regular: *moulé.) Un moulin à café* is 'a coffee-grinder'; while *une moule* is 'a mussel' and *un moule* 'a mould'.

mouvement d'humeur (m). 'A fit of bad temper', 'an ill-tempered gesture'. An expression worth noting because (1) it is quite frequent, (2) the sort of *humeur* implied is always *la mauvaise,* and (3) this is as good a place as any to recall that *l'humeur* (f) is not *l'humour* (m). The first is, generally, 'mood', as in *être de bonne humeur,* 'to be in a good mood'. *L'humour* is clear enough; *avoir le sens de l'humour* is 'to have a (good) sense of humour'. The adjective 'humorous' is *humoristique; un dessin humoristique,* 'a funny drawing' or 'cartoon'.

moyennant. A preposition often found in place of *contre:* 'against', 'in exchange for', 'by means of' (a sum of money, a promise etc.).

N

nager. 'To swim'. *Se baigner,* 'to bathe', is not quite the same. *Baigner quelqu'un* or, more commonly, *donner un bain à quelqu'un,* is 'to bath someone else'.

The art of swimming is *la natation*, but the act itself is *la nage*. *Traverser la Manche à la nage*, 'to swim across the Channel'. 'A swimming pool', however, is *une piscine* (*couverte* or *en plein air*); 'a swimsuit', *un maillot de bain*.

To indicate the various strokes, you say *nager le crawl* (*sur le dos*, *sur le côté*): 'to do the crawl, backstroke, sidestroke', but *faire la brasse*: to do the breaststroke. You can also say, *faire le crawl*. *Plonger* is to dive, and *le plongeoir* is, of course, the 'diving board'.

In conversation you may hear, *je nage*, 'I'm lost', 'I don't understand'. But someone *qui sait nager* is someone who can stay afloat in business, who knows how to get along.

naître. This verb has an active form that is missing in English: *un enfant naît toutes les deux secondes*. 'A child is born every two seconds.'

navet (m). 'Turnip', but often used to express 'flop', e.g. of a film.

n'est-ce pas? In English, you are so allergic to the double negative that a sentence like *Il n'est pas parti, n'est-ce pas?* ('He didn't go, did he?') may strike your ear as a flagrant error, whereas it is just as correct as *Il est parti, n'est-ce pas?* ('He did go, didn't he?'). The matter of 'question tags'—'have you?', 'shouldn't they?', 'aren't I?', and so forth—so troublesome to people learning English, is simplicity itself in French; they are all *n'est-ce pas?* You can even add *n'est-ce pas?* to a phrase which at first glance appears a double or triple negative all by itself, like *aucun billet n'est plus valable*. 'All tickets are invalid.'

N'est-ce pas? is also a matter of personal style in conversation; many speakers will interrupt their own train of thought with it, just as you might say 'don't you see?' or 'right?'

non plus. Often used by itself, and in repetition to express a series of 'neither', 'no more do I', and the like.—*Avez-vous vu votre oncle? —Non. —Votre tante? —Non plus.*

O

obligatoire. 'Compulsory.' Used much more often than you would say 'obligatory' in English. *Obligatoirement* denotes an imposed or legal necessity; *forcément* and *nécessairement*, an internal or natural necessity. *C'est obligé*, 'it's unavoidable, natural in view of the circumstances'.

In terms of the highway code, *un sens obligatoire* is the opposite of *un sens interdit*; that is, 'a one-way street *or* road' which you have to take, as opposed to 'a no entry'.

occasion (f). First of all, 'a chance'. *Nous avons eu l'occasion de lui parler plusieurs fois*. 'We had occasion (*or* a chance) to speak to her several times' (*v.* CHANCE). *Par la même occasion*, 'at the same time', 'while one is at it'.

And sometimes, 'a lucky chance' or 'find'. *J'ai vu une de ces robes! Alors, j'ai sauté sur l'occasion!* 'I saw such a marvellous dress! I jumped at the chance.'

Acheter d'occasion is 'to buy second-hand'.

occuper. *Etre occupé*, 'to be busy'; can be said as well of a person as of a telephone line. *La ligne est occupée*.

S'occuper de is one of those expressions which may not occur to you on the first try, since it differs so much from the English: 'to take care of', 'to look after (something)'. *Je vais m'en occuper.* 'I'll take care of it.' In a shop, an attentive salesman will ask: *Monsieur, on s'occupe de vous?* 'May I help you, sir?'—literally, 'is someone (else) already taking care of you?'

œuf (m). 'An egg'; you pronounce the *f* as in *bœuf*. But the plural, *œufs*, works like the plural *bœufs*: the *f* is forgotten, so that *œufs* is pronounced like the pronoun, *eux*.

Un œuf brouillé: 'scrambled egg'
—*à la coque*: 'soft-boiled'
—*mollet*: 'medium-boiled'
—*dur*: 'hard-boiled'
—*poché*: 'poached'
—*sur le plat*: 'fried'
Une omelette: 'omelette'.
Le jaune, 'yolk'. *Le blanc*, 'white'.

L'épicier will often mark the eggs he sells, *œufs coque*, meaning 'extra-fresh eggs', for soft-boiling.

on. You know that the impersonal pronoun is most often translated by the passive voice: *On lui a dit de le faire*. 'He was told to do it.' But a good deal less stigma attaches to constructions with *on* than to the use of the passive in English. In the active, *on* is a handy catch-all, a lazy way out of remembering the verb forms that go with more accurate pronouns. For instance: *On ne savait plus quoi faire, alors on est allé au cinéma*. Whereas you mean, *Nous ne savions plus quoi faire, alors nous sommes allés au cinéma*. Also, along with *ils*, *on* is the equivalent of the mysterious 'they' in English. 'They've announced', *on annonce que*. . . .

OPEP (f). *L'Organisation des Pays Exportateurs de Pétrole*, i.e., 'OPEC'.

ordinateur (m). 'Computer.'

oui. Even if you have a flawless accent, your French is not totally authentic until you can deal with *oui*. It is often more of a gasp than anything else, a soft sharp *ssshing* inhalation or exhalation of breath, neither '*voui*' nor '*ouish*' but somewhere in between.

OVNI (m). *Un Objet Volant Non-Identifié*—in other words, 'a UFO'.

P

pain (m). One of the most celebrated things about France. When you buy it at *la boulangerie* or in certain *pâtisseries*, you indicate whether you want *une baguette* or *une ficelle, un bâtard, un saucisson, une couronne, une petite* (or *une grosse) boule,* depending on the shape and the size; *un pain de campagne, un pain de seigle, un pain brioché, un pain moulé, fariné, bien cuit, pas trop cuit,* and so on.

   Le pain grillé is 'toast'; *un grille-pain,* 'a toaster'.

   Avoir du pain sur la planche, 'to have a lot of work lined up', 'to have a lot to do'.

   Un pain can also be 'a cake' (*de savon*) or 'a lump' or 'loaf' (*de sucre*). *Avoir quelque chose pour une bouchée de pain* means 'to buy it for a song, for next to nothing'.

pantalon (m). 'A pair of trousers *or* pants' is called simply *un pantalon;* and 'a pair of shorts', *un short.*

papier (m). The first thing to remember is that *le papier* can refer to any sort of paper but the newspaper, which is *le journal.*

   Papier à lettres par avion, 'air-mail paper'
   —*de brouillon,* 'scrap (first draft) paper'
   —*carbone,* 'carbon-paper'
   —*crépon,* 'crêpe paper'
   —*pour doubles* or *papier pelure,* 'onion skin', 'flimsy'
   —*d'emballage* (or, *kraft*), 'brown wrapping paper'
   —*à en-tête de la maison,* 'letterhead stationery'
   —*hygiénique,* 'toilet paper'
   —*pour machine à écrire,* 'typing paper'
   —*de soie,* 'tissue paper'
   —*timbré,* 'official stamped paper' (for documents)

papillon (m). 'Butterfly'; also, any small detachable slip of paper, and especially, the pet name for the parking fine placed on the windscreen of your car. *Un nœud papillon* is a man's 'bow tie', as opposed to *une cravate,* an ordinary 'straight tie'.

parages (m. pl.). Used in *dans les parages* 'in the neighbourhood', 'near here'. *Je l'ai vu passer tout à l'heure, il doit être toujours dans les parages.* 'I saw him go by just a minute ago, he must still be somewhere around here.'

parc (m). One way of saying 'park', although *le bois, le jardin, le square* may occur as frequently: *le Bois de Boulogne, le jardin des Tuileries. Amener un enfant au square,* 'to take a child out to the (small) park'. 'A square', as in 'Trafalgar Square', is translated by *une place.*

   Un parc may also be 'a baby's play pen'.

   'A car park' is *un parking.* There is a curious expression which you may think means 'a car park' but which means in fact the total number of cars in France: *le parc automobile*.

parent (m). Both a *Vrai* and a *Faux Ami*. *Un parent* is indeed 'a parent'—but also any other relative. The word *relations* (q.v.) does exist and is even a very vital part of your vocabulary, but it has nothing to do with 'relatives'.

You must use caution in approaching all relatives beginning with *beau-* and *belle-*, since these prefixes are used both for 'step-' and for '-in-law'. *Un beau-père* is your 'father-in-law', or your 'step-father'; *belle-mère* works the same way. So do *beau-frère* and *belle-sœur*, *beau-fils* and *belle-fille*, although in these last two cases you can get around the difficulty by using *gendre* (m) and *bru* (f), respectively, when you mean the -in-law sort. *La bru* is hardly used nowadays, however; and *marâtre*, the alternative for 'step-mother', still less. Today, *marâtre* has come to mean 'a bad *or* wicked mother', *une mère indigne*.

part (f). *De la part de* is a very vital little phrase: 'from So-and-So', 'on behalf of So-and-So', 'with the recommendation of So-and-So'. *Je vous écris de la part de M. Untel*, when you write to request a favour, helps your cause immeasurably: 'I come to you recommended by Mr So-and-So.' *Il m'a remis ce mot de la part de sa tante*. 'He gave me this note from his aunt (at her request).' *Dites-lui de ma part* . . . 'Tell him from me . . .'

When it comes to cakes, and to certain cheeses, *une part* is 'a portion'.

partance (f). 'The departure' of a boat, train, or plane. At the *gare de chemin de fer*, there may be a *guichet* ('window') marked, *En Partance*, for those who have to buy their tickets in a hurry because their train is to pull out in a few minutes.

particulier. 'Private.' *Un particulier*, 'a private individual'. *Une maison particulière*, 'a private house'.

partition (f). 'A musical score.' 'A partition (wall)' is *une cloison*.

pas mal. 'Not bad!', or 'a fair number' etc. *Il y avait pas mal de monde*. 'There were quite a lot of people' (*v*. MAL).

passer. A verb with manifold uses: *passer un examen* does not mean 'to succeed in an exam' but merely 'to sit for (take) it'.

Passons, like *glissons*, can be very fatalistic: *Il ne m'a jamais rendu l'argent que je lui ai prêté, mais enfin, passons*. 'He's never paid back the money I lent him, but let's not talk about it any more' *or*, 'never mind';

passer une visite médicale is 'to have a medical examination';

passer quelque chose à quelqu'un is either 'to hand *or* lend someone something', or 'to forgive someone something': *Il l'aime à la folie et lui passe tous ses caprices*. 'He's mad about her and puts up with all her whims.'

Se passer de quelque chose is 'to do without something';

. . . *et j'en passe et des meilleurs*, very colloquial, means, 'I know a lot more about it but I'll spare you the details', or, 'not to mention . . .'; and *passer chez quelqu'un* or *passer voir quelqu'un* is the nearest thing to 'to drop in on someone'.

passible. The adjective which expresses one type of 'liable': the legal sort, meaning 'punishable by', 'subject to'. *Toute personne jetant des papiers sur la voie ferrée sera passible d'une amende.* 'Littering the railway tracks is punishable by a fine.'

But the 'liable' which expresses probability or likelihood requires different treatment altogether. 'The boss is liable to come and criticize your work': *Il y a de fortes chances pour que le patron vienne critiquer votre travail*; or, *Il est probable que le patron viendra . . .*

'Not likely!' can be handled in several ways: *Ça m'étonnerait! Vous n'y pensez pas! Invraisemblable!* among others.

passif (m). 'The passive voice'; also, 'debits'. *Avoir quelque chose à son passif* is 'to have a blot on one's copybook', as *un séjour en prison. Avoir quelque chose à son actif*, 'to have something to one's credit'. *Ce jeune metteur en scène a déjà trois pièces à son actif.* 'This young director already has three plays to his credit.'

pâté maison (m). An item which may—and should—appear on the menu: a *pâté* made by, or in the style of, the restaurant itself. Not to be confused with *le pâté de maisons*, 'the block of houses'! *Je vais juste faire le tour du pâté de maisons.* 'I'm just going for a walk around the block.'

Une pâtée is 'cat- or dog-food'.

patienter. Simply 'to wait' (patiently), as in a doctor's waiting-room. *Faites-le patienter un instant.* 'Please ask him to wait.' Or on the telephone: *Le poste ne répond pas, voulez-vous patienter?* 'The extension is not answering, will you wait?'

patron (m). Corresponds quite accurately to 'boss', which means that it is widely used and also very casual. So if you are being interviewed or summoned by your superior on a white-collar job, you don't call him *Patron* but, *Monsieur le Directeur.*

Un patron being the 'pattern' used in sewing, it is also a way of indicating average or medium size in certain types of men's clothing, especially pyjamas and underclothes; you have *demi-patron*, *patron* and *grand patron*.

pavés (m.pl.) 'The paving blocks or stones' making up *la chaussée*, the surface of the road. If you mean 'pavement', in British English (or 'sidewalk', in American English), then you say *le trottoir*.

pays (m). You may have trouble getting used to the idea that *un pays* is just as often a small region or even a town as a political nation or country. *C'est un petit pays, mais bien joli.* 'The region is small, but pretty enough.' *Il y a un poste d'essence à la sortie du pays.* 'There's a petrol (gas) station at the edge of town.' *Il est le seul médecin de tout le pays.* 'He's the only doctor in all the country round', 'in these parts'.

Less often, *un pays* can even be a local fellow, a native of one's small home town; *une payse* is the feminine equivalent.

peine (f). Some very useful expressions you should know how to wield readily:

se donner la peine de, 'to go to the trouble of (doing something)'. *Je vous remercie de toute la peine* (or *de tout le mal*) *que vous vous êtes donné(e)*. 'Thank you for going to so much trouble.' *Ne vous donnez pas la peine, je vous prie.* 'Please don't bother.' A much less formal version of which is *non merci, ce n'est pas la peine. Cela ne vaut pas la peine* (*ce n'est pas la peine*) can be used quite differently, indicating 'there's no point in doing that', 'it's no use'. *Ce n'est pas la peine de le gronder, il ne travaillera pas pour autant.* 'It's no use scolding him, it won't make him work.' *Faire de la peine à quelqu'un*, 'to hurt *or* disappoint someone'. *Une situation pénible* is 'an embarrassing *or* a morally *or* emotionally difficult situation'. (If you mean 'physical pain', then you need to say *la douleur*, and *douloureux*.) *Il est pénible, ce garçon!* 'What a boring (*or*, hardly bearable) chap he is!'

pencher, se. A common expression with a rather striking image is, *se pencher sur la question*: literally, 'to lean over the matter at hand'. Said most often of *les experts, les savants. Depuis des années, les médecins se penchent sur le problème du cancer.* 'For years doctors have been making a close study of cancer.'

pense-bête (m). A reminder to do something, such as a string tied around your finger or a knot in your handkerchief.

penser. We want to call your attention to the nuances of *penser* with *bien. Les gens bien pensant* are 'right-thinking people', an expression sometimes used with irony, becoming downright pejorative.

Penser bien (or *bien penser*) is a frequent, more emphatic form of the verb, as may be the case with *sembler* and *croire. J'ai bien pensé* (or, *il m'a bien semblé*) *qu'il était gêné.* 'I had the distinct impression that he was embarrassed.' *Mais je pense bien!* means 'I should think so!' or 'but definitely!'

And as you surely know, whereas the Englishman will say 'I think so', the Frenchman more readily 'believes so': *je crois que oui*—or, if he is contradicting something you've said in the negative—*je crois que si.* 'I don't think so', *je crois que non, je ne crois pas.*

permettre. *Vous permettez?* (*tu permets?*) is the most common, and indispensable, formula for 'may I?' when, for instance, you want to share a seat with someone on the bus or reach for the salt. You may also hear, *puis-je?*, but this is a good deal more casual and may even sound rude or comical, and so is better avoided.

Pérou (m). The South American country, yes; but far more importantly, 'Eldorado', 'riches', and always used in the negative: *ce n'est pas le Pérou.* 'It's nothing to get excited about, it's no fortune.'

personne (f). 'A person' of either sex. This word provides you with a ready-made means to discretion when the occasion calls for it: *une personne a téléphoné* can mean that either a man or a woman has telephoned. But you must be careful: when you use *personne* in the negative—*je n'ai vu personne*—it becomes grammatically masculine, although for all practical purposes it is still asexual. *Personne n'a téléphoné, personne n'est venu.* 'Nobody called, nobody came.' *Personne n'est parfait.* 'No one is perfect'. You hear *les grandes personnes* far more often than *les adultes*, to mean 'grown-ups' or 'adults'.

petit(e) ami(e). 'Boy- *or* girl-friend', as the case may be, or 'sweetheart', if you prefer an old-fashioned term.

petitesse (f). Physical 'smallness'; more often, however, and like *mesquinerie* (f) and *bassesse* (f), a 'moral smallness *or* meanness'.

petit-fils (m). Just a reminder that this does not mean 'little son' but 'grandson'. One's 'little boy' is one's *petit garçon*, or simply one's *fils*. The confusion may be greater with *petite fille*, which means not only 'granddaughter' (written *petite-fille*) but also 'little girl' or 'very young daughter' (your own or anyone else's). A great-grandson obviously cannot be '*un grand-petit-fils*'. You say, *un arrière-petit-fils*. Similarly, for 'great-granddaughter' as well as 'great-grandfather' and 'great-grandmother'—*arrière-petite-fille, arrière-grand-père, arrière-grand-mère*. But 'a great-aunt *or* -uncle' is *grand-tante* or *grand-oncle*, and *arrière* enters into the picture in this case only when you need to express 'great-great-uncle (-aunt)', *arrière-grand-oncle (-tante)*.

pétrole (m). 'Oil', 'petroleum'. *Un pétrolier,'* 'oil tanker'. *Un puits de pétrole,* 'an oil well'. Salad oil and motor oil, however, are both *huile* (f).

photographe (m). 'The photographer'. 'Photography' or 'photograph' is *la photo(graphie)*.

pied (m). 'Foot', of course; and if you want to say how tall you are, you could say *5 pieds 11 pouces*, '5 feet 11 inches'.
    Pied is found in so many idioms and set phrases that you may lose your own footing at first. Look for instance at (*a*) *Faire des pieds et des mains* (*pour avoir quelque chose*); (*b*) *Faire les pieds à quelqu'un*; and (*c*) *Se faire la main*. The first is 'to move heaven and earth (to obtain something)'. The second, rather *familier*, is 'to give someone his just deserts': *Tu n'as qu'à partir sans lui; ça lui fera les pieds!* 'Why don't you just leave without him; that'll serve him right!' The third, quite proper, is 'to get one's hand in', 'do a bit of apprenticeship', 'get used to something new'.
    Faire un pied de nez is 'to cock a snook'; *faire le pied de grue* is 'to be made to wait for someone', 'to dance attendance'. 'To take something literally' is *prendre quelque chose au pied de la lettre*. And 'to blunder' is *mettre les pieds dans le plat*; more *familier* than *faire une gaffe*.

Travailler d'arrache-pied is 'to work very hard', while *travailler comme un pied* (or, *comme un sabot*) is 'to work badly', 'to botch one's work'. And finally, *partir les pieds devant*, 'to kick the bucket'.

pile (f). Any sort of 'electric battery'; but the battery of a car is called *la batterie*, as is the complete range of kitchen utensils, including *les casseroles*, *le tamis*, *le batteur à œufs*, *les passoires*, *les râpes*, *les poêles*, and so forth. *La batterie* also means the percussion instruments in a band or orchestra.

Pile ou face, 'head or tails'. 'A pile' of something is, generally speaking, *un tas*.

pilote. Translates as 'key', 'leading', 'pilot' or 'experimental'. *Une école pilote*, 'an experimental school'. *Une industrie pilote*, 'a key industry'.

piraterie aérienne (f). The hijacking of aircraft, also termed *le détournement d'un avion*. *Le pirate de l'air* is the hijacker. The key words here are *pilote* (m), the pilot; *équipage* (m), crew; *hôtesse* (f) *de l'air*, air stewardess; *otage* (m), hostage; and *rançon* (f), ransom.

piston (m). 'A friend in high places.' *Se faire pistonner* is everyone's cherished hope (*v*. also RELATIONS).

placé. 'In a position' (to do, know, help, etc.) *Il est mieux placé que moi pour vous renseigner.* 'He's in a better position than I am to inform you.'

plaque minéralogique (f). 'The number plate' of a car. The last two digits tell you which *département* the car comes from: 75 for Paris, 33 for Bordeaux (*la Gironde*) and so on.

plein. *En plein* is a good way to translate 'in the midst of'—*en plein travail* ('absorbed in work', 'in the midst of working'), *en pleine croissance* ('in the midst of growth'), *en plein dedans* (*J'ai voulu éviter cette flaque d'eau mais je suis tombé en plein dedans*—'I wanted to avoid that puddle but I fell smack into it'). This is not, however, 100 per cent reliable: *en plein air* is not 'in mid-air', but 'in the open (air)'; 'in mid-air' would be *dans l'air*.

You know that *il a la bouche pleine de chocolat* means 'his mouth is full of chocolate', and that *plein* here has to be feminine, since it modifies *la bouche*. But you can turn the expression around: *il a du chocolat* (or, *de la glace*) *plein la bouche*, in which case *plein* is invariably masculine singular, no matter what precedes or follows, as in . . . *plein les poches*.

plomb (m). 'An electric fuse'; but *quand le plomb a sauté*, 'when the fuse has blown', you do not call *le plombier*! He's 'the plumber'; and it's *l'électricien* you want.

pochette (f). Not only 'a small pocket', but also a couple of the articles which you can slip into a pocket: a man's breast-pocket handkerchief, and a book of matches. Also, 'the cardboard sleeve' of a record. 'The paper jacket' of a hardcover book is *une jaquette*.

poêle (f. and m.). One of those hermaphrodite words, like *mode*, *vase*, *voile*, which change meanings along with their gender (*v.* LE GENRE). *La poêle* is 'the frying-pan', whereas *le poêle* is 'the heating apparatus': *un poêle à charbon, à gaz, à mazout*. Watch out for *poil* (m)—(*v.* CHEVEUX)—which, although pronounced the same way, has nothing to do with either *poêle*.

point (m). *Etre sur le point de* is an expression to commit to memory: 'to be just about to'. *Il était sur le point de sortir quand nous sommes arrivés*. 'He was just going out when we arrived.'

Next, 'to point at someone' is not *'pointer'* but *montrer quelqu'un (du bout) du doigt, l'indiquer du doigt*. If you want to say to someone 'you've got a point there!' you'd best say, *il y a du vrai dans ce que vous dites!* Conversely, 'I don't see the point (of what you're saying)' is *Je ne vois pas où vous voulez en venir*.

Se pointer is, colloquially, 'to show up'. *Normalement il arrive avec un retard monstre, mais ce matin il s'est pointé à l'heure*. 'Usually he comes in awfully late, but this morning he showed up on time.' *Faire le point*, like *récapituler*, is an expression to which the moderator of a discussion may have recourse: *faisons le point*, 'let's sum up'.

Au point où nous en sommes (*où il en est* etc.), *autant. . .* is a good way of rendering 'since we've gone this far, we might just as well . . .' *Mettre quelque chose au point* is 'to perfect *or* finalize something *or* see to the details of it'.

ponctuation (f). You are certainly beyond the *dictée* stage by now but one can never be too sure of one's punctuation.

Une virgule, 'comma'; also, 'decimal point'.

Un point virgule, 'semi-colon'.

Un point, 'period', 'full stop'. (*Un point, c'est tout*, said in a firm tone, means 'period, that's all', 'that's my last word'.)

Deux points, 'colon'.

Point, à la ligne, 'end of the preceding sentence and start a new paragraph' (*un paragraphe*).

Un point d'interrogation, 'question mark'.

Un point d'exclamation, 'exclamation mark'.

Une apostrophe, 'apostrophe'.

Un tiret, 'dash'.

Un trait d'union, 'hyphen'.

Entre crochets, 'in brackets'.

Entre parenthèses, 'in parentheses', or 'parenthetically'.

Ouvrir (fermer) une parenthèse, 'beginning (end) of parenthesis'.

Trois points de suspension, 'ellipsis', as . . .

Entre guillemets, 'in quotes *or* quotation marks'. *Ouvrir (fermer) les guillemets*, 'beginning (end) of quote'. You will have noticed already that in French quotation marks are used less than in English and in a different way. A person's words are introduced by a dash and not by quotes at all, except in the case of consecutive paragraphs of the same person's speech. For instance: 'I will go,' he said, 'tomorrow.'—*J'irai, dit-il, demain*.

pont (m). 'A long holiday weekend' bridging the holiday itself, *le jour férié*, and the nearest weekend. *Faire le pont* when—let's say—Christmas is on a Thursday, is to have the Friday off as well, making it a four-day weekend.

porte-. Like *coupe-* (q.v.), this can prefix almost anything that in English is likely to be followed by '-holder', '-rack', or '-case', and many other items as well: *un porte-clés, un porte-cigarettes, un porte-tasses* . . . *Un porte-manteau* means 'a clothes-peg'; the sort of valise called 'portmanteau' in English is simply *une valise. Un portefeuille* is indeed 'a portfolio' in ministerial or investment terms, or else 'a wallet (US: 'billfold')', while *un porte-monnaie* is 'a (change)purse', in which you may sometimes carry banknotes as well. *Un porte-parole*, literally 'a word-carrier', is 'a spokesman'. On the same principle, you build words such as *un presse-papiers*, 'a paperweight'; and *des serre-livres*, 'book ends.'

portion (f). 'A helping' or 'serving' of food (*v.* SERVIR).

pose (f). The installation of something you've bought, such as carpeting or wall-paper. When you go to buy it, you'll find two prices: *au rouleau* (or, *au mètre*), and *avec la pose*. Furniture stores and decorators will often advertise *livraison et pose à domicile*, 'delivery to and installation in your home'.

Posé, when said of a person or of a person's voice, means 'calm', 'poised', 'under control'.

The verb *poser* ought to be paired off in your mind with *demander*, since 'to ask (for) something' is *demander quelque chose*, while 'to ask a question' is *poser une question*. You do not say, *demander une question*.

pot (m). Included here to remind you of:
　　dîner à la fortune du pot, 'to take pot luck';
　　prendre un pot, 'to have a drink';
　　manque de pot! 'Tough luck!' 'Too bad!' A good deal more casual than *dommage! Avoir du pot*, 'to be lucky'.
　　pot-de-vin (m), 'a bribe'.
　　Notice that *un pot* is not only 'a pot' but 'a jar' as well—*un pot de confiture, de yaourt* (or *yogurt*), *de moutarde*, and so forth; it may also be called *un verre. Pot perdu* marked on the bottom of the jar means that you pay no deposit on it (*v.* CONSIGNE). 'Kitchen pots and pans' are called *casseroles* (f).

pourboire (m). 'A tip' *pour boire*, 'to buy a drink', the silver with which you cross someone's palm in gratitude for services rendered or in anticipation of services requested. An inescapable angle of daily life in France as virtually anywhere else. The *chauffeur du taxi* will tell you the fare without adding the tip to it himself, which leaves it up to you to figure out 10% or 15% and to hand it over. The rule of at least 10% and more often 15% generally holds good; certainly nothing less is acceptable. *L'ouvreuse* ('the usherette') at the cinema expects it, the boy who gets your car out of the garage expects it, *le coiffeur* expects at least that. A restaurant usually makes sure of it by adding it to the fixed price of the menu: *service compris*. If you don't see this marked on the menu and you're not sure from the looks of the bill whether it's been done, it is legitimate to ask *le garçon* or *la caissière, Est-ce que le service est compris?*

Your *concierge* expects it, under the name of *étrennes* (q.v.) at New Year's time. Your *facteur* ('postman') and your local *caserne de sapeurs-pompiers* ('fire brigade'; US: 'fire-fighting squad') collect it at the same time of year by selling you a wall calendar.

poursuivre,se. Literally, 'to follow *or* to chase oneself'; so—'to go on', 'to continue' or 'to be continued'. *Les négociations se poursuivront.* 'The talks will be continued.'

poussière (f). 'Dust', of course; 'to dust', *épousseter* or *passer le chiffon*. 'The dustbin' or 'garbage pail' however is *la boîte à ordures*, or *la poubelle*; and 'the dust-man' is *l'éboueur*.

Avoir une poussière dans l'oeil, 'to have grit in the eye'.

Poussières, in the plural, is used when telling time or counting money to express informally 'and the odd bit'. 'a couple of minutes past', etc. *Il doit être deux heures et des poussières. Il ne me reste plus que treize francs et des poussières.*

pratiquant(e). *Il est catholique pratiquant.* 'He is a practising (church-going) Catholic.' Another term which goes along with this one, of course, is *croyant*: *Elle est très croyante.* 'She is very devout, a firm believer.'

presbyte. Nothing to do with 'presbytery', which is *le presbytère*, but with eyesight, since this is the word for 'far-sighted'; the condition is *la presbytie*. The opposite, 'near-sightedness', is *la myopie*, and the adjective is *myope*.

'Eyesight' itself is *la vue*, since *la vision* is not generally used for the physical capacity (*v.* VUE).

présenter. The verb you want for 'to introduce'. *Monsieur le Préfet, permettez-moi de vous présenter Mme Unetelle. Faire les présentations* is 'to make the introductions', 'do the honours'. *Introduire quelqu'un*, however, is 'to show someone in' (to a room, *dans la salle*), while *introduire quelque chose* is 'to insert something'; *introduisez une pièce de vingt centimes dans la fente*, 'insert a twenty-centime piece into the slot'. *Présenter* is followed by *à* (*j'ai présenté ma mère à la sienne*, 'I introduced my mother to his'), and *introduire* by *dans*.

présidentielles (f. pl.). The 'Presidential elections', held once every seven years. The President's term of office is *son mandat*, or *son septennat*.

prévention (f). May be a *Faux Ami* to you, as it can mean 'prejudice', like *préjugé* (m) and *parti pris* (m). *Il a une prévention contre les rousses*. 'He's got a prejudice against redheads.' *La prévention routière* does, however, mean 'road safety'.

'Prevention' may be translated by *empêchement* (m), but this is often avoided by *le fait d'empêcher, d'éviter,* or similar.

primordial. As in English, it means 'prime', 'primary', 'fundamental', but is used a good deal more often: *c'est d'une importance primordiale;* or *ce qui est primordial, c'est que . . .* and so on.

prise (f). The fact of taking, as in *une prise de contact* (*Nos conversations n'ont encore donné aucun résultat mais elles ont au moins servi de prise de contact*: 'Our talks have not yielded any result but at least they have allowed us to meet'); *une prise de position*, 'a statement of opinion', the fact of taking a stand; and *la prise de conscience des grands problèmes de notre temps*, 'awareness of (awakening to) the great problems of our era'.

Une prise is also 'an electric plug' (*v.* BRANCHER).

prochain. It is well to bear in mind that this means not only 'next' as in a succession of things (*la prochaine fois*, 'next time'), but also, 'immediately forthcoming' or 'imminent'. So, *Jean m'a fait part de son prochain mariage* does not necessarily mean that Jean has already been married and is about to re-marry, but merely that he is about to be married soon. Cinemas will advertise: *prochainement* —'coming soon'.

If you need to express 'next' *or* 'then' when telling a story, you need *ensuite*, or *puis*: 'next, he knocked at the house next door'; *ensuite il frappa à la maison d'à côté*. 'The lady next door' is simply *la voisine*, or *la dame qui habite à côté*. And when you are standing in line or sitting in the doctor's waiting room, the next person's turn will be announced by *au suivant* or, *la personne suivante!* since *le prochain*, as a noun, is 'one's neighbour' in the Biblical sense. *Il faut aimer son prochain*. 'Love your neighbour.' But you're safe in using the adjective *prochain* for the 'next' time, the 'next' train, the 'next' meeting, etc.

produire, se. A verb which is not likely to occur to you at first when you want to express 'to happen' or 'occur' or 'take place'; and yet it is used as often as *se passer*. *Qu'est-ce qui s'est produit* (or, *s'est passé)?* 'What happened?' *Je venais juste de rentrer quand il s'est produit une violente explosion*. 'I had just come home when a violent explosion occurred.'

Like *se manifester*, *se produire* can also mean 'to appear', 'to show up' and 'to make a stage appearance'.

professeur (m). Not only 'the university professor' but also 'the secondary-school master *or* teacher'; as distinct from *l'instituteur* (*-trice*) or *le maître* (*-esse*), 'the elementary-school teacher'.

There follow some of the terms that loom largest in the pupil's or the student's vocabulary:

admissible, être: 'to have passed a written exam' successfully; this gives you the right—and the obligation—'to attempt the oral', *se présenter à l'oral. Un bi-admissible* is the candidate for the *Agrégation* (the ultimate in university *concours*) who has been lucky enough to pass the written exam twice, in two different years but has not yet *réussi l'oral. Bi-admissible* is considered quite a worthy title in itself;

baccalauréat (m), abbreviated *bac* or *bachot*. The examination which signifies completion of secondary studies and allows a pupil to become a university student;

bizuther: 'to rag (US: haze)' a new student in one of the *grandes écoles*; these schools are on the level of the *facultés*, or beyond, but entrance is determined by a *concours*;

chahuter: 'to be rowdy in class', 'to heckle *or* create a disturbance';

collège (m): you may be misled by the British or American use of the term 'college'. In France this is a 'private secondary school', as distinct from the State *lycée* (m);

coller: 'to fail a student in his exam'; *être collé*, 'to fail';

composition (f): a 'term exam' in secondary school;

concours (m): 'competitive exam';

consigne (f): 'punishment'; especially, being kept in on Saturday;

faculté (f) or *fac*: 'college' of a university. *Faculté des Lettres et Sciences Humaines, Faculté de Médecine, Faculté de Droit*;

matière (f): 'subject of study', as '*philo*,' '*les maths*', etc.;

mention (f): 'special praise on an exam', 'honours', ranging from *Assez Bien* to *Bien* to *Très Bien*;

merde à la puissance 13!: distinctly a student way of saying 'good luck!';

moyenne (f): a passing grade or mark, *10 sur 20* or *20 sur 40*, since *examens* and *dissertations* are usually marked on the basis of 20, not of 100. A grade of 20 is unheard of except in maths; 18 is pretty awesome, and 15 is very respectable;

polycopié (m): a mimeographed copy of a professor's lectures or of assigned texts, etc.

promotion (f): the year of one's graduating class in a *faculté* or, especially, in a *grande école*;

reçu, être: 'to pass one's examination';

thème (m): 'translation from one's own language into a foreign one';

version (f): 'translation from the foreign tongue into one's own'.

propre (m). *C'est du propre!* corresponds to 'what a dirty trick!' Said with a certain indignant vehemence, it means the opposite of what it would seem to, since the adjective *propre* itself means 'clean', 'right', 'decent', 'fitting'. One washing-machine company made a neat play on words by claiming that its machine was *le propre du propre*; the very nature of cleanliness.

Propre can also mean, of course, 'own'; and you can remember this together with *le propriétaire*, 'owner', and *la propriété*, 'property'. ('To own', however, is *posséder*.) *Chacun croit que ses propres enfants sont des merveilles.* 'Everyone thinks his own children are wonderful.' Beware of mixing up *la propriété*, 'property' and *la propreté*, 'cleanliness'. The English word, 'propriety', is best translated by *les convenances* or *la bienséance*.

province (f). Anything outside Paris. This would seem simple enough; but in order to understand the first thing about France, from housing to traffic to culture, you must remember to what extent the country is still centred on Paris and realize the indifference that some Parisians can put into the terms *province*, *provincial*, *provincialisme* (m). (There is, however, a healthful tendency towards *décentralisation* in all fields.) *Cette fille ne connaît rien en dehors de sa petite province*—she's a real rustic. *Débarquer de la province*, 'to come up from the provinces', 'to leave the farm'. *Monter à Paris* is the aim of many a career, whose consecration is the appointment to a post in Paris. *Provincial*, adjective and noun, is not to be confused with *la Provence* and the adjective, *provençal*.

Q

quart (m). The fourth part of anything: *un quart de vin*, 'one fourth of a litre of wine' (just over half a pint); *un quart de Reblochon*, 'a quarter of a round Reblochon cheese'; 'a quarter of an hour'. *Il est dix heures un quart*, 'it's 10.15'.

A mechanism—a car, for instance—*qui marche au quart de tour* is one which works admirably well.

quartier (m). 'Neighbourhood' or 'area' of a city. *Le quartier estudiantin*, 'the student quarter'. Also, 'a section' of an orange!

quasiment. 'Nearly', 'just about'; can be used as excessively and as loosely as 'practically' is by some people in English: *il était quasiment mort, c'était quasiment impossible*, and the like.

que. A few special uses of *que* which your grammar-book may not stress: Exclamatory: 'how many!' 'how much!' 'how long!' 'how!' *Que de choses ravissantes dans cette boutique!* 'What a lot of lovely things in this shop!'

Imperative, requiring a subjunctive: *Qu'il finisse de faire l'imbécile ou je le fesse!* 'He'd better stop his fooling around or I'll spank him!' 'If only', 'what a pity' etc. *Que n'a-t-il pu vivre cent ans!* 'If only he could have lived to be a hundred!'

quelconque. A very common way of expressing 'so-so', 'barely tolerable'. *Normalement elle se montre excellente cuisinière, mais* *ce soir, la soupe était quelconque.* 'Usually she's a splendid cook, but the soup tonight was only so-so.'

quelque chose (m). The gender is worth noticing. 'A thing' is feminine, *une chose*; yet 'something' is masculine, *un quelque chose*. *Il a un petit quelque chose qui ne me plaît point.* 'There's something about him I don't care for at all.'

quelque part. 'Somewhere'. *Aller quelque part* is a common euphemism for 'going to the lavatory', which may also be called *au petit coin, aux toilettes, aux lavabos* (*v.* also CABINETS; LAVABO).

The best way to ask is *où sont les toilettes?* In a private home, you may think you're being ultra-euphemistic by asking *où est la salle de bains?*, but be forewarned: especially in a pre-World War II house, the toilet is virtually never to be found in the bathroom but always apart.

quoi. Apart from the obvious uses of *quoi*—'which', 'what'—you'll hear it used at the end of a sentence, for emphasis, as 'what' or 'wot' used to be in English. This sort of turn of phrase is definitely casual, all right when used by students among students, but it's very easy to overdo it and so to become, perhaps unintentionally, ripe for parody. Like sticking 'like' on to the end of almost every other sentence in English. *On est sorti hier, comme ça, quoi, histoire de s'amuser un peu, quoi, on voulait voir un film, un truc drôle, quoi . . .* You see?

Il n'y a pas de quoi is quite polite, however, and like *de rien* and *je vous en prie*, means 'it's nothing', 'you're welcome', 'don't mention it.'

Il y a de quoi is rather like, *et pour cause: il s'est mis en colère, il y a de quoi!* 'He got angry, who wouldn't?' *or*, for good reason!'

De quoi can sometimes be a neat way of saying 'something to . . .' *Vous trouverez de quoi manger dans le frigo*, 'You'll find something to eat in the fridge.'

R

radin. 'Miserly' or 'stingy'. Like *près de ses sous*, this adjective is more colloquial than is *avare*. You might expect, by analogy with *malin*—*maligne*, that the feminine form of *radin* would be *'radigne'*, but no, *radine*. *Le radinisme* is the noun.

radio (f). 'An X-ray.' Or 'the radio'. But 'a radio set' is *un poste de radio*. So you should say, *Je viens d'acheter un poste de radio*, and definitely not, *. . .'une radio'*. The same thing is valid for television: *la télévision* is the system, and *le poste de télévision*, the receiving set. *La télé* is the abbreviation which corresponds to 'TV' or 'telly' in English. 'To hear something on the radio' is *entendre quelque chose à la radio. Radio-commandé*, 'remote controlled'.

raffoler. 'To love' or 'adore' something. *Les haricots verts? J'en raffole!* 'French beans? I love them!' Intransitive, as you can see: *raffoler de quelque chose. S'affoler* is 'to become excited' in a more violent way, 'to panic', 'lose one's wits'.

rafistoler. 'To mend', 'patch', 'fix up any old way'; more colloquial than *raccommoder, arranger*, or *réparer*, and the sort of work involved is more sketchy. *Le rafistolage* is the noun.

rapporter. 'To yield', 'to be lucrative *or* profitable', *être intéressant* (*v.* INTÉRÊT). *Le rapport* can be 'profit'; or 'a report'—although 'a reporter' is *un reporter* or *un journaliste*, and 'his coverage' is *son reportage*—or the connexion or relationship between any two or more things or persons. *Je ne vois pas le rapport*, 'I don't get the connexion' (*v.* also VOIR).

rapports (m. pl.). 'Relationship'. *J'ai de très bons rapports avec lui*, 'I get along with him very well'. *Rapports sexuels*, 'sexual intercourse'.

rapprocher. Not to be confused with *reprocher. Rapprocher* is 'to draw near to' (*de*), 'reconcile', 'bring together': *un rapprochement Est-Ouest est à souhaiter.* 'A reconciliation of East and West would be desirable.'

On the other hand *reprocher* (*à*) is 'to reproach'; and the noun, *reproche*, is masculine. *Elle n'arrête pas de faire des reproches à son mari.* 'She is always blaming her husband.'

ras du cou. 'Crew-necked'; for a pullover; *à col roulé*, 'turtle-necked'.

RATP (f). *La Régie Autonome des Transports Parisiens*, 'the Paris public transport authority'.

rebondissement (m). Not 'rebound', which is *rebond* (m), but an 'unpredictable development'. *La situation peut connaître de nouveaux rebondissements.* 'There may be further developments in this affair.'

recharge (f). 'A refill' of a ball-point pen, a cigarette lighter, and so forth. *Charger* is 'to load' (as, *un fusil*) or 'fill'; *recharger*, 'to re-load' or 'refill'.

recommander. 'To recommend.' Note the difference in spelling: the *e* at the end in English becomes *a*, just as in *correspondance* (f), *indépendance* (f).

recouvrer. To recover in the sense of retrieving, regaining: *elle n'a pas encore pleinement recouvré sa santé*, 'she's not got her health back completely yet'. Not to be confused with *recouvrir*, 'to cover up', or 'cover again', as with a blanket. *L'enfant s'était débordé (dans son lit), alors je l'ai recouvert.* 'The child's bed-clothes had come undone, so I tucked them in again.'

récurer. 'To scour', as in, *une poudre qui récure, nettoie, fait briller*—
'a powder that scours, cleans, polishes'.
　　But 'to scour', as a figure of speech—'I scoured the town for a
present for him'—cannot be translated by *récurer*! *Faire toutes les
boutiques, faire toute la ville, chercher partout* would be more
suitable, or *fouiller* (*fureter par*) *toute la ville*.

recyclage (m). The two main uses of this word are both eloquent of
modern times. First, refresher training, keeping abreast of and
adapting to new skills and techniques. *Il faut que je me recycle.* In
very common usage these days, especially with executives, engi-
neers, white-collar workers generally. Second, the re-processing
and re-use of paper and other products, to avoid wasting natural
resources.

réfléchir. 'To stop and think'. *Réflexion faite,* 'on second thoughts'.
Refléter is 'to reflect' as in a mirror, and the noun is *un reflet*.

règlement (m). 'The rule', or 'the regulation'. *Il faut agir selon les
règlements.* 'You must act according to the rules.'
　　Il n'a pas voulu porter l'uniforme réglementaire. 'He refused to
wear the regulation uniform.'
　　Règlement can also be 'a payment', or 'squaring of an account'.
The carpenter will mark on the bottom of his bill, after the sum
due, *en votre aimable règlement*—'which you will kindly pay!' *Un
règlement de comptes* in the underworld means 'a session of getting even *or* wiping out a grudge'. *Régler sa note d'hôtel* is 'to pay
one's bill'.
　　Le règlement is not to be confused with *le réglage*, which is 'the
regulating' or 'adjusting' of a mechanical apparatus.
　　When a decision is to be taken and an external factor intervenes,
obviating the need to decide, you say *Comme cela, la question est
réglée!* 'That's done it!' 'That settles it!'
　　Mettre ses papiers en règle, 'to put one's papers in order'.

rejeton (m). This may look like a strange term for 'child' or 'offspring',
but there it is. There is nothing pejorative about it. *Rejeton* is
simply a good deal more *familier* than *enfant* or *gosse* (*v.*
FAMILIAR, OR INFORMAL, FRENCH).

relations (f. pl.). 'Valuable connexions', people in a position to wangle
things for you. *On a beau avoir beaucoup de diplômes, si on n'a
pas aussi beaucoup de relations* . . . 'It's not what you know, but
who you know' (*v.* also PISTON).
　　Once again, *relations* does not mean 'relatives' (*v.* PARENT).

religieuse (f). 'A nun', commonly called *une* (*bonne*) *sœur* as well.
Also, a certain type of cream cake.

remaniement (m). A rearrangement. *Un remaniement ministériel,* a
cabinet reshuffle.

remise (f). *Une* (*forte*) *remise* is 'a (big) discount on a price'. *Un* (*gros*)
rabais is also 'a (big) reduction'. 'A shed' behind the main house is

une remise too.

La remise is also 'the postponement' of something, since one of the many meanings of *remettre* is 'to postpone'. *Ne remettez jamais au lendemain ce que vous pouvez faire faire aujourd'hui par un autre.* 'Never put off until tomorrow what you can get someone else to do for you today.'

Remettre quelque chose en question is 'to bring something up all over again', 'lay it open for discussion again'.

remonte-pente (m). A familiar sight to *les fervents des sports d'hiver*, winter sports enthusiasts, as it is the term for 'ski-lift'.

rendre. You are familiar with *se rendre compte*, 'to realize'. *Je me suis rendu compte plus tard que j'aurais pu l'offenser.* 'Afterwards I realized that I might have offended him.'

Se rendre is 'to surrender'; the noun is *la reddition* or, more frequently, *la capitulation*. It is also quite often used for 'to go'. *La Reine s'est rendue sur les lieux de la catastrophe.* 'The Queen visited the scene of the disaster.'

Rendre is used more readily for 'to translate' than is 'render' in English and also succinctly renders the English 'to vomit'.

rente (f). Not usually the word for 'rent' which is *le loyer*; 'to rent' or 'let' is *louer*. *Les rentes* are one's '(unearned) income', from stocks, annuities, and the like; *vivre de ses rentes*, 'to live on one's income'. *Mais c'est une rente!* 'But that's terribly dear (expensive)!'

reprendre. 'To pick up (the thread of something) again'; a useful substitute for *recommencer*. *Reprenons notre discussion.* 'Let's resume our discussion.' *Reprenons à la ligne cinq, voulez-vous bien?* 'Let's go back to line five, shall we?' Or, 'to point out mistakes'. *Il la reprend à chaque fois qu'elle fait une faute de grammaire.* 'He corrects her each time she makes a grammatical error.'

Also, 'to take in' a pair of trousers, a dress; *donner*, 'to let out'. 'An alteration' in this context is *une retouche*.

retenir. Means, among other things, 'to detain, delay'. *Je ne vous retiens pas plus longtemps.* 'I won't keep you any longer.'

retombées (f. pl.). 'Fall-out', 'consequences'. *Retombées radioactives*; *retombées politiques*.

retourner. 'To upset someone emotionally', among other more obvious meanings. *La nouvelle de son départ m'a réellement retourné.* 'I was really upset on hearing that he'd gone away.' *Faire quelque chose (à quelqu'un)* is another away of saying the same thing: *ça m'a fait quelque chose*, 'it did something to me'.

retraite (f). 'A military *or* a religious retreat'; and also, 'retirement'. *Prendre sa retraite* is 'to retire'; and the person who does so is *un(e) retraité(e)*. *Toucher sa retraite* is 'to receive one's pension'. 'To retire' or 'withdraw' from the room, however, or from the world, is *se retirer* (*de*).

réveillon (m). A very essential word in the last week of December: the Christmas Eve celebration and again, the New Year's Eve (*la Saint Sylvestre*) party. In either case, wining, dining, dancing, and noise-making. The 'done' thing is either to go to '*une surprise party*' at friends' or to go out to a restaurant or two. It is wise to book ahead. Some days beforehand, cafés and restaurants will chalk up *Réveillon* on their windows and announce their featured attractions if there is to be a show. The verb is *réveillonner*.

rêveur (m). Included here for the sake of, *cela laisse rêveur*: 'it makes you stop and think', or 'it gives you something to think about'. Said of any sort of impressive situation, enviable or chilling. *Au début il était simple employé; à présent c'est le grand patron. Cela laisse rêveur.* 'In the beginning he was a mere employee; now he's the big boss. Food for thought there.'

rideau (m). 'A curtain', theatrical or otherwise; *le Rideau de Fer*, 'the Iron Curtain'.

Also, the veritable 'iron curtain' incorporated into all self-respecting old fireplaces and lowered like a portcullis to hide the blackened hearth or to make the chimney draw better when a fire is going.

risquer. This verb does not necessarily imply danger, as it does in English. *S'il continue sur sa lancée, il risque fort de réussir.* 'If he goes on at that rate, he's got a good chance of making good.' *Nous risquons gros*, 'we're taking a big risk', 'a lot is at stake'. 'A risk' is *un risque*.

rondelet(te). The equivalent of 'well-padded', or 'chubby', when speaking of a person. Less diplomatic than (*être*) *bien en chair* but more so than *boulot(te)*.

rouspéter. A much-used verb in this land of *l'individu*, as it means 'to protest', 'to complain'. *Un rouspéteur* is the person who does so.

roux (rousse). 'Red- *or* auburn-haired'. You can, but should never, say that someone has '*les cheveux rouges!*'—he has *les cheveux roux*. *Une rousse* is 'an auburn-haired woman'. *Une tache de rousseur*, 'a freckle'.

rugby (m). American-style football, with the oval ball. *Le football* is 'soccer'.

ruisseau (m). Both the 'bubbling brook' and, as the city-dweller knows, the 'gutter'!

S

S.A. *Société Anonyme*; corresponds to 'Company, Ltd.', or 'Company, Inc.'. *SARL, Société Anonyme à Responsabilité Limitée.*

sage. One of the classic sources of confusion, as it can mean either 'good' (well-behaved) or 'wise'. Obviously when you say to a child *sois sage*, you're not saying, 'be wise', but 'be good', 'behave yourself'. Applied to grown-ups, *sage* and *la sagesse* generally have to do with wisdom—or with prudence, which of course is not too far removed from good behaviour. *Autrefois il buvait énormément, à présent il a décidé d'être sage.* 'He used to drink an awful lot; now he's turned over a new leaf.' *S'assagir* is 'to become good', 'behave better'.

    Une sage-femme, 'a midwife', plays a far more official role in France than in the US or England. In 'the maternity hospital', *la maternité,* she often presides without the doctor's help, except of course *en cas d'urgence.*

saisir. 'To seize' or 'grip' physically, like *attraper*; or mentally, like *comprendre* or sometimes, *suivre* (q.v.). *Qu'a-t-il dit? Je n'ai pas saisi.* 'What did he say? I didn't get (catch) it.'

    The present participle, *saisissant*, is often used for 'striking', 'stunning', 'thrilling'.

saison, la belle. 'Summer'; the fine weather which is supposed to correspond to *les grandes vacances* (*scolaires*), from late June to mid-September. For all practical purposes, the month that really matters is August (*v.* FERMETURE ANNUELLE).

    Assaisonner, 'to season (food)', with *des assaisonnements.*

salade (f). 'A salad'; also, 'a lettuce', otherwise called *une laitue*. 'The salad-bowl' is *le saladier.*

    Also, colloquially, a rather dubious term, meaning 'a mess', 'a bad business' (*v.* also HISTOIRE). And *le panier à salade* is not only 'the salad shaker' but also 'the Black Maria'.

sans façon. The nearest thing you'll find to 'informal', along with *simple, en toute simplicité*, and *sans cérémonie*: *Il est sans façon* (*sans cérémonie*). 'He's very informal.' *Elle nous a reçu en toute simplicité.* 'She welcomed us informally.'

    Or *sans façon* can mean 'sincerely', 'really': *Non merci, sans façon.* 'No thank you, really.'

satisfaction (f). When you want to say that someone works satisfactorily or is (fully) satisfactory, you do not say, *Il est satisfaisant*, but *Il donne* (*toute*) *satisfaction*. You can however say, *Son travail est satisfaisant.*

saucisse (f). A sausage that needs cooking before it is eaten—*saucisse de Francfort, de Strasbourg* etc.; as distinct from *saucisson* (m), already cooked and ready to be eaten cold—*saucisson d'Arles* etc. Also, a bread shaped like a *saucisson*.

Saucissonner is a disdainful term for the straightforward way in which many a French family will eat in the train or on a Sunday outing: a long loaf, a long sausage, a ripe Camembert, and a knife to cut it all up with.

sauter. 'To jump', 'leap', 'skip' and so forth. Also, 'to explode' or 'go off'. *Faire sauter* is loosely used to mean not only 'to set off', but also 'to get rid of', *supprimer*, *faire disparaître*. *Faire sauter la cloison entre deux pièces*, 'to get rid of the partition between two rooms'.

Ça saute aux yeux (or, less properly, *ça crève les yeux*) is literally, 'it's staring you in the face'; or 'it's obvious'.

sauvage. A recent use of this adjective stems from one of its root meanings: that of 'growing wild', 'uncultivated'. So it has come to signify 'unscheduled', 'unauthorized': *une grève sauvage*, *le camping sauvage* (i.e. not on an officially approved campsite).

sauver, se. A dramatic-looking verb but one which can be—and often is—used for something as everyday as 'I must be going': *je dois me sauver. Il s'est sauvé avant la fin du concert.* 'He slipped out before the end of the concert.'

savant (m). As a noun, 'scholar' and almost exclusively, 'scientist'— who, by the way, is never a '*scientiste*' but *un homme de science*. And as an adjective, not only 'scholarly' but 'knowing', 'clever', 'expert'. *Avec des gestes savants, elle se coiffa.* 'Deftly, she combed her hair.'

savoir. *Je ne veux pas le savoir* is a nearly universal *formule* for putting an end to an argument or to opposition from someone. You might translate 'that's no concern of mine', 'that's your problem', 'that's your tough luck'—*Il est impossible de terminer ce rapport pour vendredi.—Je ne veux pas le savoir, il me le faut!* 'It's impossible to finish this report by Friday.'—'Never mind, I've got to have it.'

Another common phrase is *être payé pour savoir quelque chose*: 'to know something all too well'. *Attention, c'est un escroc, je suis payé pour le savoir.* 'Watch out, he's a crook, as I learned to my sorrow.' *J'en sais quelque chose, j'en ai fait l'expérience,* or *j'en ai fait les frais* could also express this.

scientifique (m. or f.) Because this is not only an adjective but also one of those *adjectifs substantivés* discussed on page 12, it can mean not only 'scientific' but also 'a scientist'. *Littéraire* and *manuel* are other examples.

séduire. Can be less limited and dramatic than 'seduce' in English; and the same holds true, of course, for *séduisant, séduction, séducteur* (*-trice*). The idea is that of general attraction or temptation. An airline company advertised its *formule séduisante* for round-the-world trips, meaning its attractive price scales.

séjour (m) **linguistique**. A phenomenon that has burgeoned since the early 1960's, whereby individual French pupils stay—during the Christmas, Easter or summer holidays—in a family in the country whose language they are studying, chiefly England and Germany. Numerous organizations exist to select such families and convoy the pupils to them and back.

sélectionner. 'To choose' or 'select'; *fruits sélectionnés*, for instance, are 'choice *or* select fruit'. The idea is that the choice aims at quality. Merely 'to sort', as such, is *trier*, *faire un tri*.

semblant. *Faire semblant* is 'to pretend', 'to make believe'. *Prétendre* is partly *un faux ami*, as it means 'to claim' or 'to have claims' (upon something); but *un prétendant* is 'a pretender to the throne' or 'a suitor' or 'an applicant'.

sens (m). 'Sense', 'meaning', 'signification'. *Cette phrase n'a pas de sens* (*est un non-sens*): 'This sentence is meaningless.' *C'est insensé*. 'It's sheer madness.'

'Direction.' *Prenez dans ce sens-là, vous tomberez sur la Concorde.* 'Go in that direction, you'll land right in the Place de la Concorde.'

A perceptive faculty: *la vue, l'odorat, l'ouïe, le toucher, le goût*—'sight', 'smell', 'hearing', 'touch', 'taste'. *Avoir un sixième sens*, 'to have a sixth sense'.

sens dessus-dessous. 'Upside-down'; and '*dessous-dessus*' won't do, any more than 'downside-up' will in English! *Il a tout mis sens dessus-dessous*, 'he turned everything upside down, made a shambles'.

'Inside out' does not work analagously; *à l'envers* is the answer, since *l'endroit* (m) is 'the right side' (of cloth, not of the street), and *l'envers* (m) 'the wrong side'.

As *à l'endroit* also means 'right side up' and *à l'envers* 'wrong side up', *mettre à l'endroit* is 'to turn *either* right side out *or* right side up'; *mettre à l'envers*, 'to turn inside out *or* upside down'.

service (m). A few phrases to be noted with special care:

Service (*non*) *compris*, 'tip (not) included'; something you should watch for on the menu (*v*. POURBOIRE).

Rendre service (*à quelqu'un*), 'to do (someone) a favour'. Or, in place of *être utile*, 'to be useful'. *Cette table m'a bien rendu service*. 'I found that table very useful.' *Ça pourrait toujours rendre service*. 'It could always come in handy.'

Le service d'ordre, 'the police'. *Faire son service militaire*, 'to do one's national (military) service'.

servir. 'To serve', 'to be useful'; 'to help someone (at table)'. *Servez-vous de petits pois*, 'Help yourself to peas.' *A quoi ça sert?* (or, more correctly, *à quoi cela sert-il?*): 'What's the good in (doing) that?' 'What's the use?' Or, in the case of an object, 'what's it for?', 'what's it supposed to be used for?' *Serviable*, 'cooperative', 'helpful' (*v*. ARRANGER).

si. The emphatic 'yes', particularly the 'yes' which contradicts a negative.—*Vous n'y pensez pas!*—*Mais si!* 'You're not seriously thinking of doing that!'—'Oh yes, I am!' It may be used for polite insistence:—*Je ne peux pas accepter ce prêt.*—*Mais si mais si, je vous en prie.* 'I can't accept this loan.'—'Nonsense, I insist.' And there's nothing at all surprising about *Si si si si si* . . . Where you stop is up to you.

Colloquially, you can make use of *si?* as a query, replacing *n'est-ce pas?*, with the aim of confirming a negative sentence: *Il ne vient pas, si?* 'He's not coming, or is he?'

Si also means 'if'. Used in a certain way it becomes a rhetorical or explanatory 'if' which approximates to 'because': *si je me permets de vous le signaler, c'est que* . . . 'I'm taking the liberty of pointing this out to you because . . .'

siège (m). 'The seat'—of a car or any other vehicle, of a person, or loosely, 'a chair'. *Prenez un siège.* 'Have a seat.' The exception is your seat at the theatre or at the cinema, which is *un fauteuil* or *une place*. 'To get a ticket', or 'book a seat', *louer une place*.

Le siège social of a political party, business firm, or other organization is its 'headquarters' or 'head office'; 'a military headquarters', however, is *le quartier général*. *Siéger*, 'to sit', 'be in session.' And *le Saint Siège* is 'the Holy See'.

signaler. Very often used with the idea of *faire remarquer*: 'to indicate', 'point out', or 'underline'. *Je tiens seulement à vous signaler que* . . . 'I simply want to point out to you that . . .' *Le signalement* of a person is the list of his distinguishing (physical) characteristics, especially of *un homme recherché par la police*, 'a wanted man'. *La signalisation routière* is 'the system of road signs'.

sinistre (m). A noun which may catch you off balance, since it does not mean 'a sinister person' but 'a grave accident' or 'natural catastrophe'—earthquake, fire, and so forth, and *les sinistrés* are 'the victims of the catastrophe'.

As an adjective, *sinistre* simply means 'sinister'.

SMIG (m). *Le Salaire Minimum Interprofessionnel Garanti*, 'the legally prescribed minimum wage'.

SNCF (f). *Société Nationale des Chemins de Fer*, the nationalized railway system.

sortant. Most often heard in connection with elections: *le député sortant*, 'the outgoing *or* incumbent member of parliament'.

souffrant. Can be less painful than 'suffering', since it often means simply 'sick' or 'ill', and is considered more polite than the term, *malade*. *J'espère que votre mère n'est plus souffrante.* 'I hope your mother is well now.' But *la souffrance* does mean 'suffering' or 'pain', and cannot express 'illness', for which you need *la maladie* or *l'affection* (*du foie*—of the liver etc.). 'A sick person' or 'a patient' is *un(e) malade*, and if you want to wish someone a quick recovery, you send *vos vœux de prompt rétablissement*.

sous. Generally, 'under', 'below', 'sub-' (*un sous-marin*); but often needing a different translation in expressions where English uses 'within', 'in', 'at', 'before', and other prepositions. *Sous le règne de Louis XIV,* 'in the reign of Louis XIV'; *sous huitaine,* 'within the week'; *sous la main,* 'to hand'.

sports (m. pl.) **d'hiver.** 'Winter sports' in general, and skiing in particular; a term—and an industry—that have mushroomed in recent years. *Je pars aux sports d'hiver. Une station de sports d'hiver,* 'a ski resort'. *Faire du ski,* 'to go skiing'; *faire du patin à glace,* 'ice skating'; *faire du toboggan* or *de la luge,* 'sledging (US: sledding)'. *v.* also APRÈS-SKI.

stage (m). Not 'a theatrical stage', which is *la scène*; but 'a period of training *or* apprenticeship', with or without a course. *Stage de formation,* 'traineeship'; *stage de recyclage* (*v.* RECYCLAGE) *stage de ski, de guitare,* etc. A secretarial school student will *faire un stage comme dactylo chez un fabricant, un éditeur*—work as a trainee typist for a manufacturer, a publisher. He or she is *un(e) stagiaire*.

strapontin (m). 'Folding seat' in a theatre or public vehicle.

suivre. 'To follow'; and especially, 'to understand'. *Excusez-moi, je ne vous suis pas.* 'I'm sorry, I don't follow you.' 'To take': *suivre un cours de géographie.* 'To take a geography course.' 'To take care of': *C'est le même médecin qui la suit depuis dix ans.* 'She's been going to the same doctor for ten years.'

Faire suivre son courrier, 'to have one's mail forwarded'. On the envelope you mark, *Faire suivre* (*en cas de départ*).

Lire la suite à la page 12, at the bottom of a newspaper article, tells you that it is 'continued on page 12'. Conceivably, you could ask to *écouter la suite de la suite No. 5*—'to listen to the rest of the fifth suite'.

Avoir de la suite dans les idées, 'to be consistent, logical *or* persevering', 'to know what one wants'.

supermarché (m). 'Supermarket', of course. A term that hardly existed in France when the first edition of this book was written. Also called *une grande surface,* or, when it is exceptionally large, *un hypermarché. Les petits commerçants se plaignent de la prolifération des supermarchés.*

surenchérir. 'To raise the bid' at *une vente aux enchères,* 'an auction'; and by extension, 'to outbid someone' in conversation by overemphasizing what has already been said.

surlendemain (m). A term that is missing in English, as it means not only 'the day after tomorrow' but also 'the day after the next day'. *Il est arrivé le surlendemain,* 'He arrived two days later'.

symétrique. Note the spelling: *Symétrique* and *symétrie* (f) do not need two m's, as they do in English.

système (m). 'System', of course; and also, more loosely, 'set-up', 'business', 'the works'. *Il a tenu absolument à me montrer son bureau—coffre-fort, classeurs, tout le système.* 'He insisted on showing me his office—office-safe, filing cabinets, the works.'

Il me tape sur le système is quite a slangy way of saying 'I can't stand him'. And of course you must not forget the justly famous *Système D* (*v.* DÉBROUILLER, SE).

T

tabac (m). Either 'tobacco', or 'the tobacconist's'. If the latter, *un tabac* is generally *un café* at the same time, distinguishable from the *cafés* which are not *tabacs* by the traditional sign of the red carrot, since a roll of tobacco leaves used to be called *une carotte*. The sale of tobacco is regulated by the SEITA (*Société pour l'Exploitation Industrielle des Tabacs et des Allumettes*, or state *régie des tabacs*) (*v.* also EDF, RATP and SNCF). You can buy postage stamps in a *tabac* as well as *à la poste*; or *un billet* or *un dixième* (q.v.) *de la Loterie Nationale*, or *la vignette* (q.v.) for your car. Some *tabacs* sell the official stamps, *timbres fiscaux*, needed to validate certain documents.

tabatière (f). Called *un vasistas* as well, when it means the prop-up window in the severely gabled wall of many a sought-after *chambre de bonne*. In Paris, maids' rooms house fewer and fewer maids, and more and more students. *Une tabatière* is also 'a snuff-box'; and *le tabac à priser*, 'snuff'.

table des matières (f). 'The table of contents' of a book. Generally placed at the end of the volume.

taille (f). Your 'height'; your 'waist'; and your 'size' in general. *Il est bien taillé*, 'He's well built.' *Il est de taille moyenne.* 'He's of average height.' *Il (elle) a la taille fine.* '(S)he is narrow-waisted.' *J'ignore son tour de taille.* 'I don't know his waist measurement.' In a shop: *quelle taille voulez-vous (prend-elle)?* 'What size are you looking for (does she wear)?' *Je voudrais la taille en dessus*: 'I'd like the next largest size'; *la taille en dessous*, 'the next smallest'. In the case of shoes, socks, stockings, and gloves, however, size is expressed not by *la taille* but by *la pointure*; and certain men's articles, pyjamas and underclothes particularly, are measured by *patron*, 'medium'; *grand patron*, 'large'; and *demi-patron*, 'small' (*v.* PATRON).

Il n'est pas de taille à réussir cela. 'He's not up to (capable of) doing that successfully.'

tailleur (m). In spite of its gender, strictly 'a woman's suit', never a man's, which is *un costume. Une veste* is either a man's or a woman's 'jacket', and may be more *fantaisie*, 'non-classic'—in colour, cut, and material—than *un veston*, which is always of cloth and always for men. Needless to say, *un tailleur* is also the person responsible for the clothes: 'the tailor'.

tant. You might add to what your grammar-book tells you about *tant*, these expressions: *Tant qu'à faire, autant* . . . 'While we're at (about) it, we might just as well . . .' *Tant qu'à faire, autant tout faire refaire en même temps.* 'While we're at it, we might just as well have everything re-done at once.'

Tant et tant: 'such and such sum *or* amount'. *Mettons que je gagnais tant et tant.* 'Supposing I earned such and such.'

And that curious expression (no use in trying to make sense of it word for word), *Vous m'en direz tant.* 'You've just said a mouthful', 'there's nothing left to add'.

tapis (m). 'A rug', Oriental or otherwise, as distinct from *un tapis cloué* or *une moquette*, which means '(wall-to-wall) carpeting'. *Une carpette*, contrary to what you might expect, is 'a small rug'; and so is *la descente de lit*, 'the small bedside-rug'. *Un tapis de bain* is 'a bathmat'.

La tapisserie is more likely nowadays to mean 'upholstery' than 'tapestry', just as *un tapissier* is more likely to be 'an upholsterer'. *Tapisser les murs*, however, is quite simply, 'to put up wall paper', which is called *le papier peint*.

tel ou tel. 'Such and such a'. *Il nous racontait jusqu'aux moindres détails de son voyage, qu'il avait mangé dans tel ou tel restaurant, qu'il était descendu dans tel ou tel hôtel, et ainsi de suite.* 'He told us about his trip down to the smallest details, about eating in such and such a restaurant, staying at such and such (an) hotel, and so forth.'

tel quel. 'Just as it is' (they are, etc.). *Au lieu de ranger ses papiers, il les laisse toujours tels quels.* 'He always leaves his papers just as they are, instead of putting them away.'

temple (m). 'A Protestant church'—the building. *L'Eglise protestante* refers to '*the* Protestant Church', that is, the religion. *Une église* is 'a (Catholic) church'. while *l'Eglise* is 'the (Catholic) Church'. *Une mosquée*, 'a mosque'.

'A Jewish temple' is *une synagogue*.

tenir. Another of those multi-purpose verbs that often seem to go far afield from the basic meaning: 'to hold' or 'to keep'.

Il tient de son père. 'He's like his father.'

Je le tiens de lui. 'I have it (learnt it) from him.' 'He's the one who told me.'

Tenir en place, 'to stay still'. *A partir de 5h du soir, les élèves ne tiennent plus en place.* 'Past five in the evening, the pupils simply can't sit still.'

Tenir à quelque chose, 'to value something', 'care a great deal about it'. *Attention à ce vase, j'y tiens.* 'Be careful with that vase, it means a lot to me.'

S'en tenir à quelque chose, 'to put stock in something', 'to believe'. *Je ne sais plus à quoi m'en tenir.* 'I don't know what to believe any more.'

S'en tenir là, 'to refrain from going further'. *Tenez-vous-en là!* 'You'd better stop there!'

Tiens! tenez! 'Well well!' 'Hallo!' 'Hey! What's this!' 'Just think!' etc.

Tenir debout, 'to ring true', 'to be plausible', said of a story. *Son histoire ne tient pas debout.* 'His version doesn't hold water, won't wash.'

terre-plein (m). In town, a paved square or the centre strip of a boulevard or roundabout; you may, sometimes, park your car on it. On the *autoroute* (f), 'the centre strip of grass'.

tiquer. Among horses, to have a vicious habit of biting; and in human terms, by extension, 'to wince' or 'show one's reaction of annoyance'; and so, broadly, 'to be irked *or* displeased'. *Ce qui m'a toujours fait tiquer, c'est . . .* 'The thing that's always annoyed me is . . .'

tirer. Still another of those verbs that crop up everywhere:

S'en tirer, 'to manage' or 'muddle through'. *Il s'en tire à peu près.* 'He's just about getting along.' *Je ne m'en suis pas tiré si mal que ça.* 'I got out of it pretty well.'

Il n'y a rien à en tirer. 'It's (he's) a hopeless case, there's nothing to be done about it (him).'

Tirer quelque chose au clair, 'to bring something out into the open', 'to clarify something'.

Tirer les conclusions, 'to draw a conclusion'.

Tirer (toucher) à sa fin, 'to draw to a close'.

toc! A rather elastic little exclamation, expressing anything from 'knock knock!' on the door, to the recognition that a remark has struck home or the announcement of some event: 'there!' 'so there!' 'well said!' 'there it was!' or whatever the context calls for.

tomber. Gives rise to a number of expressions which, translated word for word, are quite comical:

Tomber à l'eau (said of a plan or idea), 'to fall through', 'not to work'. *Ses projets pour dimanche sont tombés à l'eau.* 'His plans for Sunday have fallen through.'

Tomber bien, 'to occur at the right moment'. *Tu tombes bien, nous nous mettons à table à l'instant.* 'You've come just at the right time, we were about to sit down to table.'

Tomber mal is, of course, just the opposite: *Ça tombe on ne peut plus mal,* 'it's come at the worst possible moment'.

Tomber sur quelque chose, 'to find something directly', sometimes with an element of surprise. *Je suis tombé sur sa maison du premier coup.* 'I found his house on the first try.'

Laisser tomber—anything, from a cup to an idea to a subject of conversation to a person—is, 'to drop' or 'abandon'. ('Let's drop the subject' or 'let's change the subject', however, is *parlons d'autre chose*.)

Tomber (or, *donner*) *dans le panneau* is colloquial: 'to be taken in by something', 'to fall into a trap *or* for a trick'.

toujours. Does not always means 'always', that is: 'forever and a day'. It can mean 'anyhow' or even, 'just in case'. *Je ne crois pas que ça va marcher, mais essayez toujours.* 'I don't think it's going to work, but try anyhow (you can always try, there's no harm in trying).' Obviously not the same sort of *toujours* as in *vous êtes mon amour pour toujours*, or in *ils se connaissent depuis toujours*: 'they've known each other all their lives'.

tour, faire un. 'To go (come) out for a walk (*or* a ride).' *Je vais juste faire un petit tour.* 'I'm just going out for a walk.' *Un tour en voiture*, 'a drive' or 'a ride'.

Not to be confused with *jouer un tour à quelqu'un*, 'to play a trick on someone'.

When *tour* changes gender, *une tour*, it means 'a tower'.

Toussaint (f). *La Toussaint* is 'All Saints' Day', 1 November; not a sad day in itself but immediately followed by *Le Jour des Morts* ('All Souls' Day'), 2 November—a day for placing wreaths on, and visiting, family graves.

tracasser, se. 'To worry' or 'fidget', like *s'en faire* or, in more formal terms, *s'inquiéter*. *Que de tracas!* 'Such a lot of problems!' *Ne vous tracassez pas!* 'Not to worry!'

Une tracasserie is less serious than *un tracas*.

traitement (m). 'Treatment', medical or otherwise; and also commonly used to mean 'salary'.

tranquille. What looks like a solely feminine form of the adjective is in fact the only one; and the -*ille* is pronounced like that in *ville*. *Etre tranquille* can mean not only 'to be quiet' but also, 'to be alone', 'at ease', 'away from other people's noise or worries'. *Soyez tranquille, Monsieur, je m'en occupe.* 'You've nothing to worry about, sir, I'll take care of it.' (*Se*) *tranquilliser* goes along with (*se*) *rassurer*. *Tranquillisez-vous*: 'calm down', 'rest assured'. *Un tranquillisant* is 'a tranquillizer'.

travailler. Chiefly, 'to work', as you know. In a particular context, it can be used quite like *jouer*: 'to work', 'to warp'. And in another, colloquial one—*Qu'est-ce qui vous travaille?*—you have to translate by 'bother' or 'get': 'what's bothering you?' (*v.* also TRACASSER, SE). Speaking of work, you must remember that *labourer* is definitely not a synonym for *travailler*, as *labourer* is 'to till the soil' or 'work the land'; it follows that *un laboureur* is not any sort of worker in general but 'a tiller of the soil', 'farm labourer'. 'A worker' or 'labourer' is *un(e) ouvrier(ère)*, or sometimes, *un travailleur*. But *un travailliste* is a member of *le parti travailliste*, 'the Labour Party'.

travailleur, -euse immigré(e). 'Immigrant worker', chiefly from former French colonies in Africa and from Portugal and Spain.

traversin (m). The cylindrical pillow, or bolster, that goes across the width of the bed; very common in France. Usually accompanied by the smaller square *oreiller* (m), 'pillow'.

tricolore. The French flag is *le drapeau tricolore*, whose colours are always listed in order: *bleu*, *blanc et rouge*, the opposite of the American and English 'red, white and blue'.

tromper. A notorious verb: 'to be unfaithful in marriage': *tromper sa femme, tromper son mari*. Infidelity itself is *l'infidélité*.
   But you should not lose sight of the overall meaning, 'to deceive' or 'mislead'. *Se tromper*, logically enough, is 'to deceive oneself': in other words, to be wrong or mistaken. And it follows that *trompeur* is the adjective you want for 'deceiving' or 'misleading', since *décevant*—from the verb, *décevoir*—is a *Faux Ami*, meaning 'disappointing'. Thus *quelle déception!* is 'what a disappointment!' while, *quelle erreur!* means 'what a mistake!' 'how wrong he was!' etc.

trouvaille (f). 'A find', whether it be a 'buy', a lucky discovery, or a clever idea (*v.* also ASTUCE).

truc (m). A close cousin to *machin* (q.v.); but *truc* sometimes has the additional meaning of cleverness, 'a hint' or 'tip'. *Elle m'a indiqué un truc pour réussir la mayonnaise*. 'She gave me a tip on making mayonnaise.' Definitely *familier*.
   Truquer is 'to fake', 'cheat', 'fraudulently alter'—*truquer une photo*, or *les résultats du scrutin*, 'the election results'.

tutoyer. To call someone *'tu'*. The big problem is when to do it and when not. The simplest answer is that you start out with *vous*, except with small children and domestic animals; then you wait to see how the situation and your personal taste evolve. Students, *entre eux*, use *'tu'* very readily. But in general the French, when conversing with or receiving a stranger, are far less casual and off-hand than, for instance, Americans; so that to be called *'vous'*, even after months or years of acquaintance, is not necessarily a sign of coldness. And you must remember that the plural of *'tu'* is *'vous'*; so, in case you think someone is being unnecessarily cold or stand-offish in addressing you as *'vous'*, stop first to think how many of you there are! In some families, the children *vouvoient leurs parents*.

tuyau (m). A meaning which has become so widespread that it isn't even slang any more is that of 'a hint', 'a tip', 'a direct lead'—an extension of the basic meaning, 'a pipe' or 'tube'. (*La tuyauterie de la salle de bains*, for instance, is the whole plumbing installation in the bath room.) *Il cherche du travail et m'a demandé des tuyaux.* 'He's looking for work and asked me to give him some leads.'

TVA (f). *Taxe à la Valeur Ajoutée*, i.e. 'VAT'.

U

une (f). The front page of a newspaper. *Cela mérite un gros titre à la une.* 'That's worth a big headline on page one.' Normally, of course, you do not say, *la une* nor *le un*, but: *l'une* and *l'un. Ils se regardaient l'un l'autre.* 'They looked at one another.' *De deux choses l'une.* 'One of two things is possible.' *L'une des deux sœurs est jolie.* 'One of the two sisters is pretty.'

un tel (or, **Untel**). 'So-and-so'. *Supposez que vous rencontrez Madame Unetelle (Monsieur Untel).* 'Suppose you meet Mrs. So-and-So (Mr. So-and-So).'

urnes (f. pl.). Ballot boxes. *Aller* (or *se rendre*) *aux urnes*, 'to vote'. 'The voting booth' itself is *l'isoloir* (m).

V

valable. First of all, 'valid'. In the Métro: *Au-delà de cette limite les billets ne sont plus valables.* 'All tickets are invalid beyond this line.' *Il n'a pas d'excuse valable.* 'He has no valid excuse.' Closely linked to another meaning, 'worthwhile'. *C'était une expérience valable.* 'It was a worthwhile experience' (or experiment: *v.* EXPÉRIENCE). But this is not the way to translate 'valuable', which is *précieux* or *ayant beaucoup de valeur*. 'Valuables' are *des objets* (or *effets*) *personnels de valeur*.

valide. Can have the same meaning as *valable* but also, and especially, means 'sound': *les personnes valides*, as opposed to 'the crippled', *les invalides*. Yet the verb, *valider*, and its contrary, *invalider*, have nothing to do with health but rather with contracts, bills and tickets: 'to validate' and 'invalidate'.

ventiler. Especially common in these days of opinion polls and surveys, marketing and advertising: *ventiler les chiffres par catégorie*, 'to break down the figures *or* statistics by category'. Can also mean 'to ventilate, to air'. *Un ventilateur (électrique)* is 'an electric fan'.

verser. 'To pour a liquid'; also, 'to pour money'—that is, 'to pay'. 'A payment' can be called *un versement. Cette somme est à verser à la banque.* 'This sum is to be paid into the bank.' *Je paie ma voiture en neuf versements mensuels.* 'I'm paying for my car in nine monthly instalments.'

vignette (f). Among other things, a sort of car licence—not the driver's licence, which is *le permis de conduire*—which you have to renew every year around November. You buy it in a *bureau de tabac*, and its price varies according to the year and horsepower of your car.

Or again, a minuscule tab of gummed paper, with or without the price marked, on the outside of any package of medicine whose cost is partly reimbursed to you by *la Sécurité Sociale*. You have to peel the *vignette* off the box and stick it on to the prescription, *l'ordonnance*, which you send in to the *Sécurité Sociale* along with a *feuille de maladie*, or doctor's certificate.

virgule (f). 'The comma' in a sentence, and 'the decimal point' in a number. Conversely, where English uses a comma in numbers—as, to separate hundreds from thousands—French uses points: *23.987.654,01 (vingt-trois millions neuf cent quatre-vingt-sept mille six cent cinquante-quatre virgule zéro un).*

visite (f). 'Visit'; and *rendre visite* is 'to visit', 'call upon' someone; whereas *visiter* applies mostly to edifices (*visiter les Invalides à Paris*) and countries. You cannot *rendre visite à un monument*; conversely, *visiter* is rarely used for persons except when they are looked at from an institutional point of view: *visiter des orphelins*.

Passer une visite médicale is 'to be given a medical examination'.

voir. You might add these expressions having to do with 'see' and 'see about' to those you will find in a dictionary:

Cela n'a rien à voir là-dedans (or, *avec cela*): 'That has nothing to do with it, that's beside the point' (*v.* also RAPPORTER).

C'est tout vu, 'it's all decided', 'no argument'.

Il ne peut pas les voir en peinture. 'He can't stand them.'

Avant d'agir, je préfère attendre et voir venir. 'Before doing anything, I'd rather wait and see how things shape up.'

volontaire. Unites two ideas which English expresses in separate words: 'voluntary', and 'strong-willed' or 'stubborn'. *Il a le menton volontaire.* 'He has a stubborn chin.' *Un volontaire* is 'a volunteer'; *se porter volontaire*, 'to enlist' or 'volunteer'.

vue (f). 'Eyesight' or 'vision' (*v.* PRESBYTE). *Avoir une bonne vue*, 'to have good eyesight'. *Avoir la vue faible*, 'to have bad eyesight'. Also, 'a view', as in *cette maison a vue sur la mer*. 'This house has a view of the sea (overlooks the sea).'

Or 'sight' in general. *A la vue de tant de travail, il faillit s'évanouir.* 'He nearly fainted at the sight of so much work.'

Perdre quelqu'un de vue, 'to lose sight of someone', 'to lose track of *or* be out of touch with someone'.

A perte de vue: literally, 'out of sight', 'endlessly'.

Z

zinc (m). Another term for *le comptoir*, 'the counter', in a café. *Manger (boire) sur le zinc*, 'to eat (drink) standing up at the counter'.

Special Vocabularies

Banking

action (f): 'stock-market share'.

barème (m): 'table', 'scale' (for calculating rates etc.).
billet (m): 'banknote' (US: 'bill').
bordereau (m): 'statement', 'paying-in receipt'.
Bourse (f): 'stock market', 'Exchange'.

caissier (m): 'cashier'.
carnet (m) **de chèques** or **chéquier** (m): 'cheque-book'.
change (m): 'exchange of currencies', 'rate of exchange'.
chèque (m) **de voyage**: 'traveller's cheque'.
coffre-fort (m): 'strong-box', 'safe', 'safe(ty)-deposit box'.
compte (m): an 'account'.
courtier (m): 'stock-broker', 'Exchange agent'.
créditer (débiter) un compte: 'to credit (debit) an account'.

encaisser: 'to cash' or 'collect a cheque' (from a bank's point of view).
endosser: 'to endorse' a cheque, like this: *Pour acquit, à Paris, le 30 Juin* 1980, *Jean Dupont*.
être à découvert: 'to be overdrawn'.

intérêts (m.pl.): 'interest'.

monnaie (f): 'change'. *Les monnaies étrangères*, 'foreign currencies'.

pièce (f): 'coin'.
placer (son argent): 'to invest one's money'; *placement* (m): 'investment'.
prélever (sur un compte): 'to deduct' (from an account); *prélèvement* (m): 'deduction'.

relevé (m) **trimestriel**, 'quarterly statement'.
retirer, 'to withdraw'.

somme (f), a 'sum'.
souche (f), 'stub'.

taux (m) **de change**: 'exchange rate'.
toucher (un chèque, une somme), 'to cash' a cheque (from your point of view).
traite (f), 'draft' (as, credit payment deducted from your account).
transfert (m), 'transfer'; *transférer*, 'to transfer'.

verser, 'to pay', 'to pay into an account'.

Banks are generally open from 9 a.m. to 4·30 p.m. (*de 9h à 16h30 sans interruption*), from Monday to Friday; in the suburbs, and *en province*, sometimes from Tuesday to Saturday.

False Friends

You will have noticed that every so often in the main text, we have accused certain words of being *des Faux Amis*, 'false friends'. A *Faux Ami* looks so much like a word in English that you are sure it means the same: and there you are headed straight for disaster in the form of *un contre-sens*, 'a nonsensical translation'; *une gaffe*, 'a blunder'; or *un malentendu*, 'a misunderstanding'.

Still other words are traitors only some of the time. *Accuser*, for instance, does mean 'to accuse'; it also, when referring not to people but to things, means 'to underline', 'stress': *des traits accusés*, 'sharp features'; *des jaunes accusés dans un tableau*, 'strong yellows in a painting'. And *accuser réception* (of a letter) is 'to acknowledge receipt'. The following list, including only some of the more recurrent or more bothersome cases, is perhaps dangerously succinct: you are advised to take it merely as an invitation to look into each case more thoroughly. Intransitive verbs are given with the appropriate prepositions.

accommoder: to accompany with a sauce

accomplissement (m): achievement, completion

actuel: present, current; **à l'heure actuelle**: at the present moment;
  les actualités: cinema or television news

agenda (m): memo book

apologie (f): praise;
  faire l'apologie de quelqu'un: to praise someone

application (f): applying something to something else

apprécier: estimate

argument (m): reason, justification; plot of play

assistance (f): audience, public (*also* aid, Welfare)

assister à: to attend

attendre: to wait

axe (m): axis

blesser: to hurt

box (m): garage

---

accommodate: loger, caser, contenir

accomplishment: talent (m), art (m)

actual: vrai, véridique, réel

agenda: ordre (m) du jour

apology: excuses (f. pl.);
  to apologize: faire ses excuses à quelqu'un, s'excuser

application *(request)*: demande (f)

appreciate: reconnaître la juste valeur de; **to be appreciative**: être reconnaissant

argument: discussion (f), querelle (f), dispute (f)

assistance: aide (f), secours (m)

assist: aider, venir en aide à, porter secours à

attend: assister à

axe: hache (f)

bless: bénir

box: boîte (f)

111

boxe (f): boxing
brigadier (m): corporal

brigadier general: général (m) de brigade

caméra (f): motion-picture camera

camera: appareil (m) photo

canapé (m): sofa, couch
candide: gullible, creduloud
car (m): coach, bus
case (f): box, compartment; hut
casque (m): helmet
casquette (f): cap
cave (f): cellar
charte (f): charter
commodité (f): comfort, convenience
conférence (f): lecture, speech

canopy: baldaquin (m), voûte (f)
candid: franc
car: voiture (f), automobile (f)
case: cas (m); procès (m); étui (m)
cask: tonneau (m)
casket: coffret (m); cercueil (m)
cave: grotte (f), caverne (f)
chart: carte (f); graphique (m)
commodity: article (m), de consommation courante
conference: congrès (m), réunion (f)

confidence (f): secret;
   faire une confidence à: to confide in
confusion (f); embarrassment; (*also*, confusion);
   être confus: to be embarrassed;
contenance (f): amount contained, capacity
contrôle (m): check-up, surveillance;
   contrôler: to check on, verify

confidence: confiance (f);
   to be confident: avoir confiance, être confiant
confusion: chaos (m), désordre (m); *also*, confusion (f)

countenance: visage (m), figure (f)
control: direction (f), discipline (f);
   to control: guider, diriger, être maître de

courtier (m): broken; agent

courtier: courtisan (m)

décevoir: to disappoint
délai (m): time limit
délayer: to dilute, stir in
détenir (le pouvoir, la vérité etc.): to possess *or* keep
disgracieux: awkward, graceless, ugly, disagreeable

deceive: tromper
delay: retard (m)
delay: retarder
detain: retarder, arrêter

disgraceful: honteux

énerver: to annoy, irritate
entretenir: to maintain, keep (up)
éventuel: possible, conceivable;
   éventualité (f): possibility;
   éventuellement: in the event, if need be
expérience (f): experiment; *also,* experience;
   expérimenté: experienced

enervate: affaiblir, amollir
entertain: amuser, divertir
eventual: tôt ou tard

experience: aventure (f), expérience (f)

fabrique (f): factory
faute (f): (moral) fault *or* blame;
  sans faute: without fail
figure (f): face

fournitures (f. pl.): supplies

fabric: tissu (m), étoffe (f)
fault (*defect, flaw*): défaut (m)

figure (*shape*): ligne (f)
figure (*number*): chiffre (m)
furniture: mobilier (m);
  an item of furniture: meuble
  (m)

génial: ingenious, clever
grappe (f): bunch (of grapes etc.)
gratuit: free, gratuitous
grief (m): grievance, grudge
groom (m): pageboy

genial: sympathique
grape: raisin (m)
gratuity: pourboire (m)
grief: douleur (f), chagrin (m)
groom (*wedding*): marié (m);
  groom (*stable boy*): garçon
  (m) d'écuries

habit (m): formal evening wear
habits (m. pl.): clothes
hardi: bold
heurter: to run into, collide with

habit: habitude (f)

hardy: robuste
hurt: blesser, faire mal, offenser

important: big; *also*, important

incessamment: very soon
informations (f. pl.): news (*as on*
  radio, *etc.*)
inhabité: uninhabited
injure (f): insult
intoxication (f): poisoning

important: significatif: *also*,
  important
unceasingly: sans arrêt
information: renseignements
  (m. pl.)
inhabited: habité
injury: blessure (f)
intoxication: ivresse (f)

large: wide
lecture (f): reading
limonade (f): lemon soda
lunatique: fickle

large: grand
lecture: conférence (f)
lemonade: citron pressé (m)
lunatic: fou (m)

malice (f): mischief;
  malicieux: mischievous

malice: méchanceté (f);
  malicious: méchant

nappe (f): table cloth
nègre: nigger; *i.e. is pejorative*
nouvelle (f): short story;
  nouvelles (f. pl.): news (*often
  replaced by* **informations**
  and **actualités**)

nap (*sleep*): somme (m)
Negro, black: noir
novel: roman (m)

office (f): pantry

office: bureau (m)

pâte (f): dough
pet (m): fart

paste (*glue*): colle (f)
pet: animal favori (m)

photographe (m): photographer

photograph: photographie (f); **photography**: photographie (f)

physicien (m): physicist
pomme (f) **de pin**: pine cone
préjudice (m): a wrong done to someone
prétendre: to claim, assert

physician: médecin (m)
pineapple: ananas (m)
prejudice: préjugé (m), parti pris (m)

pretend (*make believe*): faire semblant, faire mine de

prune (f): plum
pulvériser: to vaporize (liquid); *also*, to pulverize

prune: pruneau (m)
pulverize: écraser, réduire en poudre

raisin (m): grape
reste (m): remainder:
  rester: to remain
résumer: to summarize;
  résumé (m): summary

raisin: raisin sec (m)
rest: repos (m);
  rest: se reposer
resume: reprendre, poursuivre

sensible: sensitive; *also*, marked, pronounced, *as*, **une hausse sensible**
store (*shop*): awning, blind, shade

sensible: sensé, raisonnable

store (*shop*): boutique (f), magasin (m)

supplier: beg, beseech
sympathique: congenial, nice

supply: fournir, ravitailler
sympathetic: compatissant

trouble (m): disturbance, anxiety;
  troubler: to disturb, make uneasy;
  eau trouble: unclear water
truculent: outspoken, vigorous, colourful (style, person)

trouble: ennui (m), difficulté (f), (avoir) du mal

truculent: féroce, sauvage, cruel

usage (m): custom;
  usager (m): user (of public transport)
user: to wear out

usage: emploi (m)

use: se servir de, employer

versatile: unstable, fickle, unreliable

versatile: ayant de multiples dons (ayant plusieurs cordes á son arc)

voyage (m): any sort of trip;
  voyageur (m): traveller

voyage (i.e. *sea trip*): traversée (f), voyage (m) par mer

wagon (m): car, coach (of train)

wagon: charrette (f)

Courtesy

It is an old story that French is the language of politeness, and even today, the outward forms, the standard phrases have been preserved to a far greater extent than in English. You must learn them off pat and be able to handle them with assurance. This makes it sound as though they are necessarily hypocritical: they are not. They are simply built in; and without them, the average conversation, introduction or—especially—letter would fall apart.

In the Paris Métro, for instance, a sign will tell you that you may not go down on to the tracks *à moins d'y avoir été expressément invité par les agents de la RATP*: 'unless you have been expressly invited by representatives of the *Régie Autonome des Transports Parisiens*'. The use of *inviter* is quite unexpected to the English-speaking person. And where in English you would say 'Please go out through this door', the Frenchman will say *Mesdames et Messieurs, vous êtes priés de bien vouloir sortir par ici.*

The imperative is frequently eschewed and the infinitive used instead. When you send photographs through the post, you mark on the envelope 'Do not bend'. The Frenchman will write *Ne pas plier*.

To say of someone that he is polite, you say either that he is *poli*, or that he is well-bred: *Il est bien élevé*; or, *Il a une bonne éducation*. The opposite is *impoli* or, more frequently, *mal élevé*; or again, *il manque d'éducation*.

An indication of the relative formality of French courtesy is that the *carte de visite*—visiting-card—is very commonly used for communication between friends, even very young ones and even on a modest social level. This is also the standard way of sending New Year's wishes; and you have the entire month of January to get around to doing so.

A sample conversation might begin like this:

Monsieur Lebrun, permettez-moi de vous présenter (je vous présente) Madame Leblanc. 'Mr Lebrun, allow me to introduce Mrs Leblanc.'

Enchanté, Madame (de faire votre connaissance). Comment allez-vous? 'Pleased to meet you, Mrs Leblanc. How are you?'

Très bien, Monsieur, je vous remercie. Et vous-même? 'Fine, thank you; and you?'

And on saying goodbye, let us suppose that Monsieur Lebrun has done Madame Leblanc a favour or service of some sort:

Vous êtes vraiment trop aimable, Monsieur, je suis confuse. Merci mille fois (or, tous mes remerciements). 'It's really too kind of you, Mr Lebrun; I'm most embarrassed. Thank you ever so much.'

Mais, je vous en prie (or, il n'y a pas de quoi), c'est tout naturel. (More colloquially, Mr Lebrun could say *de rien*: 'not at all', 'it's nothing really'.)

Au revoir, Monsieur. 'Goodbye, Mr Lebrun.'

Au revoir, Madame, je suis très content d'avoir fait votre connaissance. 'Goodbye, Mrs Leblanc. I'm delighted to have met you.'

When you step back to let someone go through a doorway or down the stairs before you, you say simply, *Passez, Madame* (*Mademoiselle, Monsieur*), *je vous en prie*. You may also hear, in this connexion, *faites*, or *faites donc*: literally, 'do'; in other words, 'go ahead'.

On entering or leaving a shop in which other customers are already waiting, you are expected to mutter, *Messieurs dames*. Well-meaning people will tell you that this is not really a proper form of address, but you never hear any other. The shopkeeper will punctuate your trans-actions with a sort of singsong: *Bonjour, Madame*. (*Qu'est-ce que*) *vous désirez, Madame? Voici, Madame. Merci, Madame. Au revoir, Madame.*

In conversation, when you are on the verge of asking a prying question (*Combien gagne-t-il? Combien l'avez-vous payé? Vont-ils divorcer?* 'How much does he earn?' 'What did you pay for it?' 'Are they getting divorced?'), you excuse yourself in advance: *Je ne voudrais pas être indiscret, mais . . .* or, *sans indiscrétion . . .*, which authorizes you to go right ahead and pry.

The equivalent of 'God bless you!' when someone sneezes is *à vos* (*tes*) *souhaits!*

When you haven't been able to hear what someone said, you have, of course, a whole gamut of expressions, ranging from 'I beg your pardon?' down to 'what?' and 'huh?' *Je vous demande pardon? Pardon? Je m'excuse? Vous dites?* (*Tu dis?*). Or simply, *Comment?* But you need to be careful of *comment*: everything depends on the tone of voice. You can make it inquire, be indignant (like, *ah mais!* or *ça alors!*), scold, joke, or merely express surprise.

When you must ask someone to keep quiet, courtesy requires *un peu de silence, s'il vous plaît*, or *un instant, je vous prie*, or *veuillez m'écouter. Taisez-vous* (*tais-toi*) is obviously much more abrupt, much less polite, and can be used only with more intimate acquaintances or inferiors: 'keep quiet'. *Fermez-la!* or *bouclez-la!* is definitely rude: 'shut up'.

The writing of a business letter is a particularly delicate and subtle matter. There are more gradations of esteem and familiarity than in English, where you have little choice outside 'Dear Mr Smith' or 'Dear John'.

In French, at the stage of greatest remoteness, or respect, you start with *Monsieur* (or *Madame* or *Mademoiselle*) on a line by itself, never abbreviated, usually near the centre of the page instead of being towards the upper left, and followed by a comma. Only very gradually, and perhaps never, will you work up to *Cher Monsieur* (*Chère Madame* or *Mademoiselle*); then, rarely to *Cher Ami* (*Chère Amie*); and the ultimate in intimacy would be *Mon cher ami* (*Ma chère amie*) or *Mon cher Jean* (*Ma chère Jeanne*). If you are addressing someone with a professional title, as Minister, Doctor, Professor, then you start with, *Monsieur le Ministre* (*le Docteur, le Professeur*).

The mode of address which you have used at the beginning will be repeated in the closing of your letter, a much more elaborate affair than in present-day English, which contents itself with, 'Best wishes. Yours truly,'. The variety of *formules* from which you may, and must, choose in French will remind you of the 'I beg you, Madam, to believe me your most humble and obedient servant,' which unhappily disappeared long ago from English usage.

Croyez, chère Madame, à l'expression, or *Veuillez agréer, chère Madame, l'expression de mes sentiments distingués (dévoués, les meilleurs)* is the most frequently found form of closing. *Croyez . . . à,* and *Veuillez agréer* are of course a little more peremptory than *Je vous prie de croire à* (or, *d'agréer, d'accepter) l'assurance* (or, *l'expression) de mes sentiments distingués* etc. And if you are writing to someone who is distinctly your superior or from whom you are asking a favour, you might use . . . *mes sentiments respectueux*.

If writing to an official for some permission or other, you may start out after the salutation *J'ai l'honneur de solliciter de votre haute bienveillance la permission de . . .*

If you are writing to acknowledge a letter, *J'ai l'honneur d'accuser réception de votre lettre du 16 courant* ('I am pleased to acknowledge receipt of yours of the 16th instant'); or more simply, *Je vous remercie de votre lettre . . .*

If you are requesting an appointment with someone you do not know, you might say *Seriez-vous assez aimable pour m'accorder un rendez-vous*, or *Je vous serais reconnaissant de bien vouloir m'accorder* etc. If, however, you are writing to someone whom you do know or who is your inferior, you may use *Ayez la bonté (l'amabilité) de m'accorder* etc. Or more familiarly still, *Vous serez bien gentil de . . .* A polite command would be *Vous voudrez bien (me téléphoner, me dire ce qu'il en est*, etc.)

Franglais

Franglais is the result of the introduction, chiefly since World War II and often willy-nilly, of English words into French where, frequently, there is no need for them or they are incorrectly adapted. As Franglais terms are more modern, to French ears, than their established French equivalent (if there is one), a certain snob value attaches to their use.

A few of the more striking examples are these:

fair play: *franc jeu*.

know-how (m): *savoir-faire* (m).

pull(-over) (m): *le tricot*; pronounced *pule-ovaire*.

relaxe: *détendu*; **se relaxer**: *se détendre*. Not to be confused with a legimate verb, *relaxer*, 'to free' (a prisoner); the noun is **relaxe** (f).

weekend (m): *la fin de semaine. Bon weekend!* has largely superseded *Bon dimanche!* and wiped out *Bonne fin de semaine!*

English words are often altered when they become Franglais:

shake-hand (m): 'handshake', *la poignée de main*; but the verb form is still *serrer la main à quelqu'un*.

solutionner un problème: instead of *résoudre*.

talkie-walkie (m): instead of 'walkie-talkie'.

Words ending in '-ing' are especial favourites, and are always assigned the masculine gender:

living: *le salon, la salle de séjour. Un living* can also mean the suite of furniture for the living room.

meeting: *une réunion, une rencontre.*

pressing: *la teinturerie* ('cleaners and dyers'); nothing to do with *être pressé*, 'to be in a hurry', or *la presse*, 'the press', 'journalism'.

shopping: *les achats, les courses; faire du shopping* implies going the rounds of department stores and specialty shops.

smoking: *la tenue de soirée*, i.e. 'tuxedo' or 'formal dinner jacket'.

standing: as in *un immeuble de très grand standing*, 'a very prestigious *or* high-class building'.

By 1966, the invasion of even administrative, medical and other vocabulary by English terms had reached such a point that the French Government issued a decree setting up the Haut Comité pour la Défense et l'Expansion de la Langue Française. In 1972, official terminology commissions were formed for the purpose of "filling gaps in the French vocabulary and proposing new terms where necessary", in consultation with the Académie Française. Since 1973 official lists have been issued "pour l'enrichissement du vocabulaire" in audiovisual techniques, construction, civil engineering and town planning, nuclear energy, oil, space technology, transport, defence, health and medicine, economy and finance, and computers (now available together in one pamphlet, no. 1468, at 16F from the Journal Officiel de la République Française, 26 rue Desaix, 75732 Paris, Cedex 15). Some of the terms are mandatory in government decrees, circulars etc., in correspondence to and from administrative departments, in textbooks used in state institutions, in work contracts etc.; use of the others is recommended.

We have room for only a few of the roughly 700 terms listed:

COMPUTERS: *matériel* (m): 'hardware'; *logiciel* (m): 'software'.

DEFENCE: *autodirecteur* (m): 'homing *or* seeker head' (of missile); *balayage* (m): 'radar/scanning'; *gros porteur* (m): 'jumbo jet'; *agent* (m) *de dissuasion*: 'deterrent'.

ECONOMICS: *capitaux fébriles* (m.pl.): 'hot money'; *marge brute* (f) *d'autofinancement* (*M.B.A.*): 'cash flow'.

MEDICINE: *stimulateur* (m): '(cardiac) pacemaker'; *axénique*: 'germ-free'; *préventologie* (f): 'preventive medicine'.

RADIO, TELEVISION, CINEMA: *palmarès* (m): 'hit parade'.

CONSTRUCTION AND REAL ESTATE: *vestiaire* (m): 'dressing room'; *niveleuse* (f): 'grader'; *cuisinette* (f): 'kitchenette'.

OIL REFINING: *tour* (f) *de forage*: 'derrick'.

TRANSPORT: *navire* (m)-*citerne*: 'tanker'; *aéroglisseur* (m): 'hover-craft'; *conteneur* (m): 'container'.

SPACE TECHNOLOGY: *capteur* (m): 'sensor'; *poussée* (f): 'thrust'.

Genders

Some genders may surprise you because the end of the word 'looks as though' it should belong to the opposite gender, or because the very meaning of the word would seem to place it in the opposite camp—as in the case of *barbe* and *moustache*. The same thing can sometimes be designated by two or more words of different genders. The face, for instance, is either *le visage* or *la figure*.

masculine
caprice: whim
chemisier: woman's shirt
espace: space
génie: genius
incendie: fire
manque: lack
musée: museum
pamplemousse: grapefruit
parapluie: umbrella
reproche: reproach
scarabée: bettle
site: landscape
squelette: skeleton

feminine
barbe: beard
calvitie: baldness
cuisson: cooking
dactylo: typist
faux: scythe
fourmi: ant
moustache: moustache
radio: radio, X-ray
recrue: recruit
toux: cough
vis: screw

And there are three celebrated words which, although masculine in the singular, are feminine in the plural:

amour: *un bel amour*; *de belles amours* (Note, however, that when *un amour* means 'a cherub' it remains masculine in the plural.)
délice: *un tel délice*; *de telles délices*
orgue: *un grand orgue*; *de grandes orgues*

Double genders:

le box: garage	**la boxe**: boxing
le critique: critic	**la critique**: criticism
le livre: book	**la livre**: pound
le manche: handle	**la manche**: sleeve; half (of game);
	la Manche, English Channel; also a *département* in Normandy
le mode: directions for use; mood (*grammar*)	**la mode**: fashion, manner
le moule: mould	**la moule**: clam, mussel
le poêle: stove, furnace; pail	**la poêle**: frying pan
le poste: job; radio *or* TV set	**la poste**: mail, post office
le solde: clearance sale; balance to pay	**la solde**: soldier's pay

le somme: nap   **la somme**: sum
le tour: a walk (around); trick **la tour**: tower
le vase: vase   **la vase**: mud
le voile: veil   **la voile**: sail, sailing

Telling the Time

Avez-vous l'heure (exacte), s'il vous plaît? 'Can you tell me (exactly) what time it is, please?'

Ma montre avance: 'My watch is fast'.

Ma montre retarde (or, **a du retard**): 'My watch is slow'.

Il est dix heures trente:
Il est dix heures et demie: 'It's half past ten' (a.m. or p.m.).

Il est vingt-deux heures trente: 'It's half past ten p.m.' You do not say, *vingt-deux heures et demie*.

Il est moins cinq: 'It's five (minutes) to', 'of'.

Il est moins le quart: 'It's a quarter to', 'of'.

Il est le quart: 'It's a quarter past', 'after'.

Il est la demie: 'It's half past', 'after'.

Il est l'heure: 'It's time' (to leave, eat, get ready, etc.).

Huit jours (une huitaine): by far the most common way of saying 'a week'. *Sous huitaine*, 'within a week', is more of a written than a spoken form. *Prière de régler cette facture sous huitaine*.

Quinze jours (une quinzaine): similarly, for 'two weeks', 'a fortnight'. *Il a remis sa visite à une quinzaine de jours*: 'He's put off his visit for a fortnight'.

En huit: 'a week from' . . . *Mardi en huit*: 'a week from Tuesday'.

En quinze: 'two weeks from' . . . *Mardi en quinze*: 'two weeks from Tuesday'.

D'ici trois jours (deux mois etc.): 'Three days (two months) from now'.

Il y a dix jours: 'ten days ago'. *Elle est partie il y a un an hier*: 'She left a year ago yesterday'.

Il était (or, **Il y avait**) **une fois**: 'Once upon a time . . .'

Tous les combien? 'How often?' This is *familier*.

Tous les six mois: 'every six months'.

Toutes les trois minutes: 'every three minutes'.

Tous les deux jours: 'every other day'.

Tous les 16 du mois: 'every month on the 16th'.

Tous les midis: 'every noon'.

Tous les deux: 'both'.

Cette nuit ('this night') is the continuation of **ce soir** ('this evening'); in other words, 'tonight'.

La nuit dernière is the continuation of **hier soir** ('yesterday evening'); in other words, 'last night'. *J'ai eu* (or *fait*) *des cauchemars la nuit dernière*. 'I had nightmares last night.' **Demain soir**, 'tomorrow evening', 'tomorrow night'.

A bientôt: 'So long', 'I'll see you soon'.

A ce soir: 'Till this evening'.
A demain: 'Till tomorrow'.
A (tout) jamais: 'For ever'.
    Jamais: 'Ever'. *Si jamais vous venez* . . . . 'If you ever come. . . .
    Ne . . . jamais: 'Never'. *Ne venez jamais*. 'Never come'.
    Jamais (de la vie)!: 'Never!' 'Not on your life!'
    Jamais, au grand jamais!: 'Never!'
    Plus jamais!: 'Never again!'
A l'instant: 'A minute ago', 'just now'. *Je l'ai vu à l'instant.*
A la prochaine: 'Till I see you again'. This is *familier.*
A tantôt, or **A cet après-midi**: 'Till this afternoon.' In certain provinces
    you can hear *je l'ai vu hier tantôt*: 'I saw him yesterday afternoon'.
Au début de la soirée: 'late in the afternoon', 'early in the evening'.
A tout à l'heure: 'I'll see you later' (in a very short while).
A tout de suite: 'I'll see you (be back) in a minute'.
Arriver à l'heure: 'to arrive on time'.
Arriver à temps: 'to arrive in time' (to prevent something, catch a train,
    etc.).

Numbers

Certain numbers keep recurring in idiomatic French; the most obvious
example is probably thirty-six: a loose way of indicating 'a lot', 'a
thousand and one', 'hundreds', and the like.

Il n'y a pas trente-six façons de s'y prendre: 'There's only one way of
    going about it.'
Elle a toujours trente-six projets en tête: 'She's always got a dozen
    different plans.'
Voir trente-six chandelles: 'to be knocked out', 'to see stars'.

The number 'four' also crops up quite often as a vague indication of
'several', 'more than one'.

Quand il a quelque chose à dire, il n'y va pas par quatre chemins. 'When
    he's got something he wants to say, he doesn't beat around the bush.'
Faires ses quatre volontés: 'to do whatever one likes' (and, the
    implication is, 'to get away with it').
Etre tiré à quatre épingles: 'to be dressed to the nines' ('down to the last
    detail').
Couper les cheveux en quatre: 'to split hairs'.
Un quatre heures (*v.* GOÛTER): 'afternoon tea *or* snack'.
Un de ces quatre matins: 'one of these fine days'.
Manger comme quatre: 'to eat a lot'.
Se mettre en quatre: 'to do anything' (for someone).

Etre à deux doigts de faire quelque chose: 'to be on the verge of doing
    something'. *Il était à deux doigts de tout plaquer*: 'He came very close
    to dropping the whole business.'
Trois fois rien: 'less than nothing', 'dirt cheap' etc. *Ils l'ont payé trois*

fois rien: 'They got it for next to nothing.'

Faire quelque chose en trois (or sometimes, **deux) temps trois mouvements**: 'to do something in the twinkling of an eye', 'before you can blink'.

En cinq sept: *à toute vitesse*, 'quick as lightning'.

Se mettre sur son trente-et-un: *s'endimancher*, 'to wear one's Sunday best'.

Passer un mauvais quart d'heure (or, **un mauvais moment**): 'to have a bad time of it'. *J'ai passé un mauvais quart d'heure chez le dentiste.*

In talking about a decade—'the Forties', 'the Twenties'—you simply say *les années* and then add the cardinal number: *les années 40, les années 20.*

Familiar, Or Informal, French

The following are a small portion of the great number of expressions which are spoken and heard far more often than they are written and read. They are not slang; since, as explained in the Introduction, we have in no way aimed at listing or translating *des expressions argotiques*. Though you may get by very well without using any of the terms of this small sampling of *langage familier*, you will frequently need to understand it—in conversation, in novels, and at the cinema. Of course the degree of familiarity or even vulgarity of a given expression depends largely on (*a*) who is saying it; (*b*) to whom; (*c*) how; and (*d*) in what circumstances.

attraper: 'to scold', 'tell off' (*v. engueuler*).

bagnole (f): 'car', 'automobile'.

bain (m): *être dans le bain* (or, *le coup*): 'to be involved'; also, 'to be in the know'.

balle (f): *le franc ancien. J'ai mille balles.* 'I have 1,000 old francs (10 new francs).'

bidule (m): 'thing'. Even more colloquial than *machin* and *truc*.

billet (m): '10 new francs'. Also called *un ticket. Ça m'a coûté 100 billets (100 tickets).* For the more general meaning of *billet v.* the chapter on BANKING.

blague (f): 'nonsense', 'sham', 'fake'. *C'est de la blague! Blague à part, blague dans le coin, sans blague!* 'no joke!' 'for real!'

blagueur (m): 'joker', 'faker'.

bled (m): adapted from the Arabic: 'an out-of-the-way hamlet', 'one-horse town'; *v.* also: *patelin, trou.*

borne (f): 'kilometre'. *Mais ça fait une petite trotte d'ici—au moins 500 bornes.*

bosser: *travailler*: 'to work'; *v.* also: *trimer.*

bouffe (f): 'food'. **Bouffer**: 'to grub'. Inelegant.

boulot (m): 'work'.

bouquin (m): 'book'; *bouquiner*, 'to read'.

bousiller: 'to ruin', 'damage', 'put out of joint'. *Sa voiture est toute bousillée.* 'His car's all ruined.'

boustifaille (f): 'food', 'grub'. **Boustifailler**: 'to grub'. More vulgar than *bouffer*.

cancre (m): 'dunce'.

casser: *Ça ne casse rien!*: 'it's no great shakes', 'nothing to write home about'. *Ça ne casse pas des briques* is a still more *familier* way of saying this. *Casser sa pipe*: '*mourir*'. *Le casse-pipe*: 'war' (from the time of the Napoleonic wars when a wounded man, operated on without anaesthetic, was given a pipe to bite on). *Casser les pieds à quelqu'un*: 'to give someone a pain in the neck'. Also, *être casse-pieds*: 'to be a real pest'.

chic: 'nice', 'generous'. *Un chic type*, 'a good chap' (*v. type*).

chic (m): 'flair', 'gift', 'smartness'.

chouette: 'great', 'fine'. *C'était chouette.* 'It was just great.' Said with ironic intention, it can mean just the opposite.

cochon: 'dirty', 'lewd'. *Une histoire cochonne*, 'a dirty story'.

coller: 'to stand up', 'be plausible'. *Son histoire ne colle pas.* 'His story won't wash.' *Ça colle*, 'It'll work, fit', 'good enough'.

copain (m), **copine** (f): 'pal', 'buddy'. More correctly: *camarade* (m. *or* f.).

cosse (f): 'laziness'. *Avoir la cosse*; *être cossard*.

costaud: 'strong', 'sturdy', 'resistant' (person, cloth, object).

coton: *C'est coton* means, *C'est difficile. C'était drôlement coton!* 'It was awfully hard.'

couci-couça: means *comme ci comme ça*: 'so-so'.

cra cra: means *crasseux*: 'filthy'. (*La crasse*: 'filth'.)

crâne (m): 'Skull', but familiarly 'head'. *J'ai un de ces maux de crâne.* 'I've got such a headache.'

croque-mort (m): 'undertaker'. Rather pejorative. More properly: *un employé des pompes funèbres*.

culot (m): 'nerve', 'cheek', 'gall'. More modern than *toupet* (m). *Etre culotté*, 'to have a lot of cheek', 'have some nerve'.

cuit: *C'est cuit*: 'it's all up', 'finished', 'no good'; like *c'est fichu*. Also, *je suis cuit, je suis fichu, je suis de la revue*: 'it's all up with me'. Also, *les carottes sont cuites*.

cuite (f): 'drinking spree'. *Prendre une cuite*: 'to get soaked', 'drunk'.

débile: 'weird', 'crazy', 'stupid', 'wild', 'far out', 'wizard'.

déveine (f): 'bad luck'. *C'est la déveine.* 'That's tough luck' (*v. veine*).

encaisser: means *supporter*, 'to bear'. *Je ne peux pas l'encaisser.* 'I can't stand him' (*v. also: peinture, sentir*). Also means, *recevoir des coups*, 'to put up with'. *Qu'est-ce qu'il a fallu encaisser!*

engueuler: 'to bawl out', 'give someone what for'. *Une engueulade*, 'a dressing-down'.

extra: '*Merveilleux*'. *v.* also *super*.

fabriquer: 'to do', 'be up to' (something). *Qu'est-ce que tu fabriques?* 'What are you doing?'

fameux, -euse: 'Excellent'. *C'était pas fameux,* 'it wasn't very good.'

fauché: 'broke', 'penniless'. Also, *être raide, être sans un. v. rond.*

flic (m): 'bobby', 'cop'. More slangily, *une hirondelle, un poulet.*

flopée, floppée (f): 'a whole lot', 'a flock', 'a swarm' (of people or things); perhaps a less desirable word than *ribambelle* (f).

foutre. Very *incorrect*—and very common. *Je m'en fous* ('I don't give a damn'), *c'est foutu* ('it's shot', 'it's all up', 'ruined' etc.) and *sa foutue idée* ('his damn idea') can be replaced by *je m'en fiche, c'est fichu* and *sa fichue idée.*

frais-frais: certain adjectives can be used in repetition like this in a negative sentence. *Ce vin n'est pas frais-frais.* 'This wine is not very cool.' *Il n'est pas riche-riche.* 'He's not very rich.'

fric (m): 'money', 'dough'. Also *la galette, l'oseille* (f).

frousse (f): *Avoir la frousse,* 'to be scared stiff'. Also, *avoir une frousse bleue.* A vulgar way of saying it is, *avoir la trouille.*

fusiller: *Se faire fusiller* means, properly speaking, 'to be shot by a firing squad'; figuratively, *se faire engueuler:* i.e. 'to get a good dressing down'.

gonflé, être: 'to have a lot of nerve'.

gosse (m. or f.): 'kid', 'child', 'brat'. Can be affectionate; much more frequent and acceptable than *môme* and *moucheron.*

gougnaffier (m): 'careless (slob)', 'ignoramus'.

goujat (m): 'lout', 'boor'.

goupiller: 'to fix', 'arrange', 'set up something'. *Se goupiller:* 'to work'. *Comment ça se goupille?* 'How does that work?'

gris, être: 'to be tight, drunk'. *v.* also: *cuite, parti, rond.*

gueule (f): 'face', 'mug'. Definitely impolite when applied to a person. *Avoir la gueule de bois* (*GDB*): 'to be hung over', 'to have a hangover'. *Les gueules noires,* 'coal miners'. *Les gueules cassées,* 'disfigured veterans'. *Gueuler,* 'to holler'; also 'to complain'. Rather vulgar. *Avoir de la gueule,* however, is complimentary: 'to be stunning'. *Ce dessin a de la gueule.*

guigne (f): 'bad luck'. More *familier* than *malchance* (f) and *déveine* (f); *v.* also *poisse.*

guigner: 'to covet something'.

lambiner: 'to dawdle'.

lapin (m): *Poser un lapin à quelqu'un,* 'to stand someone up'.

légume, une grosse: 'a big wig', 'big shot'. Note gender.

lessivé, être: 'to be deadbeat', 'dead tired'. Also, *être vanné.*

magistral: 'enormous', 'thorough'. *Il a pris une cuite magistrale.* 'He got terribly tight.' *Elle est arrivée avec un retard magistral.* 'She arrived incredibly late.'

manigancer: 'to plot', 'intrigue'; like *combiner.* The noun is *la manigance.*

maous(se) or **mahous(se):** ' enormous', 'gigantic'.

marrant: 'funny', 'comical'. *Se marrer*: 'to laugh'. *Qu'est-ce qu'on a pu se marrer!* 'How we laughed!'

marre, en avoir: 'to be fed up'. In very common use. *J'en ai marre*; also *j'en ai plein le dos, par-dessus la tête, ma claque, ras le bol.*

mec (m): 'chap', 'bloke'. Much slangier and shadier than *type* (q.v.).

minable: 'lousy', 'shabby', 'stunted'. Rather like *moche*; but you can also use *minable* as a noun when speaking of a person—*un petit minable.*

mirobolant: means *merveilleux, prestigieux*. Often encountered in the negative—*ce n'est pas une situation mirobolante*, 'that job's nothing special'.

moche: 'shabby', 'dowdy', 'dingy', 'ugly' (said of a person, room, object); 'lousy' (situation), 'bad luck'. Very common.

monstre: 'enormous'. *Soldes monstres*, 'mammoth sales'.

mouise (f): *être dans la mouise*, 'to be flat broke'; like *être dans la panade* or, more correctly, *la misère*.

numéro (m): 'chap', 'guy', 'character'. *C'est un drôle de numéro.* 'He's a funny chap, a real character.'

oust!: 'scram!' 'scat!' 'get!'

pagaille (f): 'chaos', 'total lack of organization'.

paperasse (f): 'old paper(s)', 'waste paper'; by extension, 'bureaucratic waste', 'red tape'. *La paperasserie,* 'red tape'. Very common expression.

par exemple!: like *ça alors! ce n'est pas vrai!* Expresses scepticism or astonishment. Very common and innocuous.

parti: 'drunk'; (*v. gris, rond*).

patelin (m): 'village'.

payer: *se payer la tête de quelqu'un*, 'to make fun of someone'.

pègre (f): 'the underworld'; from *la haute pègre—les gangsters, les souteneurs*—to *la basse pègre*, 'petty thieves' and 'pickpockets'.

peinture (f): *ne pas pouvoir voir quelqu'un en peinture*, 'to find someone unbearable'. *v.* also: *encaisser, sentir.*

pépin (m): *avoir des pépins*, 'to be in trouble', 'have problems'. More properly, *avoir des ennuis.*

picrate (m): bad cheap wine.

pif (m): 'nose'. *Faire quelque chose au pif*, to do something *au hasard*, by instinct, 'to follow one's nose'.

piger: 'to get it', 'to understand'. *Tu piges?* 'You get it?'

pinard (m): 'wine'.

plaquer: means *abandonner, quitter*. *Il a plaqué sa femme.* 'He's left his wife.'

poil, être à: 'to be naked'. Vulgar.

poil, être au: 'to be great', 'perfect'.

poire (f): means *imbécile*.

poireauter (or *poiroter*, or *faire le poireau*): 'to wait', or 'to be kept waiting'. *Faire poireauter quelqu'un.*

poisse (f): 'lousy luck'. *C'est la poisse.* Rather vulgar, and stronger than

déveine (q.v.).
pot (m): 'luck'. *Avoir du pot*, 'to be lucky'.
potable: 'drinkable' (*eau potable*), but also 'acceptable'.

rasoir: 'boring', 'a bore'. *Se raser*, 'to get (be) bored'.
rigolade (f): 'fun', 'amusement'. But, *c'est de la rigolade* means either 'it's nothing to be taken seriously', or 'it's easy to do'.
rigoler: 'to laugh', 'have fun'. *Je l'ai fait pour rigoler*. 'I did it just for kicks.'
riquiqui: 'skimpy', 'flimsy', 'undersized'.
rond, être: 'to be tight', 'drunk'; *v. gris, parti*. More correctly, *être soûl(e)* or *saoul(e)*.
rond (m): *Je n'ai plus un rond*, 'I'm stone broke'; *v.* also: *fauché*.

sale: 'dirty', 'dirty little', 'lousy', 'nasty'. *C'est une sale histoire*. 'It's a nasty (*or* sordid) business.' ('A dirty story' is *une histoire cochonne, grivoise*, or *incorrecte*, or *un récit salé, osé*.) *Etre dans de sales* (or *beaux*) *draps*, 'to have got oneself into a real mess'.
sentir: *je ne peux pas la sentir*, 'I can't stand her' (*v.* also: *encaisser, peinture*).
sorcier: *ce n'est pas sorcier*, 'there's nothing complicated about it', 'it's simple enough'.
super: what *formidable* was to an earlier generation.

tailler, se: 'to cut and run', 'run away'.
tonnerre (m): *c'est du tonnerre!* Means *c'est formidable*, or *épatant*: 'terrific'. *Une fille du tonnerre*, 'a very pretty girl', 'terrific looker'.
toubib (m): 'doctor'. Like *bled* (q.v.), another Arabic word.
trimer: 'to work'. *v.* also: *bosser*.
trou (m): 'hole', 'God-forsaken town'; *v.* also: *bled*.
type (m): 'chap', 'guy', 'fellow'. *Un brave type*, 'a good fellow'.

vache (f): *Ah la vache!* expresses reaction to a mean trick, a bad surprise, a nasty person. *Une vacherie* is 'a mean trick'. *Vachement*, however, is a strong, more vulgar version of *rudement, drôlement, bigrement: c'était vachement bien*.
veine (f): 'luck', 'good luck'. *Pas de veine*, 'bad luck'. *Un veinard*, 'lucky fellow'. Very common and innocuous (*v.* also: *déveine*).

Housing

One of the topics which crop up most frequently in newspapers and conversation is the housing situation.

appartement (m): 'a flat', 'apartment'.

bail (m): 'lease'. The plural is *baux*.

chambre (f) de bonne: 'maid's room'.
charges (f.pl.): 'periodic payments to *le syndic*' (q.v.).
confort (m): 'conveniences' (hot and cold running water, bathroom, heating etc.).

grand standing: 'prestige', 'luxury', 'high class' (*v.* the chapter on FRANGLAIS).

HLM: *Habitation (f) à Loyer Modéré,* 'low-rent housing estate'.

immeuble (m) en co-propriété: 'Condominium'. *Co-propriétaire* (m. or f.): owner of a flat in such a building.

locataire (m. or f.): 'lodger', 'tenant'. *Sous-locataire*, lodger to whom one sublets.
louer: 'to let' or 'rent'. *Louer à quelqu'un, sous-louer à quelqu'un*: 'to let to someone', 'to sublet'. *En location*: 'renting', 'rented', 'letting', 'let'.
loyer (m). 'rent'.

m²: *mètres carrés,* 'square metres' (measurement of floor surface).
meublé: 'furnished'.

non meublé: 'unfurnished'.

pavillon (m): 'house', especially *en banlieue*.
pièce (f): 'room'.
pierre (f) de taille: 'hewn stone'.
propriétaire (m. or f.): 'landlord, landlady'.

ravalement (m): 'repair and cleaning, *or* painting, of outside walls', now compulsory in Paris.
reprise (f): 'key money'; a lump sum which an incoming tenant must often pay to the old tenant for improvements made etc.

studio (m): 'one-room flat', 'bed-sitter'.
syndic (m): 'superintendent' charged with executing collective decisions of *co-propriétaires* on repairs, insurance, heating, maintenance etc.

villa (f): 'house', 'cottage'.
vis-à-vis (m), **avoir un**. To have too close a view of the house or flat opposite.

With this skeleton vocabulary in mind, you should find it easier to decipher the *petites annonces* (classified advertisements):

4/5 pp: four or five rooms. The *cuisine* is never counted as a room.
s.d'eau (or, **s.bns.**): *salle de bains*, bathroom.
pet.c. (or **ktchntte.**): small kitchen.
imm.g.stdg.: high-class building.

moquette: carpeting.
p.de t.: stone.
entr.: entry hall, vestibule.
s.à m.: dining-room.
gr.séjour, gr. living: large living-room.
asc.: lift (US: elevator).
ch.cent.indiv.: individual central heating.
tphne.: telephone.
gd.cft.,tt.cft.: all conveniences.
vue imprenable: splendid view.
libre de suite: available for immediate occupancy.

The Household

accoudoir (m): arm of furniture.
aiguille (f): needle.
aiguille (f) **à tricoter**: knitting needle.
alèze (f): rubber sheet.
appareil (m) **électroménager**: household appliance.
argenterie (f): plate, silver.
armoire (f): wardrobe, closet.
armoire (f) **à médicaments**:
armoire (f) **à pharmacie**:   medicine cabinet.
aspirateur (m): vacuum-cleaner.
assiette (f): plate, dish.
attrape-plats (m): pot-holder.

bac (m): basin, vat.
bahut (m): long low cabinet, sideboard.
baignoire (f): bathtub.
balai (m): broom.
bassine (f): basin, pan.
batteur (m) **à œufs**: egg-beater.
berceau (m): cradle.
bidet (m): bidet.
bobine (f): spool of thread.
boîte (f) **de conserve**: tin, can (of food).
bol (m): bowl.
bouchon (m): bottle-cap *or* -stopper, cork.
bouilloire (f): kettle.
brosse (f): brush.
brûleur (m): burner *or* ring of stove.

canapé (m): sofa, couch.
carpette (f): small rug.
carreau (m): window-pane; tile.
carrelage (m): tiling.
casserole (f): pot, pan.

chaise (f): chair.
cheminée (f): fireplace; mantelpiece; chimney.
chiffon (m): rag, cloth.
chope (f): mug.
ciseau (m): chisel.
ciseaux (m.pl.): scissors.
clou (m): nail.
commode (f): commode, chest of drawers, dresser.
congélateur (m): (deep) freezer.
conserves (f.pl.): tinned (canned) food.
corbeille (f) **à papiers**: wastepaper basket.
coussin (m): cushion.
couteau (m): knife.
couvercle (m): lid.
couvert (m): place setting.
couverture (f): blanket.
couvre-lit (m): bedspread.
crochet (m): hook.
cruche (f): pitcher.
cuiller or **cuillère** (f): spoon.
cuisinière (f): stove; cook.
cuvette (f): (wash)basin.

dé (m): thimble.
dessus (m) **de lit**: bedspread.
divan (m): couch, divan.
dossier (m): back of chair etc.
drap (m): sheet.

échelle (f): ladder.
écumoire (f): skimmer.
édredon (m): eiderdown.
épingle (f): pin.
épingle (f) **de sûreté**: ⎫
épingle (f) **de nourrice**: ⎭ safety pin.
escabeau (m): step-ladder.
évier (m): kitchen sink.

fauteuil (m): armchair.
fenêtre (f): window.
fer (m) **à repasser** : iron.
fer (m) **à vapeur**: steam iron.
ficelle (f): string.
fil (m): thread, (electric) flex (US: wire), (clothes) line.
four (m): oven.
fourchette (f): fork.
fourneau (m): stove, furnace.
fusible (m): (wire of electric) fuse.

gant (m) **de toilette:** flannel, washcloth.

glace (f): looking-glass.
guéridon (m): small round table.

housse (f): slip- *or* dust-cover.

interrupteur (m): electric light switch.

jeannette (f): sleeve ironing-board.

laine (f): yarn, wool.
lavabo (m): washstand, sink.
lave-vaisselle (m): dishwasher.
lit (m): bed.
louche (f): ladle.

machine (f) **à coudre**: sewing-machine.
machine (f) **à laver**: washing-machine.
machine (f) **à laver la vaisselle**: dishwasher.
manche (m): handle.
marteau (m): hammer.
matelas (m): mattress.
meuble (m): piece of furniture.
miroir (m): mirror.
mobilier (m): furniture as a whole.
moquette (f): wall-to-wall carpeting.
mur (m): wall.

nappe (f): table-cloth.
napperon (m): place-mat.

oreiller (m): pillow.
ouvre-boîte (m): tin- (can-) opener.

panier (m) **à salade**: salad shaker.
papier (m) **peint**: wallpaper.
parquet (m): wood floor.
passoire (f): strainer.
peinture (f): paint.
pelle (f): shovel; dust-pan.
pelote (f): ball (of string, yarn).
penderie (f): wardrobe.
petit lit (m): crib.
pichet (m): jug.
pied (m): leg (of furniture).
pince (f) **à linge**: clothes peg *or* pin.
pinces (f.pl.): pliers.
placard (m): closet, cupboard.
plafond (m): ceiling.
planche (f) **à découper**: chopping- *or* carving-board.
planche (f) **à repasser**: ironing-board.

plancher (m): floor.
plat (m): serving dish.
plinthe (f): baseboard, plinth.
plomb (m): electric fuse.
poignée (f): handle, knob.
porte (f): door.
poubelle (f): dustbin (US: 'trash can').
poutre (f): beam.
prise (f) **de courant**: electric plug, wall socket.

réchaud (m): hot-plate, small stove.
réfrigérateur (m): refrigerator.
robinet (m): tap (US: 'faucet').

saladier (m): salad bowl.
sèche-linge (m) or **séchoir** (m): clothes dryer.
serpillière (f): mop.
serviette (f) **de table**: napkin.
serviette éponge (f): towel.
siège (m): seat.
sommier (m): box mattress.
soucoupe (f): saucer.
soupière (f): tureen.
spatule (f): spatula.
surgelés (m. pl.): frozen food.

table (f): table.
table (f) **basse**: coffee table.
tabouret (m): stool.
taie (f) **d'oreiller**: pillow-slip or -case.
tamis (m): sieve.
tapis (m): rug.
tapis (m) **de bain**: bathmat.
tasse (f): cup.
théière (f): teapot.
tire-bouchon (m): corkscrew.
tiroir (m): drawer.
toit (m): roof.
torchon (m): dish-towel, dish-cloth.
tourne-vis (m): screwdriver.
traversin (m): bolster.

ventilateur (m): fan, ventilator.
verre (m): drinking glass.
vide-ordures (m): rubbish or garbage chute.
vis (f): screw.
vitre (f): window-pane.

The Post Office

For some years the abbreviation has been **P et T (Postes et Télécommunications)**; many people, however, still use **PTT (Postes, Télégraphes et Téléphones)**.

accusé (m) **de réception**: 'notice of receipt' of registered letter.
aérogramme (m): 'air-letter form'.
affranchir: 'to put stamps on';
   affranchissement (m): 'postage'.
annuaire (m): 'telephone directory'.

bon du trésor (m): 'government bond'.
bottin (m): 'telephone directory'.

cabine téléphonique (f): 'telephone kiosk' (US: 'booth').
caisse (f) **d'épargne**: 'savings account'.
centre (m) **de tri**: 'sorting centre'.
colis (m): 'parcel'.
compte (m) **de chèques postaux**: abbreviated **CCP**, postal cheque (US: checking) account;
   virement (m): payment from one *CCP* to another;
   paiement (m): payment in cash directly from *CCP* to recipient.

destinataire (m): 'addressee' of package, 'to'.

emprunt (m): 'bond issue', 'government loan'.
expéditeur (m): 'sender' of package, 'from'.

facteur (m): 'postman'.

guichet (m): 'window'.

jeton (m): 'token' for telephone.

mandat (m): 'money order';
   émettre un mandat: 'to issue, send a money order'.

paquet (m): 'parcel'.
pli (m): 'envelope', 'cover';
   sous pli séparé: 'under separate cover'.
pneu(matique) (m): 'local express letter'.

récépissé (m): 'receipt of registration'.
recommander: 'to register', 'to send by registered post'.

télégramme (m): 'telegram'.
timbre (m): 'stamp'.

Post offices are generally open from 8 a.m. to 7 p.m. (*de 8h à 19h sans interruption*) from Monday to Friday, and from 8 a.m. to noon on Saturday (*de 8h à 12h*).

Entertainment

LE CINÉMA
Some of these terms apply to the theatre as well.

acteur (-trice): 'actor', 'actress'; *acteur comique*: 'comedian'.
adultes, film pour: 'X-rated film'.

comédien, -ienne: 'actor', 'actress'.
court-métrage (m): 'short film', 'short subject'; often *un documentaire*, 'a documentary'.

dessin animé (m): 'cartoon'.
distribution (f): 'cast'.
doublage (m): 'dubbing'; *doublé*, 'dubbed'.

en exclusivité (f): said of a first-run film, *un film qui passe en exclusivité*.

générique (m): 'credits'.
grand écran (m): 'the cinema'; as opposed to *le petit écran*, 'television'.
gros plan (m): 'close-up'.

interprète (m. or f.): 'actor', 'actress'.

metteur (m) **en scène**: 'director'.

ouvreuse (f): usherette; you tip her at least *un franc*.

passer: 'to be on', 'running'. *Il y a un bon film qui passe en ce moment*.
policier (m): *Un (film) policier* is 'a detective film'.
publicité (f): 'advertising.' Makes up for the absence of advertising on French radio and the modest amount on TV.

réalisateur (m): 'director'; also '*metteur en scène*', '*cinéaste*', '*cinématographe*'. *Réaliser un film*, 'to make a film'.

séance (f): 'the show', including *court-métrage*, *grand film*, and *publicité*.
sous-titre (m): 'sub-title'.
spectacle permanent (m): 'continuous show; as opposed to, for example, *séance à 15h et à 21h*.

tourner un film: 'to make a film'; like *réaliser*.

vedette (f): 'star', of either sex.
version originale (f): in the original language (i.e. not dubbed).

LE THÉÂTRE
à bureaux fermés: *On joue cette pièce à bureaux fermés*, 'the play is sold out'.

création (f): the first time a play or rôle is directed or performed by a particular person.

entr'acte (m): 'interval' (US: 'intermission').

jeune premier (m): 'young actor in leading role'.

location (f): 'the booking' of seats; *louer*, 'to book'.

monter une pièce: 'to stage a play'.

pièce (f): 'play'.
place (f): 'seat'.

relâche (f): 'no performance'.
représentation (f): 'performance'.
reprise (f): 'revival' of a play.

souffleur (m): 'prompter'; **souffler**, 'to prompt'.
spectacle (m): 'show'. *Le spectacle commence à 20h30 précises. Le monde du spectacle*, 'show business', 'entertainment'. *Les gens du spectacle,* 'entertainers', 'show biz people'.

LA RADIO, LA TÉLÉVISION
actualités (f. pl.): 'news' on TV.

chaîne (f): 'channel'.

donner: 'to show', 'to be on'. *Qu'est-ce qu'on donne sur la première?* 'What's on on Channel I?'.

émission (f): 'programme'.
en direct: 'live'.

feuilleton (m): 'serial story'.

indicatif (m): 'theme music'.
indice (m) **d'écoute**: 'popularity rating'.
informations (f. pl.): 'news' on radio. *Prochaines informations à minuit.*

micro(phone) (m): 'microphone'.
modulation (f) **de fréquence** : 'FM'.

poste (m): 'set' (radio or TV).

réseau (m): 'network'.

speaker (m), **speakerine** (f): 'announcer'.

vidéo (m): 'video'.

western (m): 'cowboy film', 'western'.

DISQUES
cassette (f): 'cassette'.

disque (m): 'record'.

enregistrement (m): 'recording'.

haute fidélité (f): 'high fidelity'.

magnétophone (m): 'tape-recorder'; **bande magnétique** (f): 'tape'.

palmarès (m): 'hit parade'. Also called *le hit parade* . . .
plateau (m): 'turntable'.
pochette (f): 'record sleeve', 'cover', 'jacket'.

saphir (m): or **diamant** (m): 'stylus', 'needle'.

télé-commande: 'remote control'.
trente-trois (33) tours (m): 'long-play(ing) record'.

The Telephone

abonné (m): 'subscriber'.
annuaire (m): 'telephone directory'.

bottin (m): 'telephone directory'.

cabine téléphonique (f): 'telephone kiosk'.
cadran (m): 'dial'.
central téléphonique (m): 'telephone exchange'.
communication (f): 'call'.

décrocher: 'to lift' (the receiver off the hook).
donner un coup de téléphone (or, **de fil**): 'to make a telephone call', 'to ring up'.

écouteur (m): 'ear-piece', 'receiver'.

faire *or* **composer le numéro**: 'to dial the number'.

indicatif (m) **régional (national)**: 'area (country) code'.

jeton (m): 'token' for public phone.

ligne (f): 'line'.
ligne résidentielle (f): 'party (shared) line'.

opératrice (f): 'operator'.

PCV: *appeler en PCV*, 'to reverse the charges', 'to phone collect'.
poste (m): 'extension'.
avec préavis pour Untel: 'personal call for (US: person-to-person to) Mr So-and-So'.

raccrocher: 'to hang up', 'ring off'.

standard (m): 'switchboard'.
standardiste (m. or f.): 'switchboard operator'.

taxiphone (m): 'public telephone', requiring *un jeton*.
tonalité (f): 'dial tone'.

French phones in *cabines publiques* have that button which you must press immediately after you have heard your party pick up his receiver and answer you. If you don't press it he won't hear you.

Le téléphone sonne: 'The phone is ringing.'
Allo, oui? (or, *J'écoute*, or *Je vous écoute*): 'Hello, yes?'
Qui est à l'appareil? 'Who's calling?' 'Who is this?'
C'est Monsieur Dupont. Voulez-vous me passer (*Je voudrais parler à*) *Mademoiselle Dumas.* 'This is Mr Dupont. May I speak (I'd like to speak) with Miss Dumas.'
Ici Mademoiselle Dumas (or, *C'est elle-même*): 'This is she speaking.'
Monsieur X est occupé sur une autre ligne; *ne quittez pas, s'il vous plaît* (or, *un petit moment*, or *voulez-vous patienter*). 'Mr X is busy on another line, hold on please.'
Pouvez-vous (*puis-je*) *lui faire la commission?* 'Will you (May I) take a message for him (her)?'
A quel numéro peut-on vous rappeler? 'Where can we call you back?'
A quelle heure peut-on le toucher? 'What's the best time to reach him?'
Voulez-vous répéter? Je vous entends mal, il y a du bruit sur la ligne. 'I'm sorry I can't hear you, the line is bad, would you mind repeating?'
Nous avons été coupés. 'We've been cut off.'

A recorded voice may tell you: *Il n'y a pas d'abonné au numéro que vous avez demandé*: 'You've dialled a wrong number (there's no subscriber at this number).'

Cars

accotement (m): 'edge' ('shoulder') of the road.
agglomération (f): 'town', 'built-up area'.
aile (f): 'mudguard' (US: 'fender').
alcootest (m): 'breathalyser test' (US: 'drunken driver test').
allée (f): 'avenue', 'drive'. An 'alley' is *passage* (m), *impasse* (f).
amortisseur (m): 'shock absorber'.
arbre (m) **à cames**: 'camshaft'.
autobus (m): 'city bus'. Abbreviated *bus*.
autocar (m), 'coach', 'bus'. Abbreviated *car*.
auto-route (f) **à péage** (m): 'motorway with toll' (US: 'thruway').

bateau (m): depression in pavement (US: 'sidewalk') in front of *porte-cochère* used as car exit and entrance.
batterie (f): 'battery'.
boîte automatique (f): 'automatic gearshift'. *Boîte manuelle*, 'stick shift'.
bougie (f): 'sparking plug'.
break (m): 'estate car', 'shooting brake' (US: 'station wagon').
brûler un feu: 'to go through a red light'.

caler: 'to stall'.
camion (m): 'lorry', 'truck'. *Camionnette* (f): 'small van' (US: 'lorry').
capot (m): 'bonnet' (US: 'hood').
capote (f): the top of a convertible.
caramboler: 'to swerve (US: 'careen') into other cars'. *Carambolage* (m): 'multiple smash-up'.
carrefour (m): 'crossroads'.
carrossable: 'practicable' (a road).
carte-grise (f): official 'registration paper'.
ceinture (f) **de sécurité**: 'safety *or* seat belt'. *Le port de la ceinture est obligatoire depuis 1979.*
chaussée (f): 'road-surface'. *Chaussée déformée*, 'bad road'; *chaussée glissante*, 'slippery road'.
cié (f) **de contact**: 'ignition key'.
clignotant (m): 'indicator', 'turn-signal'.
clous (m. pl.): 'zebra crossing'. (US: 'crosswalk'); *traverser dans les clous*, 'to cross at the zebra crossing' (*v.* also *passage clouté*).
codes (m. pl.): 'dim lights'. *Rouler en code*, 'to drive with dim lights on'.
coffre (m): 'boot' (US: 'trunk').
collision (f): 'collision'.
conducteur (m): 'driver'.
conduite (f): 'to drive'. *La bonne (mauvaise) conduite*, 'good (bad) driving'.
contractuel (m): 'Traffic warden specializing in parking fines'. Replaced by women originally called '*les aubergines*' and now '*les pervenches*' (from the colour of their uniforms).

contravention (f): 'fine'. *Dresser une contravention*, 'to write out a fine'. Familiarly, *une contredanse*.

crever: 'to puncture'. *Avoir une crevaison, un pneu crevé*, 'to have a flat tyre'.

cric (m): 'jack'.

croiser une voiture: 'to meet a car coming in the opposite direction'.

décapotable (f): 'convertible'.

démarrer: 'to start up'.

démarreur (m): 'starter'.

déraper: 'to skid'; **dérapage** (m), 'skid'.

deux-roues (m): any two-wheeled vehicle—*moto* (f), *vélo* (m), *vélomoteur* (m).

déviation (f): 'detour'.

différentiel (m): 'differential'.

direction (f): 'steering'.

disque (m) **de stationnement**: required in the *Zone bleue* (q.v.)

dos (m) **d'âne**: 'hump' in the road.

doubler: 'to overtake' (US: 'pass').

écraser: 'to run over'; **se faire écraser**: 'to be run over'.

embrayage (m): 'clutch'. **Embrayer**: 'to let in the clutch'; **débrayer**: 'to let out the clutch'.

essence (f): 'petrol' (US: 'gas', 'gasoline'). *Faire le plein,* 'to fill up'. *Super*, 'high-grade'; *ordinaire*, 'regular'.

essieu (m): 'axle'.

essuie-glaces (m): 'windscreen (windshield) wipers'.

feu (m): 'light'. *Les feux arrière*: 'rear- (tail-) lights'. *Un feu clignotant*, 'blinking yellow light'. *Les feux de position*, 'parking lights'. *Les feux de signalisation,* 'traffic lights' (*rouge, orange, vert*). *Les (feux) stop*, 'brake lights'. *v.* also *phare*.

frein (m): 'brake'. *Le frein à main*, 'hand-brake'.

galerie (f) **de toit**: 'luggage rack'.

gas-oil (m): 'Diesel oil'.

glace (f): 'window'.

graissage (m): 'lubrication'.

hayon (m): 'luggage-compartment door', 'hatchback'.

huile (f): 'oil'.

impasse (f): 'blind alley', 'dead end', 'cul-de-sac'.

lubrifier: 'to lubricate'.

lunette arrière (f): 'rear window'.

manivelle (f): 'crank'.

motard (m): 'motorcycle (motorway) policeman'; (*fam.*) 'motorbike rider'.

moteur (m): 'engine'.

panne (f): 'breakdown'. *Tomber en panne*: 'to break down'. *Avoir une panne sèche*, 'to run out of petrol'. *La dépanneuse*, 'breakdown lorry' (US: 'wrecker', 'tow car').

papillon (m): 'parking ticket' on your windscreen.

parc automobile (m): the 'number of cars' in a given country.

parcmètre (m): 'parking meter'.

pare-brise (m): 'windscreen' (US: 'windshield').

parking (m): 'a parking area', 'car-park'.

passage clouté (m): 'zebra crossing' (US: 'crosswalk'. See *clous*).

passage (m) **à niveau**: 'level (grade, railway) crossing'.

permis (m) **de conduire**: 'driving licence'.

phare (m): 'headlight'; *les pleins phares*, 'beam lights'.

plaque minéralogique (f): 'registration (licence) plate'.

plein (m): *faire le plein*, 'to fill up the tank with petrol (US: gas, gasoline)'.

pneu (m): 'tyre'.

poids lourd (m): 'heavy lorry', 'truck', 'van'.

point mort (m): 'neutral'.

police (f): 'the police'. *Un policier*: 'policeman', 'detective'. *Un agent de police*, 'policeman'. *Monsieur l'Agent* is the polite form of address when you ask directions etc.

police (f) **d'assurance**: 'insurance policy'.

pompiste (m): 'attendant' in filling station.

pont (m): 'bridge'.

pont arrière (m): 'rear axle'.

portière (f): 'car door'.

poste (m) **d'essence**: 'filling (petrol, gas) station'.

pot (m) **d'échappement**: 'exhaust pipe', 'muffler'.

PV (m): *Procès-Verbal*. Like *contravention* (q.v.)

queue de poisson, faire une: to cut too sharply in front of another driver.

réservoir (m) **d'essence**: 'petrol ('gasoline') tank'.

rétroviseur (m): 'rear view mirror'.

rodage, en: 'running in' (US: 'breaking in').

rond-point (m): 'roundabout' (US: 'traffic circle').

roue (f) **de secours**: 'spare tyre'.

rouler: 'to drive'. *J'ai roulé toute la nuit*.

route (f): 'road' (US: 'highway').

rue (f): 'street'.

sens (m): 'direction'. *Sens giratoire*, 'roundabout', 'traffic island'. *Sens interdit*, 'no entry'. *Sens obligatoire*, 'compulsory direction'. *Sens unique*, 'one-way'.

soupape (f): 'valve'.

stationnement (m): 'parking'.

tableau (m) **de bord**: 'instrument panel', 'dashboard'.

tambour (m) **de frein**: 'brake drum'.

tonneau, faire un: 'to overturn'.
traction (f) **avant**: 'front-wheel drive'.
trottoir (m): 'pavement' (US: 'sidewalk').

verbaliser: 'to impose an on-the-spot fine'. *L'agent a arrêté un conducteur pour excès de vitesse et a verbalisé contre lui*, 'The policeman stopped a motorist for speeding and wrote him out a fine'.
verglas (m): 'sheet ice' on road.
vitesse (f): 'speed'; also, 'gear'. *La boîte de vitesses*, 'gear-box'. *En première*, 'in first gear'. *En seconde*, 'in second'. *En troisième*, 'in third'. *En quatrième*, 'in fourth'. *Passer les vitesses*, 'to change gears'. *Etre au point mort*, 'to be in neutral'. *Faire marche arrière*, 'to back up'. *Mettre en marche arrière*, 'to go into reverse'.
vitre (f): 'window'.
voiture (f) **de tourisme**: 'private car'.
volant (m): 'steering wheel'.

zone bleue (f): area in which you may park for a limited time or only on certain days of the month. The *disque de stationnement* must be placed at the windscreen to show when you arrived and when you should leave.

English—French
Cross-reference Index

Note: this might better be termed, a 'mere' cross-reference index, so as to give you a more accurate idea of its completeness, reliability and usefulness. The French word given after each English entry is meant as a suggestion of where to turn in the main French-English text; it may not even be the translation of the English word, nor the only translation possible. Where more than one French word is given, you will want to look each of them up in the main French-English text, to find which one suits which situation. And indeed, a number of items in the main text have not been cross-referenced here, because they do not lend themselves to the distorted condensation which an index necessitates.

A

abandon, to: tomber
able: habile
abortion: avortement
absent-mindedness: distraire, se
about to, to be: point
accelerator: champignon
accident: sinistre
accommodating: arranger
according to: d'après
accountant: bureau
accurate: correct
accused: chargé
acquit, to: innocenter
act, to: comédien
actor: comédien, interprète
adapted from: d'après
additional: extra
adjoining: attenant
adjust: règlement
administration: direction
administrator: cadre
adore, to: raffoler
adult: personne
advanced: évolué
advantage: intérêt
advantageous: intéressé, intérêt
advise against, to: indiquer
affair: affaire, bricole, liaison
afford, to: abordable
against: moyennant
agreed: entendre parler

agreement: accord, entendre parler
aid: concours
airport: gare
air stewardess: piraterie aérienne
air terminal: gare
alcohol: boisson
all aboard: abordable
all right: accord, ça va, entendre parler
All Saints' Day: Toussaint
All Souls' Day: Toussaint
almond: dragée
alone: tranquille
along: avec
already: déjà
also: aussi
alter: truc
alteration: retouche
always: toujours
ambitious person: arriver
amiable: abordable
amusement: distraire, se
and so on: avenant
announcement: faire-part
annoy, to: chiffon, tiquer
antiques: antiquité
antiquity: antiquité
anyhow: façon, toujours
any old way: au diable
apostrophe: ponctuation
apparatus: appareil
apparently: conditionnel

141

consider, to: interroger, s'
consistent: suivre
contact: liaison
contend, to: discuter
continue, to: poursuivre, se; suivre
contraception: cachet, contraception
convenient: commode
cook: fourneau
cooker: fourneau
cookie: gâteau
cooking pot: casserole
cooperative: arranger
cord: corde
correct: correct, reprendre
cost, to: chercher, rente
cough: graisse
countdown: cosmonaute
counter: zinc
country: bleu, pays
course: classe
coverage: rapporter
cracker: gâteau
craftsman: artisanat
cranky: grognon
crayon: bureau
cream cake: religieuse
credit: avoir, crédit, passif
credit instalment: appointements
crew: piraterie aérienne
crew-cut: cheveux
crew-necked: ras du cou
crippled: valide
crisis: crise
crowd: monde
crude: crudités
crumple, to: froisser
cuff: manchette
curate: curé
curator: conserver
cure: cure
currency; monnaie, flotter
curtain: rideau

D

dam: barrage
dance: boom
dance attendance, to: pied

dash: ponctuation
data processing: informatique
data transmission: informatique
date: échéance
dead tired: crever
dealings: circulation
dear: rente
dear me: Dieu
death's doorstep: article
debit: passif
deceive, to: tromper
decimal point: virgule
decorate, to: arranger
decree: arrêté
defrost, to: dégivrer
degree: diplôme
deliberately: exprès
delivery: arriver
demented: illuminé
demonstration: manifestation
deny, to: infirmer
department store: boutique
departure: arriver, partance
deposit: appointements, arrhes, consigne
depression: dépression
deranged: déranger
design: maquette
desk: bureau
detain, to: retenir
deviation: entorse
develop, to: mettre en valeur
development: rebondissement
devil, to the: au diable
devout: pratiquant(e)
dictaphone: bureau
didn't he?: n'est-ce pas?
die, to: crever
diet: grossir
difficult: donner
difficulty: difficilement, embarrasser
direct, to: conduire, mettre
direction: direction, indiquer, sens
dirty trick: propre
disappear, to: filer
disappoint, to: peine, tromper
discount: remise
discuss, to: discuter

in theory: en principe
in touch with: joindre, liaison
introduce, to: présenter
in trouble: auberge, bêtise
inventive: astuce
invoice: bureau
iron: coup
ironmonger: couleurs, marchand de
issue: issue

J

jacket: pochette, tailleur
jam: embouteillage
jewel-case: housse
jobhunter: chômage
John Bull: Marianne
join, to: joindre
joke: blague, farces et attrapes
jump, to: sauter
jumper: bonneterie
just: juste
just about, to be: point
juvenile delinquent: blouson noir

K

keep, to: tenir
key: pilote
keyboard: bureau
kick the bucket, to: pied
kiss, to: baiser
kitchen utensils: pile
knock: frapper, toc
knocked out: chandelle
know, to: figurer, ignorer; savoir, se
knowledge: bagage

L

label: dégriffé
Labour: travailler
labourer: travailler
lack: manquer
ladder, to: filer

lamp: ampoule
language holiday: séjour linguistique
lapse, to: échéance
last straw: manquer
laundry: linge
lavatory: cabinets, lavabo, quelque part
lavish tipping: arroser
law: droit
lay-by: garage
layout: maquette
lay out, to: mettre
lazy: cheveux, fumiste
lead: tuyau
leader: animateur
lead, to: conduire
leading: pilote
lean: graisse
learn, to: tenir
leather-goods: maroquinerie
leave: congé, déposer
left: droit
leftovers: bribes
legal age: bémol
legislature: Elysée
lemonade: limonade
lend, to: emprunt, passer
let out, to: reprendre, débrayer
let slip, to: échapper
letter-opener: coupe-papier
lettuce: salade
liable: passible
liberate, to: affranchir
licence: conduire, licencié, vignette
licenced: licencié
licentious: licencié
life on earth: au-delà
light: feu, illuminé
light bulb: ampoule
light meter: cellule
light switch: interrupteur
like: tenir
lime: limonade
line, to: double
linen: linge
listener: auditeur
literal: figuratif, pied
load, to: recharge

loaded: chargé, recharge
loaf: pain
loan: emprunt
local fellow: pays
logical: suivre
long run: échéance
look: air, coup
look after, to: occuper
look for, to: chercher
loose talk: baratin, boniment
lose weight, to: grossir
lost, to be: nager
lottery: dixième
lousy: infect
love affair: liaison
love at first sight: coup
love, to: raffoler
lower: inférieur
Ltd.: S.A.
lubrication: graisse
luck: chance
lucky: pot
lucrative: rapporter

M

mac: étanche
machine: appareil
mad: déranger
made to measure: confection
magnet: aimant
maiden name: fille
mail: bureau
mailbox: boîte
main points: ligne
main thing: essentiel
major: bémol
make, to: confection
make believe, to: semblant
make both ends meet, to: bout
make love to: baiser
make use of, to: emprunter
malicious: malicieux
man: garçon
manage, to: arriver, débrouiller, se; tirer
manila folder: bureau, chemise
manner: façon, genre
manners: éducation

march: marcher
mark: marque, ponctuation
market: marché, marcher
marry, to: marier
master: professeur
match: feu
match book: pochette
matriculate, to: inscrire, s'
matter: affaire, arriver
may I?: permettre
meagre: maigre
meaning: sens
meanness: petitesse
medical care: appointements
medical exam.: visite
medicine: ampoule
medium size: patron
mend, to: rafistoler
merger: fusionner
mess: gâchis, salade
mess about, to: bricole
metre: compteur
metric system: mètre
midwife: sage
military service: service
miner: bémol
minimum wage: SMIG
minor: bémol
mint: bêtise, frapper
miscarriage: avortement
mischievous: malicieux
miserly: radin
mislead, to: tromper
miss, to: manquer
mistake: tromper
model: mannequin
model child: mannequin
money: galette, monnaie
mood: mouvement d'humeur
moon landing: cosmonaute
mosque: temple
moth: papillon
mother country: métropole
mould, to: moudre
move, to: bouger, émotion
much more: autrement
muddle through, to: débrouiller, se
mushroom: champignon
musical score: partition

mussel: moudre
must: falloir, manquer

N

nail: clou
narcotics squad: monde
National Lottery: dixième
nature: caractère
nausea: mal
nearly: manquer, quasiment
near-sighted: presbyte
near thing: juste
necessarily: forcément, obligatoire
negligee: habillé
neighbour: prochain
neighbourhood: quartier
neither: non plus
new maths: mathématiques
   modernes
newspaper: papier
New Year: étrennes, fête, réveillon
next: prochain
next life: au-delà
nibble, to: bout
night club: boîte
nightgown: chemise
nobody: personne
no entry: double
no joke: blague
no matter how, when, etc.:
   importer
northern: méridional
not bad: mal, pas mal
not easy: évident
note: billet
notebook: bureau
no thank you: bourratif
notice: licencié, constater
not know, to: ignorer
not   likely: invraisemblable,
   possible
no use: peine
nuclear power: centrale nucléaire
nuisance: intoxication
number plate: plaque minéralogique

nun: religieuse

O

object: bibelot
obligatory: obligatoire
observe, to: constater
obstacle: embarrasser
obvious: sauter, évident
occasion: occasion
occur, to: produire, se
ocean bed: fond
of course: entendre parler
offend, to: froisser
office: bureau, cabinets, maison
officers: bureau
offspring: rejeton
oh really: ah bon
oh well: ah bon
oil: pétrole
oil spill: marée noire
oil tanker: pétrole
oil well: pétrole
OK: accord, ça va
older generation: jeunes, les
old maid: fille
omelette: œuf
on behalf of: part
one another: une
one-way street: double
only: que
on purpose: exprès
on second thoughts: réfléchir
OPEC: OPEP
opinion: prise
orchestra: conduire
or else: autrement
otherwise: autrement
ouch!: aïe!
outbid, to: surenchérir
outgoing: sortant
outlaw: droit
outlet: issue
outline, to: brosser, ligne
out of place: cheveux, dépayser
outskirts: faubourg
outspoken: franc
oven: four
overall: bleu, combinaison

reprocessing: recyclage
researcher: chercher
reshuffle, to: remaniement
resign, to: licencié
responsible: chargé
restless: bouger
restore, to: mettre
result: donner
resume, to: reprendre
retire, to: retraite
retreat: retraite
return ticket: aller
reverse: marcher
rich: monnaie
ride: tour, faire un
rider: avenant
right: correct, donner, droit, propre
right moment: tomber
right-thinking: penser
ring up, to: coup
ripe: fait
rise: carré, hausse
risk: risquer
road block: barrage
road safety: prévention
road signs: signaler
rocket: cosmonaute
room: chambre, espace
rot, to: moisir
rotten: infect
rubber-band: bureau
rubber stamp: bureau
rude: élever
rug: tapis
rugby: rugby
rule: règlement
ruler: bureau, mètre
ruling class: classe
run away, to: fugue
run, to: filer, marcher, afficher
run into, to: croiser

S

sack, to: congé, licencié
sadness: chagrin
safe: coffre-fort
saint's day: fête

salad: salade
salad dressing: dresser
salary: appointements, traitement
sale: dégriffé
sales: appointements
SALT: armements
sampling: dégustation
satisfactory: satisfaction
sausage: saucisse
scale model: mannequin, maquette
scalp: cheveux
scare: émotion
scheme: combinaison
scholar: savant
science fiction: anticipation
scientist: savant, scientifique
scissors: ciseau, bureau
Scotch tape: bureau
scour, to: récurer
scrap: bout, bribes, brin
screw, to: baiser
seabed: fond
seal: cachet
season, to: saison, la belle
seat: espace, siège, strapontin
second-hand: occasion
section: quartier
seduce, to: séduire
see, to: voir
seek, to: chercher
seem, to: air
seize, to: saisir
select, to: sélectionner
self-interested: intéressé
semi-colon: ponctuation
sense: sens
serve, to: desservir
serves you right: chercher, pied
session: siège
set fire, to: feu, incendie
set theory: mathématiques modernes
settle, to: règlement
settle out of court, to: arrangement
set to music, to: mettre
set up: système
sexual intercourse: rapports

start, to: démarrer, mettre
starter: démarrer
station: gare
stay still, to: tenir
stay too long, to: moisir
steering: direction
stenography: dactylo
step: marcher
step-: parent
stimulant: euphorisant
stingy: radin
stockings: bonneterie
stomach ache: mal
stop and think, to: réfléchir
story: histoire
stove: fourneau, poêle
straightforward: carré
strapping: brin
straw mattress: bassin
stretch, to: extensible
strike: frapper, grève
strike-breaker: bleu
striking: saisir
striking power: force de frappe
string bag: marché
stringed instruments: cuivres
strong: calé
strongbox: coffre-fort
strong person: armoire à glace
stubborn: volontaire
stuck, to be: coincer
study: pencher, se
stuffing: farces et attrapes
stupid: abruti, chameau
style: genre
subject to: passible
suburbs: banlieue, faubourg, ligne
succeed, to: marcher
such and such: tant, tel ou tel
suffering: souffrant
sugar almond: dragée
suit: complet, tailleur
suite: suivre
summarize, to: dresser
summer: saison, la belle
sum up, to: point
sunburn: coup
superfluous: double
supermarket: supermarché

supposed to: conditionnel, en principe
surrender: rendre
suspended sentence: ferme
swaddling clothes: langes
swamped: débordé
swear word: gros mot
sweater: bonneterie
sweep, to: coup
sweetheart: petit(e) ami(e)
sweets: confection
swim, to: nager
swimming pool: nager
swimsuit: bonneterie, nager
symmetric: symétrique
system: système

T

table of contents: table des matières
tablet: bureau, cachet
tailor: tailleur
take, to: emprunt, passer, suivre
take care of, to: arranger, occuper, suivre
take in, to: comédien, reprendre
taken in, to be: avoir, bleu, marcher, tomber
take leave, to: congé
take literally, to: pied
take place, to: produire, se
taking: prise
talk over, to: discuter
talk shop, to: boutique
tape: magnétophone
tape measure: mètre
taper: bougie
tape recorder: magnétophone
taste, to: dégustation, goûter
taste: sens
tea: goûter
teacher: professeur
telephone: appareil
telephone call: appel
telephone operator: bureau
telephone switchboard: bureau
television: radio
temperament: caractère

temple: temple
tenth: dixième
term of office: présidentielles
terminal: gare
that is: c'est-à-dire, bouquet
that looks: ça fait
thaw: dégivrer
theme-song: indicatif
then: prochain
there!: aller, ça y est, toc!
therefore: aussi
they: on
thin: maigre
thingumabob: machin, truc
think, to: penser
thrash, to: dérouiller
thrilling: saisir
throw off scent, to: dépister
thumb one's nose, to: pied
thumbtack: bureau
ticket: billet, espace, siège
tie: papillon
tight: juste
tight spot: embouteillage, coincer
till, to: travailler
tin: boîte, conserver
tip: étrennes, pourboire, service, truc, tuyau
toast: griller, pain
tobacco: tabac
tobacconist's: jeton, tabac
tobacco pouch: blague
toilet: cabinets, lavabo, quelque part
toilet paper: papier
token: jeton
tomboy: garce
too: aussi
too bad: pot
tool-shed: remise
toothpick: cure-dent
top quality: extra
touch: sens
tough luck: pot
Tour de France leader: bleu
towel: gant de toilette
tower: tour, faire un
town: pays
town house: hôtel particulier
trace of accent: cheveux

track down, to: dépister
trade: circulation
trade-mark: marque
traffic: circulation
traffic jam: embouteillage
traffic light: feu
tragedy: comédien
trailer: caravane
train, to: dresser, stage
trainee: stage
training camp: classe
training period: stage
translate, to: rendre
translation: professeur
transparency: diapositive
trash collector: boîte
treatment: cure, traitement
trick: astuce, farces et attrapes; tour, faire un
trinket: bibelot
trouble: bêtise, histoire, intoxication, mal
trouble, to go to: donner, mal, peine
troublesome: donner
trousers: pantalon
tube: tuyau
turnip: navet
turtle-necked: ras du cou
twine: dactylo
two days later: surlendemain
two-way street: double
type, to: bureau
typewriter: dactylo, bureau
typewriter key: bureau
typist: dactylo

U

UFO: OVNI
unauthorized: sauvage
Uncle Sam: Marianne
unconscious: chandelle
uncooperative: arranger
under: sous
underclothing: linge
underline, to: signaler
underpants: combinaison
undershirt: chemise

understand, to: saisir, suivre
understanding: arranger
understudy: double
unemployment: chômage
unfaithful: tromper
unjust: juste
unlikely: invraisemblable
unmarked: banaliser
unplug, to: brancher
unscheduled: sauvage
unselfish: intéressé
unwillingly: contre-cœur, à
upholstery: tapis
upset, to: émotion, retourner
upside down: sens dessus-dessous
up to date: affranchir
useful: service, servir
usherette: pourboire
utility: intérêt

V

vacuum cleaner: housse
valid: valable
validate, to: valable
valise: porte-
valuable: valable
value, to: tenir
VAT: en plus, TVA
vaunt, to: article, boniment
vendor: marché
very: autrement
vex, to: chiffon
vicar: curé
victim: sinistre
view: vue
visionary: illuminé
visit: visite
voluntary: volontaire
vomit, to: rendre
voting booth: urnes

W

wages: appointements
waist: taille
wait, to: patienter
wait and see: voir

waiter: garçon
walk, to: marcher; tour, faire un
wallet: porte-
wall-lamp: ampoule
wallpaper: tapis
warm, to: chambre
warn, to: gare
warp, to: travailler
washbasin: bassin
washcloth: gant de toilette
washing: linge
washing machine: linge
wash-stand: lavabo
waste-paper basket: bureau
watch out: gare
water, to: arroser
waterproof: étanche
watertight: étanche
wax, to: cirer
way: bout, façon
way out: issue
weapons: armements
wear, to: mettre
wedding: marier
weekend: pont
weight: marché
well . . .: enfin
well!: comment, tenir
well-behaved: élever
well qualified: calé, corde
what: quoi
what'shisname: machin, truc
what of it?: encore
which: quoi
while we're at it: tant
whimsical: farfelu
white: bleu, œuf
white coffee: crème
White House: Elysée
wild: sauvage
wince, to: tiquer
window: tabatière
window-shopping: lèche-vitrines
wire: brancher
wise: sage
with: avec
with difficulty: difficilement
withdraw, to: retraite
within: sous
without: avec

woman: fille
wonder, to: demander, se; interroger, s'
wood dealer: bougnat
woodwinds: cuivres
work: pain
work, to: marcher, pied, travailler
working class: classe
working day: férié
works: système
worldly: monde
worn out: linge
worry, to: tracasser, se
worthless: intérêt
worthwhile: valable
wound, to: froisser
wrestling: catch
wrinkle, to: chiffon, froisser
wrong: droit, tromper
wrong moment: tomber

X

X-ray: radio

Y

yawn, to: mettre
yes: oui, si
yolk: œuf
you: tutoyer
younger generation: jeunes, les
you're welcome: quoi
youth: jeunes, les
youth hostel: auberge

Z

zipper: fermeture éclair